HUNDRED ALTARS

JULIET BREDON

Hundred Altars © 2018 Soul Care Publishing

All rights reserved. No part of this book may be used or reproduced or transmitted in any manner whatsoever, transmitted electronically, or distributed by any means without the written permission of the publisher.

Library and Archives Canada Cataloguing in Publication

Originally published in 1934.

Published by Soul Care Publishing, Vancouver, B.C. Canada

To the everlasting people, - my friends of Hundred Altars

Table of Contents

I.	Stranger's Entry	1
II.	Hundred Altars	10
III.	The Spring Feast of Ancestors	18
IV.	Shui Ching in Search of a Son	24
V.	To Her That Hath—	33
VI.	"Hot Noise" at the Chi House	42
VII.	Ma Makes a Decision	49
VIII.	The Arrival of the Little Wife	56
IX.	The Red Thread of Tragedy	62
X.	Crossing the Year	75
XI.	What the Gods Send	86
XII.	Dangerous Years	98
XIII.	Young Tiger	107
XIV.	The Dragon's Mark	116
XV.	White Business	126
XVI.	Scandal	136
XVII.	Revenge	146
XVIII.	Chi's Relations Arrive	155
XIX.	Ma Apprentices Young Tiger	166
XX.	Red Festivities	176
XXI.	The Rain Procession	187
XXII.	Rumours	196
XXIII.	The Great Adventure	204
XXIV.	The Flight	213
XXV.	The Prodigal	224
XXVI.	Exiles	231
XXVII.	The Double Son	240
XXVIII.	The Return	246
XXIX.	The Marriage of the Dead	256

XXX.	Tientsin	264
XXXI.	The Marriage of Little Dragon	276
XXXII.	Little Dragon Comes Home	285

I. Stranger's Entry

"You have come to the right place," said the old Chinese diviner looking fixedly across the table at the merchant who sat opposite him. "This village of Hundred Altars attracts the favourable 'wind and water' influences (*fēng shui*). And if a man expects good fortune in his business it is wise for him to settle in fortunate surroundings. When the spirits are hostile, efforts are useless."

Ma, the merchant,—a short fattish man, bull-headed, with keen slanting black eyes,—listened attentively to the soothsayer's words. Because of his occult knowledge, this lean old man in his patched cotton coat and the big horn-rimmed spectacles looped over his ears with bits of string, was greatly respected in the countryside. The peasants summoned him to cast out devils, to read omens and, in general, to reveal the will of the spirits towards all their undertakings. For none knew better than he the mystic rules of those magic "wind and water influences" which the West can never fathom, but the East has long lived by. They might so easily be disturbed by a running stream, or angered by too tall a building. Such things would lead them to desert a village leaving ill-luck behind them. Or again, they might be pleased with the shape of a mountain or an outgushing spring, and gather to focus happiness upon that place. No ordinary man could tell what the "wind and water" spirits might do— or why. But the diviner was the village high priest of *fēng shui*. He knew—and under his wise direction the peasants took no chances of offending the invisible ones who dwell in every field and tree and brook. At his command the farmers burned red paper to the spirit of a tree which refused to bear fruit, or to the Well God i£ the water failed, or built a new house or refrained from building one.

"Even the neighbouring villages of this region," the old man droned on in his sing-song voice, "admit that our situation is lucky. The natural features around us are balanced and harmonious, and rightly related to produce harmony in those who live among them. The ordinary folk here are content. Over a hundred years ago a famous scholar was born in Hundred Altars. No other hamlet round about can make such a boast. He won distinction for our village by

1

securing a high degree in the Imperial examinations during the lifetime of my grandfather—a soothsayer even as I."

"That indeed is an honour to any place!" exclaimed Ma.—Merchant though he might be, he respected scholarship like all Chinese, even above the riches which he worked for. Where one successful scholar had been born, he thought to himself, the good *feng shui* might produce another—perhaps even in his own family, though as yet he had no sons. Under the Empire it was the ambition of every man no matter how humble or great to have a scholar born into his house. For though, the nation's governors Were chosen from the nation's scholars, learning was loved also for its own sake. A scholar shed lustre not only on. his kindred and on his birthplace, but was even revered throughout the land as one more jewel in that crown of culture of which the Chinese are so justly proud.

Well, Ma had come to consult the omens and they were good, —better than one could hope. So here in Hundred Altars Village he would buy land and make his home. He told the diviner so.

"But why not stay where you belong,—where you are already settled?" the old man asked suspiciously.

Ma had expected this question. He knew he must give reasons, and good ones, for coming, to a new place since "moved people" in China are always, under suspicion. Most folk prefer to die where they are born. Why, then, should a man leave home unless his neighbours forced him to because he was an undesirable member of the community? For two good reasons only;—flood or famine. In Ma's case it was a flood that had swept away the village near Tientsin where he was comfortably settled.—"The waters flowing over it like a strong tide have ruined the region," Ma explained, "it is necessary to seek a new place."

"Well, that is a reason," the diviner admitted cautiously. "Perhaps you might be accepted here."

Ma knew well enough what he meant. A stranger might be outwardly accepted, yes, and kindly treated—for a time. But residence in a rural community does not necessarily mean true membership in it. He would never be allowed to live and do business in the closed corporation of a village where most people were kin in some degree and all were friends and neighbours for generations, unless he, a newcomer, could bring guarantees of honesty and

Hundred Altars

solvency. Until people knew who he was and why he came, and what manner of man he might be, none would sell him land, or give him a voice in community affairs, or let his sons have their daughters in marriage. Ma was no fool. He realized all this. And so he had wisely taken the precaution of bringing a "recommendation letter" from a man named Chien with whom he had had business dealings.

"This letter guarantees me," he said, spreading it out on the table in front of the diviner, "You know Chien of course. He is the nephew of a man of the same name living in the village."

"Yes, yes,—Squint Eye Chien!—I know him well," the diviner answered, giving his client a much more friendly smile than heretofore. "That nephew was an earnest, hard working lad who got a good place in the town where he earns thirty silver pieces a month, they tell me, in a cloth shop."—For a few minutes the soothsayer rambled on about the Chien family; how greatly Chien himself was respected in Hundred Altars,—and all about his nephew and his nephew's wife, until Ma tactfully dammed this stream of village gossip by asking him where it would be best for him to buy land.

"Tell me first the hour and the day and the month and the year of your birth, and then I will see what animal presides over it and what element controls your fate, and whether you belong to those folk who should trade southward and westward, or whether you should direct your energies toward the south and east."—So saying the old man delicately turned the pages of the thin paper Almanac with his pointed fingers tipped with inch long nails, too fragile and too precious to be cleaned.

Ma had often seen copies of this Almanac with its quaint pictures of gods and goblins and weird animals, a book prepared each year by the Emperor's own astrologers in their musty office under the shadow of the Peking city wall. There was a copy in nearly every house and ordinary people used it as a calendar. But only a diviner knew how to interpret omens from this sacred book of the unscientific science of *féng shui*. He, and he alone, could read its secret meaning. It taught him how to interpret dreams, to cure sickness; how to decide the influences that rule men's lives, and to foretell lucky and unlucky days for weddings, funerals and building new houses. Even such seemingly trivial matters as the right date and hour for taking a bath, cutting one's hair, paying a call or buying a pig, the soothsayer was asked to look up in the Almanac.

When Ma had told what he was asked to, tell, the diviner, after carefully consulting his book replied, "The piece of land southeast of the village street, close to the Black Dragon Spring would be best for you and your purposes. Facing it is the stone lion from the holy Mount Tai Shan which forbids evil spirits to pass that way. To the north is a range of hills to protect you from bad influences that might come from that unlucky direction. Studying the omens of your life I find that there and there only you should build your house so that your affairs may prosper."

The merchant rose and bowed his thanks. For once the mystical and practical combined in his favour. Good water near at hand was a precious asset in his plans. He drew from the folds of his gown a roll of copper coins politely wrapped in paper and laid them on the table. They amounted to less than fifty cents as we count money. Nevertheless the sum was a generous fee judged by village standards. And Ma knew as well as the diviner that the latter would receive a present of like amount from the owner of the piece of land which the merchant had been recommended to buy.

"I thank you for your advice," Ma said bowing respectfully, "and now I will go and call on the chief Elder, and talk with him of my intentions."

Without his consent and the approval of the old men's council who helped him regulate village affairs, Ma could never take advantage of the good fortune that the diviner foretold for him in Hundred Altars. These men, speaking for the group, might if they chose, refuse the hospitality of the village to anyone they did not like. Therefore they, no less than the soothsayer, must be consulted by a stranger who desired to come and live among them.

When Ma rose to leave the diviner went with him to the door to see him off, not heeding his requests to "go no further, go no further. I am unworthy of your kindness."—That it was Ma's duty to say to an older man and a scholar who, though poor enough—as witness the patches on his cotton gown—commanded more respect than any merchant. But when the diviner insisted on coming as far as the street gate, Ma was greatly flattered.

The diviner's gesture was a tangible asset. Passing villagers remarked the goodbyes between host and guest. A stranger so honoured by a man with the title of "teacher" and a knowledge of reading and writing which few of them could boast, must be a person worthy of regard,—a man who might be welcome in the village. For no one but knew already of the merchant's purpose in coming to Hundred Altars. The carter who drove him out from the city of Peking—a half day's journey distant,—had inquired at once not only where he was going, but why. And Ma had told him frankly. A stranger could not hide his intentions lest he arouse suspicion. A hidden motive must be a shameful motive and every man whether carter, muleteer, neighbour or even passerby, had the right to know the business of the person he served or dealt with,—not only know it, but tell it to all and sundry. So the carter had brought news of Ma's plans to the village and discussed them at the teashop, and the peasants began judging the newcomer's *p'i ch'i* (inner nature) the moment they heard the size of his tip.

As Ma sauntered slowly down the village street, he thought it was but natural that the diviner should praise the situation of Hundred Altars. On three sides the village had a sheltering screen of mountains, and, on the fourth the hills opened and the plain with its wide horizons stretched away for a full hundred miles to the sea. This fertile tract of country where the springs never ran dry and the crops seldom failed, was cut up into fields,—squares and triangles and long ribbons of good farming land. For the most part the tillers of the soil were the owners of it, and lived in the network of villages scattered over the countryside, and but rarely in isolated farmhouses.

This great North China plain is a strong land. It is a stubborn land too, with a long hard winter and cruel spring winds laden with suffocating dust from Mongolian deserts, and short hot summers with torrential rains. But just as one is often surprised to find queer nooks and corners of unexpected tenderness in strong characters, so here one finds gentle valleys with leafy orchards lying against a background of stark, rock-ribbed hills, and wild violets and iris springing up between the stones of dry river beds.

It is indeed a strong country. So much has happened there, and it wears the air of remembering everything. For centuries it has been the stage of wars and invasions, and great dynastic changes. The mighty Tangs once ruled the whole of it. The ruined temple on the hill crest nearby is a memory of the warring Liaos. A lonely pagoda on a distant crag proclaims a victory over Tartar hordes who broke like a storm through the passes of the Great Wall which writhes along the mountain tops scarcely fifty miles distant. A half ruined Buddhist shrine on a rocky slope rising abruptly beyond the village and the thirteen lonely tombs of the Ming Emperors in the deep valley to the north speak of the coming and the passing of this last Chinese dynasty. There is something dramatic in these crumbling temples and tombs and the extinction of the great people who built them, though theirs was often only a fierce dominating feudal renown.

But Ma the merchant did not dwell on ruins as he looked about him. He was no lover of the past, but a man whose nature and ambitions were essentially of the present. Indeed for the times he lived in, he was modern minded. What interested him were the yellow roofed buildings of the Black Dragon Temple glittering in the morning sunshine on the summit of Flowering Eyebrows Hill. They had been given as an Imperial compliment by a Manchu Emperor to the Dragon God of the springs whose pure water was one of Ma's main reasons for coming to Hundred Altars.

A descendant of this great Manchu sovereign still ruled the Celestial Empire, though people said he was a weak youth and might not be able to hold on to his throne for very long. Yet he remained, so far, a power in the land, and the peasants told how now and then he came on pilgrimage through the countryside giving gifts. Indeed his Summer Palace was not far away, just beyond the spur of pointed hills that looked like a scholar's pen rest, and was another lucky omen for Hundred Altars. The Imperial Hunting Park was not far distant either, and on a clear day one could see, thirty long miles across the plain the stone freckled hill of Tang Shan, famous for its hot springs where the Emperor had a small travelling palace.

Musing on these lucky surroundings Ma presently reached the Elder's house. Two small boys were playing beside the doorway in a pile of dirt. Their hands and faces were black with it. They even had dirt on their tongues. He asked them if the Elder was at home. "He is, he is not, he is, he is not," they answered mischievously, and darted through the gate. But presently a bright-faced woman hearing the commotion appeared. "Forgive these little ones," she said in a chirping, bird-like voice. "They are too young to understand courtesy. Now if you are looking for the house-father he has just returned from the fields and is washing himself in the kitchen. Enter and I will call him."

Ma waited but a few minutes before a very dignified farmer came into the room. It was easy to see why such a man had been chosen elder for he was a natural leader of his fellows. Not that there was anything overbearing in his manner. Far from it. The wrinkles on his face were plainly the dry beds of kindly smiles, and his strong features, unlovely but lovable, showed wisdom, good judgment and integrity of purpose.

Host and guest greeted one another politely, each clasping his own hands and bowing. Ma felt instinctive and ungrudging respect for the Elder, a fine figure of a man who at seventy-five had still the body and muscles of a man of fifty.

When both were seated the woman, obviously a daughter-in-law, brought tea and Ma explained once more about the flood in his home village, and how his house had crumbled and his neighbours scattered. "I am obliged to seek a new home," he added, "and I have heard this is a lucky place."

"It is," replied the Elder quickly, "but we already have a hundred homes here, and each has its family altars and its ancestral tablets. Many of us are bound together by blood bonds and we have been established here for centuries. The record of our earliest settlers is lost. No one knows when or whence they came, but legend says they were the subjects of fairy emperors who, partly covered with fur or feathers, taught our people to cook food, build houses, and till the soil. Thus our earliest traditions have bound us to our land. The need to work it is in our blood," he added proudly.

"These things I have heard said," Ma answered bowing respectfully.

"We have our own customs too, established this long time," the Elder proceeded calmly, "our own code, and our own conventions. It might not be easy for a stranger..." he paused, then asked abruptly,—"Have you any guarantors?"

"Yes,- Chien, the nephew of your neighbour down the street is ready to guarantee me. I have a letter from him here."

"I see," Elder Chi nodded, "and what is your business?"

"I am a merchant."

"Well, we are all farmers in this village, men of the soil as I have told you, and mostly related to one another. But there might be a place for an honest merchant among us. Our fields however are not for sale," he added cautiously,—"Where did you think of establishing your house?"

"The diviner thinks I might get the piece of vacant land near the Black Dragon Spring. With that excellent water I could set up a wine distillery. I have silver to buy your millet to make wine. And in addition I would keep a shop with flour and such other merchandise as your field folk need.—So none would lose by my coming."

"It may be so," the Elder answered still a little doubtfully, "I will discuss the matter with neighbour Chien.—You've seen him already?"—Ma nodded assent.—"If he is prepared to confirm his nephew's letter saying you are an honest man and you yourself are prepared to abide by our customs, perhaps we might be willing to have you come among us."

Thus the interview ended, and Ma went back to the little local inn where he was lodged and waited calmly for the villagers' verdict. Meanwhile Elder Chi talked the matter over with Liu and Chang and Shih, his assistant headmen. And he consulted Chien. who answered frankly,—"I am certain Ma is such a man as my nephew says, a good neighbour, neighbours, and an honest trader. Besides he might, if he belonged to Hundred Altars, buy our surplus grain at better rates than those 'big stomached' speculators from the city."

Then the diviner was called in to give his opinion, and the priest of the parish temple, Trembling Sea, a large man with heavy-lidded eyes. Wu, the coffin-maker, also said his say, and the innkeeper Chin put in his word, adding shrewdly, "If we should need to borrow it might be well to have a man with silver in the village, instead of depending on the money lenders of Peking with their ruinous rates of interest."

So they all talked back and forth and after much wagging of tongues and shaking of heads the peasants agreed that Ma should be allowed to settle in Hundred Altars, though they felt this permission for a stranger's entry was no light thing to give. Indeed few outsiders ever came to disturb the peace of the village except once a year at the short season of pilgrimage to the mountain shrine of Miao Feng Shan beyond, and then they only passed by and quickly withdrew again. At all other times the hamlet lived apart, aloof from strangers and new ideas— asking only to be left in peace and guarding its isolation stubbornly. For near as it was in actual distance to the great capital of Peking, the village was miles away in spirit and the peasants, born on the land and living by it, detested towns and distrusted townsmen.

So Ma was duly grateful when he was finally invited to join the community, and at once offered a feast to his new neighbours so that he might come among them as a friend and equal. Now he could begin to bargain, dollar by dollar, for his land while silent witnesses noted that he was both shrewd and generous. And next he built his house and his shop and his distillery. Then last of all Ma again consulted the old diviner, and bade him choose a plot for his family tombs. For until Ma brought his "spirit tablets" and the bones of his dead to Hundred Altars he might not call that place his home. It was unthinkable that the ancestors should lie among strangers. Human society in this most eastern East is founded on the bond between the living and the dead. The latter still form part of the family, and care for their comfort is a descendant's first duty. Therefore, only when the graves of his forefathers were properly prepared on his own land, and their spirits had been reverently invited to enter their new home, could Ma himself and his wife dare to install themselves in Hundred Altars.

Juliet Bredon

II. Hundred Altars

Luck was the architect of Hundred Altars, which had grown haphazard through the centuries as the community slowly formed. There was nothing four square and regular about the plan of this village as about so many of the hamlets of the plain. Small lanes dodged around corners like little truant boys to houses huddled close together, their courtyards touching one another lest evil spirits squeeze in between them. No two of these lanes were parallel, no two straight except by accident, and all were so narrow that when an occasional farm cart passed by or a donkey laden with trailing millet stalks, women pressed back into their doorways with shy caution.

The main street straggled and twisted for a mile,—undrained and unpaved. It was just a long passage through the village, now high, now low, between houses which were never in line and mostly raised well above the roadway, one standing forward and another back and all hidden behind blank rubble walls. Often the street was so narrow that there was no room for a cart to turn, yet who would think to widen it for convenience sake? Bad roads were as natural as bad sanitation. The "wind and water spirits" were not concerned with such material matters. Besides the street was as much an outdoor living room as a means of getting from place to place. The swarming children cramped in their own narrow courtyards overflowed into it, and played there naked all the summer long. Peddlers halted their barrows casually for an hour or two—or three; passing craftsmen plied their trades in sunny corners, mending rice-bowls, making brooms, or shaving heads.

Householders threw refuse out of their doors, and chickens scratched in the garbage, while pigs wallowed grunting with delight in the puddles of dirty water that formed in the middle of the street. No one was offended by pools of household filth beside the gates. They were neither revolting nor repulsive to the farmers but magic gifts from the gods to fertilize the fields and make the crops grow rich, and strong. What matter if obstacles such as these obstructed the traffic?—Traffic could wait since time was no object. Between sunrise and sunset there were hours enough for all men had to do, and only devils demanded haste. So why make improvements?—Why repair what went awry? Therefore in summer, when the main street became a swift flowing river, the farm carts splashed through it up to their hubs in water, and during the dry season they rumbled past in a cloud of dust over the loose stones washed down from the hillsides by the rains. Their fathers and their grandfathers and their great grandfathers had done the same. Any improvement would imply a reproach to the ancestors and show a lack of filial piety, the highest of all virtues. Change to the people of Hundred Altars did not mean progress, and they preferred to bear their discomforts with passive indifference, believing that what has been should be.

At the west end of the street stood the parish temple within its rose-washed walls, twice a man's height, from which the plaster was peeling. It stood back from the road behind a grassy common shaded by old cypresses, and facing the main gate was an open air theatre—a single pavilion on a high stone platform. The temple gave unusual distinction to Hundred Altars because it was also a memorial shrine. Though images of the gods occupied several of its altars it had a special sanctuary set aside for the spirit tablet of the Harmonious Prince who owned much land in the neighbourhood during the early days of Manchu rule. —A good man and a good master he was so beloved by the people that when he died they petitioned the Emperor to allow his spirit to dwell forever among them, offering ground from their precious food lands—the greatest gift in their giving—to raise the temple in his honour. The Emperor, graciously consenting, made a royal contribution towards its building, and between Sovereign and people it was formally agreed that the Prince's shrine should also serve Hundred Altars for its prayers and ceremonies.

Midway along the street was a miniature temple where the doll-like figures of the *Tu Ti*, the local Earth Lord and his Lady Wife, were housed—small enough in stature but powerful in village affairs. And at the eastern end of the village on the very outskirts, because of the prejudice that strangers be kept "outside the family," was the inn. Primitive lodging might be had there in smoked stained insect-ridden rooms, sour smelling from grimy travellers. It provided stables too for beasts, and outside the door was a well and a stone drinking trough where passing carters stopped to water their animals, throwing coppers into it for payment.

After field work was over farmers could usually be found sitting at the cement tables of the inn, discussing crops and prices while mine host in a soiled apron poured tea for them. If he had by chance a good scrap of scandal to tell he did not hesitate to improve on it, and when trapped in his embroidery of falsehood he would laugh and admit the exaggeration, saying: "Well, who knows but it was like that!" or "At least it ought to have been that way!" He was a master gossip, that innkeeper Chin of the wide smile and pouched eyes. He had a rich streak of mockery and malice and was ever ready to point his stories with a witticism and a wink.

But except for the inn and the temple most of the other buildings in the village were farmers' homes. From the street really nothing of them could be seen except the roofs above the walls that screened them from the road.—Even the rare house without a protecting wall had windows only on the inner side. Some of the farm-houses were pitifully poor—just two or three little buildings made of sundried clay bricks dug from the fields, and grouped around a courtyard of beaten earth. These adobe hovels —for they were little else,—belonged to farmers who owned but four or five acres of land, and lived from hand to mouth, always half hungry, with nothing beyond what they gained by the day's labour.

If in bad years they still managed to exist, it was because they might always ask help from more fortunate relations. Every member of the family must stand by every other in times of need. The debt of one was the debt of all, and no man ate from the bowl of charity while a member of his clan lived in comfort. In the scheme of ancestral life the man inside the clan must be protected though the man outside might be considered fair prey. The poorer peasants might have a scant living and only two suits of cotton without date or fashion to wear the year round, yet they were content. They supported their fathers; their sons would work for them. And to compensate their poverty they had other things—a capacity for enjoyment in small ways, for pleasure in their rare hours of idleness, for neighbourly talk, and above all for laughter since the Chinese, despite their quiet dignity, are truly laughter loving and even a quarrel can often be softened by a joke.

Hundred Altars

Moreover the tumble down doorways and crumbling walls of the village gave a false impression of its poverty. There are not a few well-to-do farmers living there with silver to spend for private and community pleasures, and solid comfortable homes. They might not choose to waste money on road-repairs, but they were lavish on things they considered important—weddings, funerals, temple festivals and feasts.

But until Ma came to Hundred Altars the house of the chief Elder's family was the only one to rise above the general level. Standing a little apart from its neighbours, it was bigger and better built. The separate pavilions were constructed of grey brick, with solid timbers to support the roofs which extended well over pillared verandas. The summer rains did not crumble them as they did the poorer homes, for their king and queen posts were of sound wood. The courtyards were paved with flat stone slabs, and the outer walls protected by painted circles of white chalk supposed by a polite fiction to represent cannon mouths very terrifying to the unsophisticated bandits of the Empire.

For generations the Chis had been born on the land, lived by it, and believed farming to be the most honourable calling which, might occupy a man's energy,—except of course for those rare beings who had the Heaven-sent gift of scholarship, like their own ancestor the Han Lin graduate whose memory was still the village pride. But the rest of the Chis bought land instead of books they could not read. Now they held sixty good acres all in one piece,—the largest holding of any family in Hundred Altars and three generations of the same name still lived under the ancestral roof,—the Elder,— the grandfather,—his son, the .present farmer, the latter's wife and their two small boys. Contented and in peace they lived, proud of their fertile fields, proud of their scholar ancestor, proudest of all of their good old name— a byword for uprightness and honesty throughout the countryside.

Elder Chi no longer took much active part in the farmwork but as the oldest and most respected man in the village as well as the largest landowner, he was the village headman. Supported by a council of old men like himself, chosen by their neighbours he settled disputes, safeguarded village morals, arranged festivals and ceremonies, and judged and punished those who broke the village law. The Magistrate, the only government official with whom the people were in touch interfered but little with their affairs. He lived two hours donkey ride distant in the market town of Pei Yang Ho and, unless they summoned him or he had his yearly taxes to collect, he never came near the village. So Hundred Altars under its elders was a petty republic managing its own affairs—a true democracy in miniature, despite the autocratic sovereign at the head-of the State.

Apart from his power as head Elder, old Chi's reputation as a good man gave him much influence in the district round about. Even the Robbers Guild respected him. No one could make a better bargain with its chief than he. "Go elsewhere," he would say calmly to him, slipping a few pieces of silver into his greedy hand when a strolling band of petty thieves menaced the village. "We are good, hard-working-people here—and poor."—And the man would take his followers to another village where they had been less wisely bribed and less courteously treated.

Elder Chi's son, the farmer, was a tall lean man of fine physique. The land was his only interest, the good warm dark earth. In him lay the force of generations of farmers like himself who desired land of their own and inherited knowledge of how to bring the best out of it. A bitter disappointment it had been to him, as to his father, when his younger brother turned out to be a restless spirit. This second son claimed his share of the family inheritance in cash, as was his right, and then moved away to another province to the north to seek his livelihood, because he was weary, so he said, of being in the same place among the same folk season after season. His going left Farmer Chi to work the fields alone as the Elder grew older, except for hired help, while he waited for his two little sons to grow up into farmers like himself. Regardless of heat or cold he went out at dawn to his fields and stayed there till darkness came, with only a short noon day rest when his wife, Clever Needle, brought him food. Then he ate, and afterwards lay down for a brief hour to sleep under a tree with a stone for a pillow, while his mules rested beside him with drooping heads.

Like his poorer neighbours, he had the simplest farm implements—only the wooden plough and the spiked drag, a stone roller, a hoe, and a bamboo rake, and he, like they had his own ways of sowing and ploughing and fertilizing the land,—ways as old as time. Seed was sown by hand, carefully and cautiously that none might be wasted. Crops were harvested with scythe and sickle. But whatever the hardships the farmers never complained. They knew that "Heaven wills who shall be rich and who shall be poor, and who shall work and who shall be idle."— A man has only to take what Fate sends and hear it. If they did not have much they at least made the most of what they had and did not grumble, rejoicing that their lives were bound to the slowly turning wheel of Mother Earth.

Before Ma came the farmers had disposed of their surplus crops through agents from Peking. But now Ma bought their millet for his distillery, and himself sold what he did not need through his friends in the city. He dealt well and fairly by his neighbour and they learned to respect and trust him. That was saying much since peasants are by nature distrustful. Ma served them too, in other ways. He employed labourers in his distillery; his shop was a boon to the community. Hitherto the peasants had had to depend on the annual fair, and barrow peddlers passing by for oil and flour and such other necessities as they could not make at home.

Nor were the benefits of the merchant's coming all on the side of the village. The place had, as the diviner promised, proved fortunate for Ma. Business was good. Every year he grew richer. Not content with the village trade he soon spun his web wider and sent out barrow-men to other places on market days; the first and the sixth to one hamlet, the second and seventh to another, the third and eighth to another, the fifth and tenth to still another, by which time the circle of neighbourhood markets was completed. This peddling business was all built on cash— the little copper cash which forty years ago were used throughout the countryside. They were strung on hempen strings through a square hole in the centre, and it took several thousand cash to equal a silver dollar, and five dollars made a barrow load. For this cumbersome coinage Ma demanded from his men a very strict accounting and his apprentices spent hours and hours stringing and counting the little coins.

Trade is a merchant's standard as land a peasant's. The merchant with trade in his blood loved the excitement of buying and selling just as much as the farmer with the land in his, loved to toil and enrich and add to his fields. But while Chi buried his surplus silver in the ground, Ma, though not trusting his shoes of sycee to any bank in the city melted them into a great pyramid of silver which stood in the courtyard behind the distillery in plain sight of all,—a tangible security to be seen and touched, and against which he issued promissory notes.

In his heart Ma was a little scornful of his neighbours content with the day's food for the day's work, and the peasants in turn were a little scornful of his easy life. They worked themselves lean while he sat comfortably at his desk until his paunch grew smoothly rounded. Already the village wits had dubbed him "Rice Bowl" so fat and sleek he was. Moreover he had the luck rare in China to have no poor relations to eat holes in his rice bags. "It's natural," the farmers said among themselves, "that this merchant prospers easily with no large family to support!"

But, though he had no hangers on, he had no son either to continue his ancestral line,—a deep and constant grief. He was but a year married when he came to Hundred Altars and had built his house grandly like a city trader's residence thinking it would be a proud inheritance for his son.—Yet after five years he had no son, nor, indeed, any child to inherit his wealth.

Still of his fine pavilions and the big compound in which they stood Ma could be justly proud. A spirit wall inside the front gate kept devils off his premises. One large room served for the shop. At the west end stood a counter and well-stocked shelves behind it; at the east end several tables with benches around them where wine bought from the distillery might be drunk. Though there were many patrons it was seldom that a man took more than he could hold.

Behind the shop stood the distillery, the stables for the mules who ground the grain, and the sheds for the great grind stones which these patient blind-folded animals turned hour after hour. Still further back was one pavilion with an upper story where Ma entertained his merchant friends from the city and the market towns. This was the only double storied building in the village, and a source of pride to all the inhabitants.

The living quarters were apart in their own courtyards, surrounded by a high wall with a moon gate. The big guest-hall facing south occupied one whole side of the first courtyard. Its furniture was of heavy carved blackwood. A few heirlooms— good pictures and bits of fine porcelains—which Ma had inherited from his father and grandfather who had been traders also and travelled men, added to the dignity and beauty of the room. Ma's own latest acquisitions in which he felt great pride as rarities were an English enamel shaving mug with a wreath of forget-me-nots painted on it, and a coloured lithograph of Queen Victoria's coronation. Such things appealed to the merchant because they were strange. Less conservative than his neighbours, he needed outside interests to keep him in touch with the world, for he was unwilling to regard the village and its life as the be-all and end-all of existence.

Shui Ching, his wife, felt otherwise. She was a peasant woman, daughter of a rich farmer and fitted naturally into Hundred Altars. She lived contented in its little world where the naively calculating and the idyllic mingled: where devils bewitched children and the personal interest of the Earth God was invoked at every turn. She saw life, as her neighbours did, in sharp contrast of fun and sorrow, success and failure, birth and death— but all within the narrow compass of their sheltered valley. There were hardships, yes,—but then no one was too poor to laugh at a joke, and if the daily food was crude and coarse, there were feasts now and then; and if the daily life was dull there were still dramatic moments and quick shifts of emotion. By no accounting was all grim labour and grimmer child-bearing. In the world she knew the hard work of the home and the fields was lightened by singing, and the scatter-witted shepherd lad played upon a flute as he led his flocks through the village to pasture on the cloud-shadowed hills beyond.

Juliet Bredon

III. The Spring Feast of Ancestors

The morning of Clear Brightness, the Spring Feast of Ancestors, no farmer worked in his fields. Duty bade him go forth and worship at his family graves instead. To serve the spirits of the dead was the strongest instinct of the Chinese race. Filial piety dictated such loving care. Family love was rooted in it. Loyalty was based upon it.

Shortly after their morning meal the Chis, like all their neighbours went off to visit their tombs, walking in single file, as peasants do from the long habit of treading the narrow furrows of their fields. Grandfather Chi strolled ahead setting the pace,— the privilege of age. Next came his son the farmer, Chi the Second, and Clever Needle, his wife, followed behind as women do when they walk with men. Her two small sons, Chin-tzu,— Real Gold—and Yin-tzu, Real Silver,—trotted beside her. Between them they carried the grave offerings; silver paper money, bundles of incense sticks, a pot of tea, a jar of wine, and a basket of food.

They loitered along slowly, stopping to chat with neighbours now and then. A stout matron standing in her doorway called out to Clever Needle,—"Have you eaten?"—the usual greeting of one Chinese to another for in that question lies the root of an undernourished nation's need.—"I have eaten to repletion," was her polite reply.—To be full fed proved that all was well with her. So many people went half hungry all their lives long.

"Are you going to your tombs?" called another woman as she threw a pailful of dirty water out into the street, narrowly missing the legs of Elder Chi.—She knew perfectly well where the Chis were going and why, but the obvious question is a politeness and the obvious answer no less a courtesy. "Yes, we are going out," replied Clever Needle, "and, of course, you are also?" —"Yes, we too a little later," the woman screamed after her as the family passed by.

To stop and chat in this casual manner was not unseemly despite the nature of their errand. For they did not think it sad. Mourning clothes and mourning manners would be out of place. In fact, actually, it was a gay and happy occasion. The peasants were doing a duty they liked to do, not fulfilling a gloomy task. In a sense unknown to us, their dead remained alive, seeing their every act, knowing their thoughts and hearing the words they spoke, and so companionship with them was natural.

The promise of spring was in the air. The first buds were on the willows, and the peach trees on the lower foothills were bursting into blossom, looking like delicate pink mists against the rocks. Lark songs were heard. A few early butterflies lived their little lives gaily as if knowing them all too brief. There was a scent of growth abroad, a promise of harvests to come.

A few days earlier Chi the Second had been out to sweep his tombs which stood like little brown tents in the midst of his own fields and not in any common graveyard. Wind and weather had crumbled the mounds since the last spring festival and he must put them in order. Though no stones marked their resting places he knew where each ancestor lay, for there was a rigid order of precedence in burial. The central and largest mound belonged to the oldest member of the clan whose bones were long ago dissolved into the forgiving earth.

Now as the whole family arrived before the tombs they laid their offerings on the newly swept earth in front of them,—the wine cups and food bowls, each with a pair of chop-sticks beside it as for a human guest. It was the duty and right of the Elder as the head of his house to light the incense sticks, make the food offerings, and burn the paper money before each grave, thus solemnly recognizing the obligation of the present to the past,— the living to the dead. For the past lives and has its being in the present, and the present in the past.—The two are one, and thus the dead and the living family form a unity.

Bending his stiff old knees, Chi knelt and bowed three times before each grave, and his son and his son's wife did the same. Even the little grandsons followed the example of their elders, looking very serious and grave like full grown men and behaving in a respectful and modest manner as they had been taught to do. Far and near across the fields other little blue gowned groups cheerfully set out similar offerings and followed similar rites before the resting places of their forefathers. Only here and there before the grave of one newly dead a woman knelt, leaning her head against the dry brown earth and sobbing.

While the ancestors consumed the spiritual essence of the food spread before them, their children sat about in silence waiting respectfully. Well-nourished and tenderly remembered the dead would continue to protect their living descendants from the shadowy world. Only if neglected they might become revengeful.

Once their simple rites were over the Chis squatted on the ground before their graves and made an alfresco meal from the offerings. It was all very formally informal, for these simple folk did all things simply, feeling it must be pleasing to their dead to feel their graves were scenes of hospitality in which they shared! As the Chis ate with hearty peasant appetite they chattered merrily. The farmer looked proudly and contentedly over the edge of his rice bowl on the springing winter wheat already a good six inches high, striping his fields with emerald green. His keen eye detected his neighbours also examining their land with more or less satisfaction. But there was no one, he noticed, at the Ma's grave plot.

"The merchant has not yet come," he observed to his father.

"Is there any wonder that he should not be out early?" the old man asked, "He will wait until we have all gone home. How should any man without a son come with his neighbours to worship at his fathers' graves and be shamed openly?"

Ma guessed exactly what his friends were saying. They were right. It was a bitter day for him, the bitterest day of the year. Cut off, isolated from the community, he sat behind closed shutters trying doggedly to apply himself to his accounts and wasting lamp oil. There was silence in the shop. Today was a holiday and all the workmen were away. There was silence in the village now. No sound of children playing or of passing carts. Everyone had gone out to the graves. He had heard them go, family parties passing in procession down the street in the early morning. It made him sour and jealous when the prattle of the children reached his ears. Their voices interrupted his work. He was angry because he could not control his thoughts. Yet when he tried to work again his ledgers only proved to him that in these last years he had made profits, great profits, and his wealth called loudly for a son to inherit it. What irony that these poor neighbours should all have sons while he who was rich, had none!

When it was. within an hour of noon and the rest of the villagers had come home, his wife Shui Ching—Clear Crystal—appeared in the doorway with the basket of offerings in her hand.

"Husband, everything is ready," she said, "let us go."

He looked up at her and sighed heavily. Such a healthy woman she appeared, the very type for child-bearing. Why did she not give him the son his heart yearned for? He felt resentful as if she had failed purposely. And yet he knew she suffered the shame of her barrenness no less deeply than he did. This spring day winter was in her heart as in his. No glorious season of renewal of life for them, no budding or bloom.

Both were thinking that to slip out of their house like this was a loss of face. Still they must avoid folk who would regard them with curious covert glances,—sometimes a look of wondering speculation, at others ill-hidden scorn. The merchant rose silently and walked before his wife across the courtyard and out into the street, thence by a winding path across the fields to their tombs—richer and finer than those of their farmer neighbours. A low crescent wall of brick surrounded them to keep off evil spirits, and one tall stone tablet marked their site, its base a tortoise, its crown a band of twisted dragons.

As he lighted the incense Ma muttered to himself:

"The chain of creation is bound up with the chain of worship. If the chain extends backward, so also must it reach forward. How shameful for a man to let that chain be broken!"

Afterwards he and his wife ate the offerings in silence. This lonely pair did not feel the happy picnic spirit of a "complete family." Still Shui Ching waited upon her master dutifully, filling his wine-cup when he wished to drink, seeing the choicest morsels of the little feast found their way to his bowl. She was slow in movement as she was slow in words. As she finished her own food for which she had small appetite, she observed her husband moodily. A fear she had long feared suddenly grew strong filling her heart with dread,—the fear that he was nearing the end of his patience with her barrenness.—For five years now they had been married and no son had been born to them. And well she realized that to be the mother of men was a wife's first duty. Every girl in China knew by heart the saying of the Sage:

"Is any blessing greater than to give unto your husband, a son, man's prime desire by which he and his name shall live beyond himself;—a foot for him to stand on, a hand to stop his falling, so that in his son's youth he shall be young again, and in his strength be strong?"

In fact a childless wife might be divorced since the continuity of the family must be carried on, and male descendants provided to worship the ancestors, no matter at what cost to helpless women.— Yet Shui Ching felt sure that her husband would not divorce her, even though the law allowed. He was a good man, too kind to shame her publicly by sending her back to her father's house, since in all other ways he was well content with her. But there was something else he might desire to do—and that was to take a Minor Star, a concubine.

She hated the thought not so much from jealousy—for old-fashioned Chinese women were used to sharing their menfolk with "little wives"—but because she knew the written word for discord means "two women under one roof." But if he so decided she could not dispute his decision.—No wonder his patience had grown thin after five years! One last appeal however she could make—and did— to forestall his decision. Gently and meekly she addressed him:

"Next month is the month of pilgrimage to the shrine at Miao Feng Shan where the Heavenly Lady of Birth who gives sons is worshipped. May I go as an 'incense guest,'—a pilgrim— and promise her a new satin robe if we are sent a male child?"

"Go if you wish," Ma answered kindly after a moment's thought. "It is time indeed we had a son,—but I have never had any favours from the gods whatever I promised them."

The woman's voice trembled as she answered:

"The pilgrimage will be a big expense. I shall have to have a chair for myself, and another for the amah to carry us there and back—and gifts for incense and tea, and food money.—But I have heard it said that the Goddess is very good. She has already sent a boy to one wife in this village, a woman barren for many years whose husband, grown impatient, planned to take a concubine. But she persuaded him to wait, and within the twelvemonth after she went and prayed, she had a fine male child, fair and sound.—If others can succeed then why not I?"

Ma smiled doubtfully.—"It may be so,—go if you wish, but keep the expense within bounds. I do not believe in the Heavenly Ladies, but since you do, perhaps they are worth trying."—In his heart he was more than a little distrustful of the gods and their miracles. Could they, even if they would, interfere with men's affairs? But Shui Ching did not doubt their power or mercy, and hopefully next day she began to make her plans to go on pilgrimage believing that if she prayed in faith to the Goddess of Birth her prayers would certainly be answered.

Juliet Bredon

IV. Shui Ching in Search of a Son

It was deep full springtime now, praying time in China when people go on pilgrimage. For several days pilgrims from distant places had been straggling through Hundred Altars towards the mountain shrine of Miao Feng Shan,—some on foot, some in carts, and those who could afford them in sedan chairs. But more than half of the "incense guests" were humble toilers trudging through the dust carrying their food in boxes swung from carrying poles across their shoulders.

Each passerby had his own reason for visiting the shrine of the three Heavenly ladies who dwell on the holy hill. Many were sick, they went to ask for healing, some were blind; they went to beg for sight. Fathers, mothers, brothers, sister, journeyed to pray for loved ones too ill to go themselves. A few sought pure pleasure only, the excitement of the crowd, the gay comradeship of the road, the miracle of spring after the long, hard winter and its confinement within doors. By far the greater number, however, were women asking for a son from the Goddess of Many sons, and Shui Ching was one of these.

All the past month she had been making preparations and looking forward to her pilgrimage, comforting herself that the Heavenly Lady could not fail to answer prayers sincere as hers.

And now the lucky day for starting on a journey according to the Almanac had come. At the gate of the Ma house two wooden pilgrim chairs, borrowed from the parish temple, stood ready to carry her and Amah Wu, her maid, to the shrine of the Lady of Birth. Eight sturdy local farm lads who worked as chair coolies during the brief season when the "mountain was open" squatted in the dust beside the doorway chatting and spitting as they waited for their fares.

Presently Shui Ching appeared at the gate, a little shyly because of the watching neighbours who, knowing her childless state, guessed her purpose, and stared pityingly. She stepped heavily into her chair, settled herself and smoothed her best blue silk coat down over her knees. A square, solid woman,—large hipped, full-bosomed—she seemed, even to the most casual observer, built to be

Hundred Altars

the mother of sons. But in such matters one can never tell. There was Wong the blacksmith's wife, for example, a little slip of a narrow woman who bore six sons in seven years...

The amah followed her mistress closely and stowed the bed-quilts and provisions carefully about her feet. What could not be put in the chair was tied in blue cloth bundles to the carrying poles. But the silver for their expenses and the cash for the beggars who flock to every temple festival the amah held wrapped in two separate handkerchiefs on her lap.

Now the bearers raised the chairs, settled the poles solidly on their shoulders and, with a word from the leaders to mark the step and set the pace, jogged off down the village street. The day was warm, almost summery, with bees tumbling among the lilacs in every little garden. The sky was cloudless, the air so clear that the world seemed a thousand miles wider than usual.

Beyond Hundred Altars the road wound westward across the plain towards the foot of the mountains. There was no sound except the rhythmical creak of the chairs as their wooden arms rubbed against the carrying poles, or an occasional grunt from the coolies as they shifted the weight on their shoulders, lifting the poles an inch or two to ease their bare flesh.

Every few miles they passed villages whose earth-coloured houses did not jar the pattern of the countryside. The peasants built by intuition to harmonize with Nature, earth upon earth, so that their homes seemed actually a part of the landscape. They felt instinctively—these field folk—that Nature was peaceful and harmonious and that they must fit their lives and dwellings into her design so as not to disturb the guardian spirits of the earth and air. A great quietness was the result of this understanding. It seemed incredible that a landscape so heavy with people should be so quiet.

As the path turned upwards beyond the Temple of the Great Awakening, Shui Ching had a clear view of a landmark setting the direction of the pilgrimage. It was an old pagoda caught upon the ridge of hills and stuck there somehow to the rocks— the *Liu Liang T'a*, or Tower of the Sixth Wolf. In bygone times a famous Chinese warrior, sixth son of a still more famous general surveyed from the tower the movements of his troops fighting the northern barbarians on the plains below. Then its upper stories had little stiff rooflets flying outward like the skirts of a dancer when she whirls swiftly in the dance, and from its pointed eaves hung wind bells which tinkled softly in the breeze. Now nothing remained but a shapeless pyramid of worn stone wreathed in summer morning glory vines.

Yet Shui Ching knew that ghosts of yesterday still haunted the narrow boulder-strewn pass that leads to the ancient ruin, gathering in that shadowy canyon by which messengers brought battle tidings to the Sixth Wolf Cub. The peasants believe—she had often heard them say so—that at twilight the spirit of Liu Liang on his beloved horse still toiled up the rock-strewn path to survey the countryside. And often they thought, tricked by the wind playing through an aolian harp of rocks that they heard the shouts of the Khitans as they swept across the plain,— wild nomads knowing no law but the sword, no home but the saddle, no faith but the black magic of their Shaman priests.

Beyond the wild, dark valley the stone flagged pilgrim road began. People of all kinds and conditions toiled in steady procession up the mountain. Amah Wu was near to stare her eyes out at the wives of high officials, handsomely dressed, and the sleek monks in grey gowns and the nuns with tight fitting black skull caps over their shaven heads, and the laymen loaded with chains to expiate some heavy sin, and the devout pilgrims who climbed on their knees in fulfilment of a vow.

"Look mistress," she called out in her surprise, "look at that girl yonder how she prostrates herself at every step,—standing and falling, and rising again and again!"

"Doubtless she comes in true belief," Shui Ching answered, "to ask that a sick parent may be cured!"

"And those people further on with their yellow cloth knapsacks and banners and the merry bells jingling on their food boxes, who may they be?" the amah asked curious as a child in strange surroundings, pointing to a group of country folk travelling together in a cheerful company just as Chaucer's Canterbury pilgrims did.

"Those are doubtless neighbours from the same village, members of a 'Mountain Society.' Their flags proclaim it!"—her mistress told her, "They have drawn lots for who should come and who should stay at home and these are the lucky winners banded together for the sake of companionship.—But now," she added kindly, amused by the old woman's curiosity, "don't forget you look about you to get the coppers ready for the 'want-food persons.'— Here they are!"

Amah Wu, recalled to the duty of giving alms for her mistress whom etiquette forbade to give them for herself, untied the handkerchief of copper coins, and began distributing them to the endless chain of beggars by the road-side, each one of whom had bought the right to beg along a few yards of the path, and. jealously guarded his preserve. "Give lady, give kind teacher, give—give!" whined these poor maimed or sightless wretches, as they huddled on their mats with begging bowls extended in claw-like hands. And passersby were careful to throw a cash to each and everyone. On pilgrimage charity has no merit unless all share in it alike.

Up and up the road mounted curving and twisting, ever steeper ever wilder as it climbed towards the highest pass. Rocks stuck out here and there at corners, sharp as needles some of them. Others lay tumbled about in fantastic groups. Some were like houses, some like great beasts lying down, and some formed natural, gateways crossing the path.

Here and there a halt was made to catch one's breath, sip a cup of tea, and burn an incense stick at one of the little shrines clinging to the mountain side,—shrines where the walls were newly painted and the gods freshly gilded, and many worshippers went in and out. As they rested travellers chatted to one another with easy manners and natural dignity, frank and friendly, with the perfect democracy of the road where people share and share alike. Even in those Imperial days great ladies in their silks and satins were not offended by the good-natured jostling of rough peasant women. Nor were rich merchants too proud to drink tea with chair-bearers who sat beside their masters with perfect equality yet without presumption. Better than any other people the Chinese understand the right harmony of human relations,— a hard lesson learned by generations of living crowded together.

They show it in their grading of society. Knowledge not birth or wealth is the measure of the superior man. An unlettered coolie may wholeheartedly respect a master who can read the classical books, and he, in his turn, respects the dignity of an honest labourer.

Juliet Bredon

With such solid standards, envy and class hatred were unknown. After a full three hours of climbing, Shui Ching's bearers set her chair down before a matshed eating house at the top of the pass where bowls of steaming macaroni stood ready to refresh the weary travellers. The way had been rough and very steep, the work for the coolies very severe, and here at the highest point of the journey they stopped for ten minutes' rest. Instantly they all squatted in a row and brought out their pipes and began to laugh and chat among themselves. Shui Ching visited the peddler's booths nearby where pilgrim staves with carved dragon heads were sold, and butterflies of red chenille to stick in the hair. Such souvenirs, costing but a few coppers each were popular with the pilgrims. Amah Wu stood spellbound near a group of acrobats by the roadside. To her their simple tricks were marvellous. But Shui Ching, once her purchases were made, preferred to look over the plain in quiet meditation. It spread out below her—a giant panorama of many coloured fields, warm brown where they were newly ploughed, tender green where the young crops were springing up, and bright emerald around the wells close to the bat-wing brown villages.

Presently the coolies announced: "Time to go on.—We are ready and dusk is falling."

Now one by one a long time of torches were set blazing up that long mountain road to light late comers on their way, for many of the pilgrims were too weary to make the haste required to reach their goal before darkness fell, and the temptation was strong: to linger in the valley between the hills where the roses that perfume the tea grown on the Holy Mountain pour out their incense with the evening dews.

But Shui Ching's coolies, eager to show their strength, attacked the last steep flight of steps leading to the temple with shouts of "Eiyah!—Aiyah!" and, pushing past the lingerers, rushed her chair up at a quick trot and set her down before the guest pavilion.

The place was crowded to overflowing, but Shui Ching had wisely sent ahead to reserve a room. Her generous offering also assured a small corner of the temple kitchen where Amah Wu could prepare their food. And no sooner had they eaten than the two women, tired from the long day's journey spread their wadded quilts and lay down to sleep.

"Let us rest while we may," Shui Ching said to her maid, "for at the first gong stroke after dawn we must be at the shrine! They tell me, those who should know, that the first prayers said are the ones most likely to be answered."—A moment later Shui Ching had fallen asleep, and was dreaming that she held a manchild in her arms while Amah Wu snored loudly.

Meanwhile the shrines on the mountain top was closed for the night. They stood peaceful and quiet now with the bright moonlight shining on them, like birds with their silver wings folded.

The doors were shut. The ever-ringing bells were silent. The priests slept heavily. Even the goddesses on their carved and gilded altars were wearied, like their mortal worshippers, with the day's prayings. Except for this two weeks' pilgrimage they were accustomed to a quiet life. Only an occasional worshipper came toiling up the heights to ask an occasional boon. So the unusual bustle of the crowded pilgrim season tired even these Immortals. Now night had come they welcomed the respite from petitions, and the chance to gossip together unheard by mortal ears. For Chinese goddesses are very human and like to talk things over as earthly ladies do.

The Lady of Birth, especially, was worn out for the majority of the "incense guests" that day had come to ask favours of her — favours which her kind heart hated to refuse.

"You would think that all these seeking women might realize," she protested a little sadly to her neighbour the Lady of Good Sight, "that I have only a certain number of souls to send as guests to longing mothers' hearts. Boys, too, they all want. What of the girl children waiting to be born? What shall I do with them? Indeed I would so willingly please all my believers, but sometimes the Gates of Birth are closed. Ah! I am weary of asking mothers!"

"And so am I, quite worn out also," said the Lady of Heavenly Flowers, otherwise known as the Smallpox Goddess, from the opposite altar. "'People come to me to cure the hopeless cases, at the last minute, too! And many of those who pray have not much faith in me but only wish to leave no stone unturned, no shrine untried, to cure their sick children."

"Now were you in my place," interposed the Goddess of Good Sight, "would you give instant healing to that round-faced boy with sore eyes who came this morning? I noticed he wore spectacles and of a kind that proves he has seen barbarian doctors before he came to me!"

"No, I should not!" the Smallpox Goddess answered, "He does not really believe in you or he would have come long before.

Let those foreign doctors make him well— IF they can."

"No, nor I," added the Birth Goddess nodding with fatigue. "For those who do not reverence us I have small pity. Let them learn that the old ways are best. I'll wager he's the type of boy who shows no duty to his parents and neglects the gods unless he wants a favour."

"Not unlikely.—Still it hurts me to see blinded eyes unhealed. But what do you propose to do yourself about granting the prayer of that unbelieving merchant's wife who lives in Hundred Altars ? I am told she arrived this evening to ask you for a son."

The Lady of Birth sighed heavily.—"A difficult case that, a difficult case indeed! My heart pulls me one way and my duty as a goddess pulls another. For her sake, poor woman, I would so gladly send a son. The home is most desirable,—money and comfort, and a good woman to bring up the child.... But alas, the husband scoffs at us. Grudgingly he offers me a robe in exchange for a son and not even a bead hat to match.—At many a Mah jong party he wastes fifty silver dollars on his pleasure. Yet twenty-five is all he is ready to give for a gown for me! Bah, I hate petty bargaining for heavenly favours! Were he a beggar able to give only one stick of incense but gave it in deep faith, I'd be content. But as it is I cannot send that stiff-necked man a son—not till he learns to ask not only with his lips, but with his heart."

"It is too bad," the other goddesses agreed, "that his poor wife with her simple faith should suffer for his lack of it. But in dealing with such folk as this merchant and that boy who shows his eyes to foreign doctors and the woman, too, who had her child pricked with needles in a new fashioned hospital to ward off smallpox, we goddesses must stand by one another. Supposing we do not,—why soon no one will rely on us at all, but seek favours elsewhere!"

"Yes, so it must be," said the Lady of Birth with a deep sigh, "and yet, for the sake of the woman, I wish it were not so. To make her suffer for her husband's sins seems cruel. But I must find some way to save my face and yet send comfort to her poor trusting heart.

Tomorrow I will think of a way. And now, Ladies, no more decisions for tonight. I am tired, so are you both. Let us rest."

Hardly had the cock crowed next morning before worshippers were waiting at the shrine of the goddesses for the doors to be opened by the sleepy-eyed priests. It seemed as if all the world was set on praying, and especially the world of women. Princess and peasant pressed forward together to place flaming bunches of incense in the great iron burners, to light their candles and offer their piles of spirit money and their prayers. And Shui Ching with the amah behind her, was among the first. Her face shone with hope, and in her hand she carried a red cord to tie about the neck of one of the clay babies that stood on the altar of the Goddess in the shrine of Numerous Children.

She approached the altar reverently, sure that the Lady of Birth would take pity upon her, given the full depths of her devotion. Then she knelt and prayed with her whole heart.— "Lady Goddess, grant me a son. In faith I come to you knowing that you have sent a son to many a sonless wife. If you have any love and pity, I beseech you to grant me a male child. And if you hear my prayer I will bring you a new embroidered robe as a thank-offering. The one you wear now is unworthy of your beauty!"

The painted clay face of the Lady of Birth gave no sign that she knew the woman who knelt before her was one whose belief was fervent. Her soft serenity, the passionless kindness of her expression remained unchanged. It was her duty so to appear before the high as before the low, the virtuous and the unvirtuous alike. No one must guess how and when she would answer.

But Shui Ching having knocked her head reverently three times on the kneeling mat before the Goddess went out into the rosy dawn with contentment in her heart. Her duty was done. She and Amah Wu wandered happily through the temple courtyards, kneeling here and kneeling there, giving due worship to all the other goddesses until it was time to start on the homeward journey.

When Shui Ching reached home again Ma said to her jokingly:

"Well, have you brought back a son?"

"Oh, husband," she answered gently, "I beg you do not mock the gods! I have made my prayer, and the Lady of Birth knows that my faith is real. Trust and be patient."

"Patient!—Patience I have had for five long years," he grumbled, "If twelve months hence ..."

"I know, I know," she interrupted him, "but I know too that once before her virtue drew her up to Heaven my Goddess was a mortal, and a woman. She understands an anxious wife's heart. —I am no longer troubled."

V.   To Her That Hath—

Scarcely a week after her return from the mountain pilgrimage Shui Ching had another opportunity to ask her favour of the gods, but this time of Kwanyin, the Buddhist Giver of Sons. None thought it strange that she should beg her help after having already petitioned the Taoist Lady of Birth for the same boon. The goddesses, although of different faiths, were not jealous of one another, and the broad tolerance of their creeds permitted prayers to both.

Now one could, of course, pray any day at the local temple. Its gates were always open to the people. But the best time for asking favours there was springtime—at the annual festival held in Kwanyin's honour for then she might be expected to grant special mercies.

Trembling Sea, the parish priest made ready some days ahead for the stream of worshippers whose gifts were his chief source of revenue. The jars of pickled cabbage, the baskets of dried peas that, with irreverent familiarity, he usually kept in the sanctuary were moved into his own bedroom by his little orphan acolyte. The lacquered coffins that the richer farmers stored until needed in the temple, were pushed into a corner to make room for the expected crowd. Meanwhile Elder Chi and his helpers took charge of the business arrangements for the fair held in connection with the festival. It was the custom to thus combine trading and religion. Mortals and immortals had the same tastes for feasting and the drama, and neither despised a bit of bargaining. So while Trembling Sea prepared his charms and dusted his altars, the headmen allotted stall space in the outer courtyard to petty traders, and engaged a troupe of actors to play in the open air theatre facing the main shrine, so that men and gods might make happy holiday together.

In fact the village as a whole prepared for visitors. Matshed booths sprung up overnight on the outer common beyond the temple gates. Ovens were dug deep in the ground so that it seemed as if large moles had burrowed there. The fair was to last three long exciting days, and consequently the innkeeper mended his torn paper windows, and patched the roof of his stables. The housewives also got ready to receive guests since it was usual for relations to descend upon them at fair time whether invited or not. Uncles and aunts and in-laws had the right to demand hospitality and come they would even if they guessed they were not wanted.

The day the fair opened Farmer Chi's wife was up as soon as the first grey fingers of dawn touched the paper windows. On holidays like this there was no late lying abed especially with an aunt and two cousins staying in the house. Clever Needle threw aside the wadded quilt and slipped off the k'ang, the brick platform on which the whole family slept. Night clothing being a luxury unknown to peasant women, she simply buttoned the inner day jacket which she had loosened when she lay down to sleep, tightened the girdle that held her trousers, re-tied her ankle bands and slipped on her shoes.

Before the rest of the family awoke she had done all the duties of a woman who has the care of a household on her busy hands, placed an incense stick before the Kitchen God's shrine, and lighted the fire in the primitive brick stove fed with dry grass through two small openings in the front. While the flames flared- up hotly she measured the millet or "small rice" for the breakfast gruel into a deep pan fitted with a wooden cover, and them filled the kettle with water for tea. A long wisp of hair fell over her face as she worked. She pushed it back into place. Later she would smooth and dress her hair in the other room, but never in the kitchen. To use a comb in his sight was displeasing to the Hearth God who was affronted if long black hairs sullied the food.

Presently she carried two cups of tea into the sleeping room dutifully offering the first to the Elder, and the second to her husband. The old man rose, yawning, and shook himself like a dog thus settling his garments into place, while the farmer drank his tea slowly to the last drop, and then hitching up his trousers and shuffling into his coat remarked:—"Ha, I must be off early to the fair. Provisions will have to be bought for our father's eightieth birthday feast.—That will soon be coming now."

"Pity our old cow died of sickness last spring instead of this," observed Clever Needle as she roused her two sleepy sons. "There would have been meat and to spare on hand."

"Yes, yes," the Elder agreed regretfully—for the Chis were a saving race, "When the beast died we had to buy nothing from the butcher's barrow for a month, skin, flesh, bones and blood served us for so many meals. True for some time afterwards, I had a pain in the east side of my stomach, but that was nothing compared to all the money we saved."

"Still it would never do to skimp for your eightieth feast," his son said grandly, "even if we had a dead cow at this very time. People would say we were not offering them the best, nor doing you sufficient honour. No, we must have fresh meat, first quality too, whatever it costs. I will buy a fat pig and perhaps a sheep also."

"That's a good son," chuckled the old man, "and be sure you are not cheated," he added slyly.

"Trust me, father!" Chi the Second answered with a grin. He cheated—, he the best bargainer in the village! Not likely. In fact neighbours would be sure to stand round and watch him buy because they admired his talent for getting things cheap. A cent saved, they argued, was two cents gained and one close bargain set the standard for another.

When Clever Needle had placed the bowls of steaming gruel on the kitchen table she shouted loudly: "The rice is open. Come and eat!" Her aunt and cousins came at once, bowing politely to the Elder before they sat down. Such family meals were rare. More often the men took their food out to the gate and squatted on the door step bowl in hand, chatting with the nearest neighbours while they ate. But today it was more convenient to eat together though without waiting for one another. Chi the Second, shovelled his gruel into his mouth with his chop-sticks as fast as he could work those "nimble lads," then rose, scrubbed his calloused hands and long bony face in the kitchen and wiped them dry on a square of dingy calico hanging above the stove. "Esteemed one," he said to his father, "have you eaten well?"

"I have eaten to repletion," belched the old man. "Let us be off without delay——for I, too, have business at the fair." The Elder felt he must be on hand to attend to the hundred details referred to his wise judgment.

Before her husband left Clever Needle asked him for money to buy a silk coat to wear at the birthday feast. "What?" he exclaimed, "is cotton no longer good enough for you?" but handed her three big round silver dollars nevertheless while pretending to grumble at her extravagance.—"Spend wisely, woman, and get the best!"

Juliet Bredon

Her guests went off early, too, anxious to miss none of the fun of the fair, but Clever Needle was not able to go herself till nearly noon, for she took her housework heavily, and never allowed pleasure to upset her routine. She liked to do everything with her own hands, cook and wash and sew and spin. "I'd rather be a frog in a well," she sometimes said to her husband in answer to his suggestion that she have a slave girl to help her, "than bear an interfering woman in my house. Servants waste and they break. Not one remembers to pour the tea back into the pot to be reheated. Besides they wear out clothes and brooms too—"

Old Liang Nai Nai wife of the cake-maker, known as the village shrew, never failed to comment caustically on Clever Needle's industry. "*That* woman!" she said, "I am tired of hearing her held up as the model housewife! She washes and turns her coats so often that she wears them out as quickly as I do mine by keeping them always on my back. I get all the strength out of them while she wastes it on the washing stones. But not a man can understand that! Not a man but tells his wife what a pattern of industry she is!"

Yet Clever Needle who did everything herself always had time for everything but gossip, and when she went out on holidays like this she looked neat as a new pin. Her ankle bands embroidered by her own hands were, spotless, and her shoes did not turn under at the heel as so many of the women's did. As for her two small sons they were as trim as their mother in long clean cotton coats with their hair neatly braided into five pigtails that stuck out like spiked haloes round their heads.

As the little family made its way. down the street, carters and , muleteers shouted "Lend me your light!"—meaning "give place for us to pass." The road was crowded with fairgoers and Clever Needle steered the children carefully with quick wren-like gestures. There was indeed something brown and bird-like about this serious-faced little mother, as if at any moment she might spread protecting wings over her brood.

Presently she spied Shui Ching with Amah Wu ahead. When she caught up with her neighbour she remarked amiably:"What a sight! No one would recognize Hundred Altars today! All these people from near and far... all these matsheds. The common looks like a second village!"

Hundred Altars

"So it does," responded Shui Ching. "Clutch your purse tightly who knows what bad characters may be about,—and the beggars too are especially greedy. How hideous they look! It is pitiful to think that some of them are maimed or blinded in childhood to touch the heart of charity!"

"Yes, pitiful indeed,—and see how the dogs snarl and sniff round them distrusting their staves yet hoping to steal a morsel from their bowls!"

The crowd which had brought them together now pushed the two women apart again and Shui Ching joined the stream of people going into the temple to pray. Trembling Sea saw her coming, and his eyes dulled by incense smoke, peered greedily.— The rich merchant's wife might be counted upon to make an offering large enough to provide him with his only luxury, an occasional opium pipe.—Leaving his poorer customers to light their own incense sticks, he came forward and offered to beat the fish head drum to call the attention of the goddess to her petition. "Please do so," Shui Ching said simply.

After the dazzling hot sunshine outside the semi-darkness of the great hall was cool and comforting; after the noise and bustle of the fair the figure of Kwanyin sitting there so calm upon her throne with the candles blinking before her and clouds of incense floating to the roof seemed soft serenity personified. Shui Ching received the lighted incense torch the priest put into her clasped hands, and kneeling upon the woven straw mat before the altar murmured her prayer,—"Mother of Mercies,—send sons, send sons, send sons,"—while Trembling Sea watched her bored with her bowings. The gods to him were images, nothing more. He gave them lip service in order to earn a living. He had neither knowledge nor faith and simply mumbled sutras all day long without even understanding the words he droned. Kwanyin to him was a meaningless wooden idol. But to Shui Ching she was a living goddess, not a lacquered figure with an inscrutable smile. Wise men call statues symbols. But women know better than this. They believe that faith can make the gods alive. Have they not hearts and lungs like human beings, replicas in silk of what we need to breathe and feel compassion? Have they not each one a little living creature, a tiny sparrow or snake or spider, prisoned in their breast to give the vital principle? Are they not set upon their altars with bandaged eyes and given sight in a mystic ceremony when they "come alive"? Certainly Kwanyin lives in many a loving heart. Surely she hears a mother's prayers. Only a fool and an image-maker refuses to believe in the gods,—a fool because he is a fool; an image maker because he knows of what stuff they are made.

Meanwhile Clever Needle who needed to waste neither time nor money praying for sons, flitted from stall to stall making her purchases. At the cloth peddler's she feigned interest in printed cottons. It would never do to let the shrewd merchant think she wanted silk lest he judge her a wealthy woman and put up his price. But all the time she had her eye on the very thing she needed and was mentally cutting out the piece patterned with orchids long before she even asked the cost.

"Now mother," the wily salesman tempted her pulling his stuffs between his fingers to show how strong they were, "buy this flowered cotton for your boys," or "Buy that for your good self,—or "here's a fine bit to make a holiday gown for your 'outside'!"—meaning, of course, her husband. But Clever Needle too wise to be flattered at last took up the length of silk and said:

"This and no other if the price is right!"

Thus they haggled and bargained to and fro till finally she paid a little more than she had hoped to give, and he got a little less than he had hoped to receive. Then she was impatient to be at home and get her needle into this fine new stuff, but those little sons of hers loitered and lingered at the toy stalls and the sweet sellers. Chin-tzu, the eldest, even insisted on stopping to look at baskets and spades and rope harness and plough shares, since even at his young age he had the farmer's instinct for such useful things. Finally at the stall of the spectacle mender they met the Elder.

"Daughter-in-law!" the grandfather greeted Clever Needle, "I see the old and the young buy from different merchants. I am on my way to the 'Upright Tooth Remover' yonder while my grandsons here have been buying from the candy man. One leads to the other in the end!" He chuckled at his own joke. "Meanwhile my son is bargaining for new hoe handles to fit our blades which are still strong, and new shovels to fit our sound handles. I wonder if he had yet bought the pork,—the meat seems good this year. Look yonder at those fine pigs for sale, their sides propped open with bamboo skewers so one can see what one is getting!"

After a short chat which gave the Elder a chance to make the little jokes he loved, Clever Needle went her own way, and the Elder his. Now that her purchases were made she could not resist consulting the fortune teller sitting at his table under the sign "Averter of Calamities." This lean old man with the great mole on his chin from which half a dozen hairs sprouted, never lacked customers since most people, the world over, want to know whether happiness or bitterness is in store for them.

In return for a small coin he handed Clever Needle the bamboo jar of tally sticks, and holding it firmly in both hands she shook it up and down until one stick fell out.

"Ha!" he said reaching for it with one hand while with the other he thumbed his well-worn book of omens. "Hear now what Fate has in store for you!—Aiyah!"—he looked at her sharply,— "It is *increase*!" There was a twinkle in his old eye, as he went on, "From the Almanac it would appear that the numbers six and twelve are unlucky for you, while seven and twenty eight point directly to your good fortune. The willow is a tree you must avoid. But should you meet a lame man carrying a chicken with one wing—that will mean fortune.—Yes, on the whole luck smiles upon you.—My last customer had to shake the sticks three times 1 before she received an answer even moderately propitious."

"And was that customer a woman and a merchant's wife?" Clever Needle asked with a knowing smile.

"She was," he answered slyly for he was well primed with village gossip.

And Clever Needle, as she turned away from his table, laughed a little noiseless laugh.

Suddenly strident gong strokes and the shriek of high falsetto voices warned fair goers that the drama was beginning. Visitors from a distance had already drawn up their carts in a semicircle around the stage. Their mules, unharnessed, but tied loosely to the wheels dipped contentedly into their nose-bags while their owners sat cross-legged on the carts, as proud as if they owned a private box. Clever Needle chose a corner near the theatre where for a few cash she hired a backless bench in the midst of a group of poorer neighbours who, for economy's sake squatted on the ground.

It was only a poor troupe of travelling mummers who filled the stage with a clatter of noise and a rainbow of colour. There was no scenery except for an embroidered backdrop and boys and men acted the women's parts. But the audience was not critical. Trained to use imagination, they themselves supplied the deficiencies of the players and the stage settings. A riding whip sufficed to suggest a horse to them. An oar called up the picture of a boat floating upon a summer sea. A piece of painted calico was an unscalable city wall, and in the flourish of a horse hair switch, they recognized the magical powers of an Immortal.

Of course the peasants knew the plays by heart, old favourites given year after year—and if the classical language was a bit above their heads, the costumes that marked the characters gave them the clue to scenes and motives. No one could mistake the comic man because the white patches on his nose proclaimed his role, nor the hero with his red painted mask, nor the general with the long pheasant feathers attached to his helmet, nor the bold warrior stepping high across the enemy's defences, nor the rebel villain swishing his whip to show that he was riding forth to battle.

Never tired, never impatient, the people sat entranced watching the unending plays, dazzled by the glorious world of unreality unfolded before their eyes, swept far away to realms of fancy where virtue is all gold and wickedness all black. Here was escape for them from drudgeries and disappointments. Here was drama that appealed to the dramatic instincts crushed out in everyday life by the super-imposed ideal of self-restraint and self-control. Here was the theatre as the theatre ought to be, not realistic but imaginative, a place of dreams come true, where justice triumphs over wrong-doing, and virtue is rewarded.

For three long afternoons Hundred Altars and its guests lived in this happy world of unreality. Then suddenly on the fourth day it crumbled as quickly as it had sprung into being. The matshed
booths came down like card houses, the ovens were filled in and sodded over, and the actors, now indistinguishable in their everyday clothes from ordinary folk packed their properties into a shabby cart while the "master of the chest" stood by with his list and called out,

"One trunk of cast off rags for beggar characters, the mask of a murderer in a cardboard box, a coal, black beard, a fairy crown with ten big beads missing, a scholar's hat, a sea consisting of a dozen large waves, one a little bigger than the rest and a trifle damaged!"

The fair was over till next year.

Juliet Bredon

VI. "Hot Noise" at the Chi House

On the fifteenth day of the fifth moon—about the middle of May—Elder Chi had his eightieth birthday. No one was invited to congratulate. That would have been bad taste. But not a soul in the village missed the occasion. People must go. Besides they wanted to go and wish luck to their beloved patriarch.

Everyone had seen the matshed makers putting up the awnings, gay with lucky bats and longevity characters, over the Chi courtyard, since the house was too small to receive so many guests. Everyone knew that Chi the Second, whose duty it was to do the honours for his father, had bought a whole pig and a sack of white rice at the fair. Everyone felt sure that a fine *jéh nao* was preparing—still another reason why nobody would fail to be present. An eightieth birthday feast was not an everyday occurrence.

Ma was, of course, going though he had little heart in it. Twinges of envy spoiled the party for him. The subjects of descendants and ancestors was a sore one to a childless man.

"Strange!" he said to his wife, "How easily that man Chi gains face!—how Fate seems always ready to help him! Here he has two sons already, and a father old enough to be called Ancestor under his roof. And now he has a chance to show off his filial piety to all the village by offering a fine feast!"

"Yes, but that means spending much money," Shui Ching said comfortingly.

"Bah, money is only silver after all. But face is gold!"

In speaking thus Ma voiced the sentiments of all his countrymen. From highest to lowest they valued the appearance of things more than reality. It was face that mattered.—Everyone, even the humblest beggar, must have face. There were humiliations that no man might inflict even on such as he without outraging an age-old ethical code, for to deny a man face is worse than stealing his purse or his wife, since losing face he loses dignity, credit, the respect of his fellow men,—and worse still self-respect. What looks well is well in China. What glitters must be gold, and sham honour is valued when real honour cannot be had.—Witness the District Magistrate who as a special favour was executed in his official robes.—Losing his head he nevertheless saved his face.

So the eyes of all his neighbours were focussed on Chi the Second. The amount he spent on the feast offered to his father's friends would mark the high peak of his filial piety. Chi was well aware of this. He bade his wife not stint on anything, but call the cook from the inn and young Liang, the cake-maker, to help her so that on the great day she would be free to entertain the women guests.

"The best is not too good for the eldest-born of the house of Chi," the farmer boasted proudly as he surveyed the victuals laid out in the kitchen. There was enough and to spare,—fat dishes made of pork, dumplings stuffed with cabbage and redolent with garlic, and quantities of "long-life noodles" that Clever Needle had specially prepared herself. They symbolized the great age of the Elder and were indispensable for the birthday feast.

Very early next morning Clever Needle was up and finishing her cooking, last flavourings must be added, and she had no intention of letting outside cooks meddle with her own special dishes. When she had seasoned all her last sauce Chi's wife left the kitchen to take one more look around the main room. The floor of stone slabs was spotlessly clean. The k'ang was neatly covered with a new mat, and on the long hardwood table stood the well-polished family treasure— a large foreign style clock with huge pink roses painted on its dial. It ticked loudly with a beat as cold and devoid of feeling as the utterance of a philosopher whom nothing on earth could move. Once more the careful housewife flicked her feather-duster over the carved wood shrine with Kwanyin's picture in it, and set the clumsy chairs and stools in pairs against the wall to give the maximum dignity to the room. Though heavy the furniture was not unsightly, but in a sense lovable with the quality of things made entirely by the human hand.

Presently her husband called her to bow before the Longevity Altar draped with a red-embroidered apron. As they looked up at the picture of the God of Long Life with his favourite deer beside him and a peach of immortality in his hand, they whispered a hope of longer life for their beloved Elder.

Meanwhile old Chi looked over his gifts from his neighbours with childish pleasure. Most people had sent eatables since it was not polite to go to a birthday feast without contributing a share of the food, though no one need send a third of what he could and did eat.

"A pity," said the Elder as he fingered the steamed cakes made in the shape of peaches and painted in natural colours, "that there are only three and not five generations living in this house, for were there five the Emperor himself would send a gift—perhaps a scroll of good wishes written by his own hand to hang upon our wall."

Before midday the whole family dressed in their best to receive their guests. The weather was warm now and even the Elder took off his wadded clothes and wore a thin silk coat cut neatly to fit his long thin body. A folded fan, thrust in his collar at the back of his neck, stuck out like a stiletto behind his right ear. Chi the Second, newly shaved and his thick queue well-oiled, wore a new blue cotton robe, and his two small sons were miniature replicas of their father, in their long gowns like grown up men and round black silk caps. As for Clever Needle, she had made up the silk bought at the fair into a short jacket and trousers. Her silver bangles jingled as she moved, and the chips of jade in her earrings showed leaf green in the sunlight.

The neighbours arrived by twos and threes. The Changs were early. They could always be depended upon to come first and stay last since their appetites had never yet been fully satisfied and they feared to miss so much as a sun-flower seed to crack between their eager teeth. Old Liang the cake-maker, who had heard from his son that much good food might be expected, was on time too, and, for once, his shrewish wife was smiling. Wong the blacksmith and Chien with their families arrived together with Bent Neck, Ma's trusted man-of-all-work, who when he walked down the village street with a carrying pole over his shoulders bent his head so far forward that he looked like a headless man. Late comers, like Chin the innkeeper and his wife and their four girl children who ate so voraciously that their contribution counted as nothing against their appetites, trooped in with other neighbours—farmers smelling of earth and large and roomy women. They overwhelmed the house and the mat-covered courtyard where the tables hired for the feast were spread. Their talk was loud, a coarse flood of earthy words and outbursts of broad humour. Their laughter shook the place. They seemed to have risen bodily out of the soil, the soil that clung to their ears and their dark hair. It lay black and rich under their nails. They smelt of it and of sweat.

Last of all came Ma and Shui Ching with more worldly manners and richer clothes than the farmers, and bringing with them a finer present than the others could afford.

All the guests went first to the inner room and congratulated Elder Chi, respectfully knocking their heads three times on the ground before him. But Chi the Second acted as proxy, for his father in returning the congratulations. It would have been too tiring for the old man to make so many bows himself.

Afterwards folk crowded into the courtyard to begin the serious business of eating—the main pleasure of all Chinese gatherings? When the neighbours came to take their places at table the usual polite confusion reigned. None could admit his right to the seat of honour though Chi begged all to seat themselves "in comfort and not to stand on ceremony." But still they hesitated,—it was good manners. Finally taking Ma by the sleeve Chi pushed him into the place of honour beside the Elder at the "high table" in the centre of the courtyard. Then, as host, Chi went the round of all the other tables, holding a wine cup in his hand and saying to the senior man at each:

"I pray you to be seated, neighbour!" lifting his cup to drink with him.

And the honoured guest replied: "I take a great liberty in sitting in the best place!" meaning that he tacitly assumed the task of seating the other guests of his table.

When the hot dishes of food began to appear,—in pairs alternately sweet and sour,—Chi rose again from his place and with his own chop-sticks lifted a dainty morsel of pork and put it in the saucer set before the principal guest at each table. This was the signal for eating to commence, and everybody dipped his own chop-sticks into the well-filled bowls with gusto, expressing his pleasure as he ate with loud sucking noises. More and more dishes followed one another in slow oriental succession.

"Eat plenty, eat plenty!" urged the host. But most of the guests needed no urging. Most of them, also, drank no less deeply than they ate. In fact there was only one, the priest, Trembling Sea, who felt called upon to refrain from wine:

"Though I eat well my wine capacity is poor," he excused himself turning to Ma, "so I appoint you my substitute to drink for me!"—following the custom which permits this. Religious scruples had nothing to do with his abstemiousness.

"Very well!" shouted Ma with a hearty guffaw, fully aware of the humour of the priest's words, "But when I've had enough I too shall get a substitute and he may take one also!"

Trembling Sea. chuckled: "You will be emptying your cups and drinking healths at the women's table with all this wine flowing!" This was a broad joke since men and women did not mix at parties, and amid general laughter all set to again with added appetite.

At the arrival of the sixth of the eight delicacies Wu the coffin-maker, now thoroughly warmed with food and wine, called out; loudly above the din to old Chi:

"Congratulations elder brother! You have lived long enough to understand harmony and to have earned idleness! At your time of life a fan and umbrella are the only things with which you need burden yourself!"

It had taken him some time to think up this fine speech and he got it out proudly. "Good!—good!" shouted the other guests applauding him with thumbs turned up as they would praise an actor at a play. Others now complimented the farmer, saying: "How lucky you are to have your father still with you, and how filial to serve him so generously!"—"This is a most expensive feast,—The food must have cost a great deal I am only sorry I can eat no more for already I am replete!" Loud hiccoughs punctuated these appreciative phrases.

Not until late afternoon was the white rice served—the customary sign that a feast was over. By this time the guests had, for once,, eaten so much that they could scarcely touch their bowls. Still all were constant to the wine cup. But much as they drank Chi urged them to drink more—

"Drink friends," he said, "we need not think of moderation today. Put yourselves entirely at ease and enjoy your wine."

Some men. overheated with food and drink now threw off their outer garments and sat bare to the waist. Others set their feet more squarely on the floor, knees well apart, and tucked the skirts of their long gowns about their waists. Now the time had come when the finger-game might be indulged in.—A merry game it was where every player must guess the number of fingers his adversary would show suddenly as he opened his fists. Whoever lost must drink—"Kanpei!" bottoms up. Whoever remained sober longest won the game.

Ma was an expert at "guessing the fist." He had much practice on his frequent jaunts to Peking where he combined business and pleasure. Five times running he won by a canny play.

"I show the Eight Immortals!" he shouted holding up eight fat fingers, and old Chi bowed in acknowledgment of this subtle way of wishing him long life.

The women seated at special tables in the inner courtyard were less boisterous, but they too chattered and giggled with delight as each new dainty was served. What a pleasure to eat food they had not themselves prepared, to have meat and white rice without counting the cost instead of the eternal bean jelly and millet and vegetables!

"A good cook you are indeed, Clever Needle!" they complimented her. "Nobody's sesamon sauce is as tasty as yours!"

And she was flattered and proud and urged them to eat more and more, till at last even Chang Nai Nai hiccupped happily, "I am fit for bursting, fit for bursting!" That was a rare admission. Seldom in her fife had Mother Chang said she had eaten all the food she craved.

At dusk, just as it was time to leave, hot towels were handed round to wipe sticky hands and damp faces. Then each guest rose heavily to make polite farewells to their hosts, and once again congratulated them on the success, and, above all, on the great cost of the feast. To their remarks Chi answered according to custom:

"You are all too polite!—I have treated you rudely.—I have not given you enough."

Though Elder Chi was not expected to see off any of the neighbours, Chi the Second must accompany them all to the outer street gate, where he said politely:

"Seeing you must go, and neither wind nor rain has come to force you to remain with us longer, take care, walk slowly. Mind your step,—and come again!"

So well fed and wined, the villagers returned home to talk over the feast and go to bed, somewhat in drink and heavy with so much eating. By the time all were gone it was black dark. Grandfather Chi was nodding with sleep, but the farmer and his wife sat together in the main room talking over the party.

"Aiyah!" sighed Chi proudly, "there was a good crowd to congratulate!"

"Well, the neighbours don't get an eightieth birthday feast every day," she said drily.

"And the presents too were good!" said the farmer.

"But how much did we spend for it all?" Clever Needle asked anxiously.

"Nearly fifty silver dollars—but then there were the presents. Neighbour Chien, who kept the lists told me he wrote down eight dollars in cash, and twenty eight boxes of noodles, and twenty plates of peach bread, and eight packages of tea leaves, four baskets of fruit, and Ma gave twenty bottles of wine!—a good gift that saved us a lot and didn't cost him too much!"

"The seasonings were very expensive," Clever Needle said with a yawn,—"I had to spend three and a half silver dollars for them, I couldn't get enough for less. Aiyah, how they cost! Sweet oil,—more than a dollar, and six cents for pepper alone, besides salt, yellow bean sauce and vinegar!"

Still, as Chi the Second insisted, the feast was not too dear. It had to be given and it must be given lavishly to make a proper impression—for face-sake. "The guests certainly had well-filled bellies!" he said, "and the Elder was proud and happy. Let us hope the Longevity God was also satisfied. We offered him the best sandalwood incense and food fit for an Immortal.—Surely he was pleased!"

VII. Ma Makes a Decision

Once more winter had stripped the trees bare and April sunshine clothed them with green. Another year's larks, another season's pink foam of blossoms had come since Shui Ching's pilgrimage and her visit to Kwanyin. Yet neither the Lady of Birth nor the Lady of Mercy had sent a son to the Ma household. So once again the merchant and his wife were obliged to go alone to worship at their graves. For again it was the Spring Feast of Ancestors and the Emperor's Edict commanded the people to put off their wadded winter clothes and fulfill the duties proper to the season of re-birth.

On this holiday morning Ma spent the time before going out to make his offerings by looking over his property, thinking glumly to himself that the neighbours must be gossiping about his childlessness even more than usual, and making coarse jokes about his wife's failure with the goddesses. Year by year such contemptuous talk grew harder to bear and made him more irritable. Now he spoke sharply to his garden coolie Jung-erh— Woolly One—chiding him for wasting the water that he drew from the well in a reed bucket. Jung-erh was a stalwart lad with a shining set of teeth. He had charge of the vegetable garden. Now he had stripped off his jacket and worked bare to the waist showing the ripple of his well-developed muscles. Except when Ma was in a bad humour he was well-pleased with the lad who had a knack for growing things. Already the garden beds protected by reed screens from the force of the northern winds were brilliant green. It was great luck to get a gardener like Jung-erh, —young, strong, devoted to his task, an orphan too with no family to teach him a better paying trade. And Jung-erh who for years had made a meagre living by doing odd jobs around the village was pleased to work for Ma. His labourers were fairly treated. They received small wages, true enough, but everything was "found," and they were decently housed. The master even provided feasts for them at the great festivals of the year.—So when Ma yelled at the coolie:

"Son of a turtle, why do you waste water by pouring it so fast: into the irrigation trough and letting it overflow into channels where it is not needed?"—Jung-erh accepted the insulting epithet and the unjust reproof good-humouredly. He knew Ma was irritated—and why.

Ma was subject of late to sudden angers which arose from his bitter thoughts and made him hard on his workmen and disagreeable to Shui Ching. On a day like this which marked the disappointment of his childlessness most heavily, he was more than ever out of humour with her.

When he had finished bullying Jung-erh he called out to her to bring his tea and water-pipe into the courtyard. She came obediently, handed him his filled cup, lighted his pipe with a coarse spill of brown paper, and stood beside him waiting for what he might be pleased to say to her.

"Wife,"—he spoke irritably— "It is now many moons since you prayed at the temples and there is no hope of a son. (The tone of his voice implied "I told you so!") If you are truly barren... he paused significantly,—surely she could not fail to understand. It is never the oriental way to blurt out the blunt truth bluntly.

At first she did not grasp his meaning for she answered brokenly:

"I know very well that you despise me, husband, and I wish I had borne you sons. Unlucky was the day I left my father's house!"

"Unlucky indeed!" he exclaimed sourly, angry that he must make his words still plainer. "But since you cannot bear me a son, and a son I must have to continue our line—what is to be done?"

Though she was a woman of slow perception she knew what he meant—had long seen what was coming,—the shadow on the wall—and had deliberately turned her eyes away. But the shock now that at last she was face to face with the problem of every childless Chinese wife was no less great because she had so long expected it.

"What if we should die," her husband went on, "who is to offer sacrifice to my tablet or to yours? Who will tend our graves? Answer me wife!" he asked impatiently.

Shui Ching, always easily alarmed by the need for sudden decision could not think what to say quickly. Fear drove her to temporize, as women will.

"Ah," she cried out bitterly, "I am still a young woman! Could we not wait a year or two longer before... before..." That was all she said to him. The rest of her words remained hidden deep within her.

Ma shook his head silently, angry that she should try to turn him from his purpose. Man-like, he resented that she did not make it easy for him to have his way. She knew as well as he that the time had come when he must take a second wife, a Minor Star, to bear him sons and that without his first wife's consent and her outward approval at least, he could not do so decently.—"If your wife is against it do not take a concubine," runs the proverb. She MUST consent. Whoever heard of a wife setting herself up in obstinacy against her husband?

He turned angrily and stared full at her. Never in the six years she had been about his house had he known Shui Ching to look like that, so set and hopeless,—though in her words she tried to cling to hope. Suddenly she appeared twice her age, ugly and plain, her square brown face hardened, to a wooden mask, her large mouth pale, her wide eyes dull. That she suffered deeply, he could see, but her unhappiness left him unmoved.

Surely she, a woman—an inferior being—could stand suffering better than he!

"You know what you should do," he said sternly, "You have guessed my will.—Obedience is a wifely virtue."

His words recalled her sharply to her duty. How had she dared to cross the master even in thought, forgetting her mother's teaching: "A wife must be silent when a husband speaks, must smile upon him if he censures her, must coax him when he is ill-tempered, must thank him when he chastises her, must love him when he scorns and hates her."

The shrill voices of children going along the village street with their grave offerings echoed through the courtyard. Shui Ching's whole body trembled. Her teeth chattered as with cold. But she made the sacrifice her master asked of her without complaint.

"Husband," she said humbly, "I see your desire plainly at last. A Minor Star, a little wife, must be brought into our home. Since it is your wish what can I be but willing?"

"Rightly spoken woman," Ma answered with a deep sigh of relief now that the tension was broken and the matter settled once for all. "But do not be distressed.—Surely you cannot feel hurt at my doing what I cannot help doing?—Nor do I reproach you for what you cannot do!"—Having got his way he smiled arid spoke agreeable words: "And I shall give you the right of the respected first wife," he went on, "to choose my Minor Star. Choose someone with whom you are in agreement and whose temper is good. For my part, I ask only that she bears sons."

"But what if the new one is forever in and out of my kitchen all day long," said Shui Ching dubiously, "forever borrowing something, or tattling to the servants?—Such women are like that! Aiyah,—henceforth our house will be a house of intrigue!"

"You are the mistress of my home," Ma replied pompously. "It is for you to control the little wife and keep the peace. But I shall build her quarters of her own and she can remain within her courtyards. Though you belong to the same family you shall eat from separate stoves so there will be no excuse for quarrels between you."

Shui Ching fell silent. She was thinking whom she should ask to join their household. In fairness it must be someone agreeable to her husband and yet obedient to her. There was a cousin's daughter who might be willing to come, and it would be more pleasant to have a woman of her own family than a stranger.

The girl was healthy, true,—but pockmarked. "Pretty women," Shui Ching thought bitterly, "do not bear sons more frequently than plain ones, and after all she is neither bald nor a half wit."

—But no, she would not ask this girl. The master might be displeased at the suggestion.

Ma was thinking the same thoughts for he interrupted her by asking a little shamefacedly: "Who could you find to fill the place?" and relief showed in his face as she answered thoughtfully.

"There is no family in this village who will give their girl as little wife.—I could go to Pei Yang Ho—the nearest market town—and get someone there. Perhaps a healthy slave girl might be bought for a reasonable price."

"Perhaps," he agreed.

"If only we may still have peace in this house," Shui Ching repeated wearily. "So often the more women in a home, the more trouble there is. I can remember what my mother told me about my father's friend, the District Magistrate, whose concubines were always quarrelling.—His 'nine black pearls' he called them.—Many a time my father found the great man seated at his table quite unable to attend to business, and when my father inquired: 'Great lord, what troubles you?' he answered sadly, 'My nine black pearls are fighting one another behind the Orchid Door!—Who can make them live at peace with one another?'"

"Don't be a fool!" snapped Ma irritably, "I propose to take one little wife, not nine!—And in this house it will be for you to keep the peace!"

Shui Ching might well comfort herself with the thought that though Ma was determined to have his way he was not unreasonable. Many a rich merchant,—indeed almost every rich city merchant—brought expensive singing girls into their homes,— greedy, rapacious creatures forever asking for jewels and satin robes. Wives were neglected while these arrogant maidens catered to the master's pleasures. But Ma, at least, was taking a woman into his house for no reason of ugly lust. The neighbours might criticize him because two wives were unusual in the country, but Ma must have sons. They knew that. As for Shui Ching herself she would still command their respect since she was to choose the Minor Star. Yet all this knowledge did not make her happier, nor take the bitter sting from the fact of another woman coming to her house. Alone in her own room she sat down on the k'ang and bowed her head in her hands.

Thus her old amah, who had come, with her from her father's house when she married, found her weeping bitterly:

"Daughter of my honourable old mistress—what troubles you!" she inquired with deep concern.—Long years of faithful service entitled her to ask questions when it pleased her, and to give advice too.

"The .master," sobbed Shui Ching, "needs a Minor Star to bear him sons. He bids me bring one here, and soon."

"Aiyah!" the old woman exclaimed, trembling with excitement from head to foot. She looked grotesquely ugly with her queer pear shaped face and resentment glittering in her usually dead eyes. "Why, oh, why, did the Goddess of Birth fail to answer our prayers! Where shall we find room in this house for little wife?"

"There will be a new building, the master says," Shui Ching answered, "for he knows that there must be a place where the new one can be separate, and a kitchen for her own use. It is but right!"

"Money wasted!" the amah sniffed, "If the woman bears no sons she is useless, and if she has a male child she will rule us all—The master is mad."

"No, no!" Her mistress answered gently taking her husband's defence, "the master is right and he knows best. He is wise too and his silver is not foolishly spent.—Why should you grumble if I do not?" But Amah Wu was deeply hurt for her lady's sake, and could find no better way to show her affection and sympathy than by complaining.

"I have enough to do to wait upon you, my mistress," she said crossly, "How shall I serve a strange woman?"

"Because boys there must be in this house and if I can not give them to the master someone else must. You know that as well as I!"

"I know, I know mistress," the amah was almost in tears,

"When you were a tiny child I nursed you, and I have waited long and patiently to receive your manchild in my arms."

"It seems that such a joy is denied us," Shui Ching said resignedly, "but rest your heart. Surely the master who is good and kind will get another maid to wait upon the new woman if I ask this favour of him."

And so. for an hour and more the two women talked together, comforting each other more like friends than mistress and servant. Three days later Shui Ching, astride her husband's black riding mule led by a small boy and accompanied by Amah Wu on a donkey, went to Pei Yang Ho where she hoped to buy the girl she wanted. But she did not find a girl to suit her immediately. One who looked likely had narrow eyes set close together, as Amah Wu was quick to observe. "Don't take her, mistress,— eyes like that are a sign of bad temper," she whispered. A second girl Shui Ching rejected because she appeared delicate, but finally she found a house where the farmer's wife had two slave girls to offer. The eldest was too old for Shui Ching's purpose. But the second seemed suitable, small-boned but wiry and judging from her smile, sweet-natured.

There was much talk between the two women concerning this maid. And more between her owner and his wife. But finally the farmer agreed to sell her for twelve pieces of silver, a fair price.—He was a good man pleased to get a good home and future for the girl.— "You may have her," he said, "she is too pretty to be a slave anyway, and for half what you have paid I can get an ugly one who will do my work as well."

As for the girl herself when Shui Ching promised her two gold-washed rings, a pair of earrings, and a new gown, she was happy to enter the merchant's home.

So it was agreed that on the first propitious day after the work of the early harvest was over, the slave, Lilac Blossom, should come to Hundred Altars and bring with her a little serving maid. This pleased Amah Wu greatly. It would have a loss of face for her to wait upon the Minor Star.

"Your business was not so easy to arrange," Shui Ching told her husband on her return. "But now a choice is made, and the girl will come as soon as she can be spared from field work."

Ma would have liked to ask her how the maid was, tall or short, fat or lean, ugly or pretty, but pride and decency forbade him. Shui Ching for her part having picked out one she knew would please him felt virtuously righteous.—"As you desired, so I have done," she ended a little unctuously.

"Good!" Ma exclaimed, hoping for the best. No matter how much a man desires sons it is pleasant that the girl who bears them be not unpleasing, and a woman does not always judge her sex quite as a man does.

Juliet Bredon

VIII. The Arrival of the Little Wife

Ma was a man of prompt action. He had what his countrymen so often lack—a sense of the value of time, and when his mind was made up he neither hesitated nor havered. The new house for the new wife must be begun at once even if she was not expected before midsummer. So he consulted the diviner promptly about a lucky site for it. Though he had little faith in the gods,—and less than ever since Shui Ching's failure with them—the merchant did respect the "wind and water influences" and would not risk offending the Earth Spirits.

When the soothsayer decided that a piece of Ma's precious kitchen garden must be used for the new buildings Shui Ching remarked tartly, "Imagine wasting valuable food land to house a Minor Star!" Yet the diviner's decrees were beyond dispute, and his recommendations must be followed without question.

Besides Ma was not a man to be influenced by women's words, and he went on calmly with his plans.

First he visited the Earth God's shrine, burned incense, and announced his purpose. It was a duty he could not well neglect since the whole of the vast land of China is in charge of local Earth Gods, and every man is expected to report—each to his own god—what happens in his family. If he marries a wife he must tell the guardians of the village, and if a son is born to him, or if a parent dies, he must do the same. There is no question of religious faith involved. The Earth God typifies a kind of spiritual constable whose right it is to know what goes on in his own bailiwick.

This done, Ma sought out the village carpenter—an eccentric who had never married though he could well afford to take a woman. In a world where eccentrics were rare and uniformity the rule for all good people, men looked a little askance at him. They often joked at his expense and because of his large head and outstanding ears he was nicknamed "The Elephant." It was generally admitted however, that, despite his peculiarities, he knew his business thoroughly, and could, if workmen failed, dig a well or put up a building with his own two hands.

An hour's talk between Ma and "The Elephant" sufficed to settle the details of the new house which must be built in such a way that its main gate faced south since "only the Dead may safely turn their faces to the North." Each beam, each door, each window had its price, and "The Elephant" was known as a hard bargainer though he met his match in the merchant.

"Agreed," he said at last with deep respect for a customer who could so shrewdly, yet not without many a cheerful joke, bargain him down.

So on the first lucky day after this interview work was begun and three weeks later it was ended for the house needed no deep foundations and was quickly built. Ma provided the usual feast to Lu Pan, God of Carpenters with special green candles for his altar table,—green because red candles might suggest fire,—and "prosperity dumplings" and, as a great delicacy, the delicious "Before the Rain" tea. And when together they had thanked the Craft God for his help, the workmen went away content, and Ma looked over the new place with pleasure muttering to himself:

"A good house, a sound house—a fitting birthplace for my son-to-be!"

Then he had a white cock killed and its blood sprinkled in every room, and incense lit lest the spirits who dwell in the darkness take up their abode in the empty rooms. The furniture he had ordered was afterwards moved in with due regard to the points of the compass—good plain chairs and tables, besides few ornaments pleasant to look at and yet not costly.

Then Ma sent a messenger to tell the girl's master all was ready for her, and after the first harvest he let her go as agreed.

There was no great ceremony made for a Minor Star's coming to a new home. She was only a bought woman, a little wife, after all—not a first wife entitled to be carried to her husband's home in the bride's red chair. The slave girl and her little maid left Pei Yang Ho astride two small grey donkeys one late afternoon for it was already full summer and too hot to travel earlier in the day. The kao liang—great millet—soaked in sunshine, was tall now—higher than a man's head. Melon peddlers carried trays of ripe red fruit from which they drowsily whisked the flies now and then. Cicadas shrilled late into the warm evening. The mountains cut into the metallic sky, their crests like points of thin sharp steel.

When mistress and maid reached Hundred Altars passing villagers made ribald jokes at their expense. "Who is this slave woman coming to a house where there is already a wife?" they asked—though they knew well enough.—A few small boys even followed the women right up to Ma's gate, grinning from ear to ear and giggling , which annoyed the merchant who could hear them plainly from his upstairs study where he sat waiting. It was an uncomfortable moment for the girl and some half grown louts who loitered in the street, burst into loud guffaws to see her blush. How happy she was when once she had passed the gate and heard it shut behind her, screening her from their impertinent eyes!

In the first courtyard she got stiffly off her donkey and let the little maid lead her towards the inner quarters, where according to custom, Shui Ching was waiting to receive her. Before the lady of the house Lilac Blossom bowed low, and offered her greeting in a soft voice with modest downcast eyes:

"Here I am, house-mother, and ready to serve you loyally,"

Shui Ching acknowledged her greeting and then led her to her apartments. The maid followed behind with bulging eyes. She had never seen such a grand place in all her life before, this little girl, younger even than her mistress,—an elfin creature in her faded blue trousers and jacket faded almost white because they had gone so often to the washing pool.

"Here is your house," said Shui Ching, "the master awaits you. Obey him in all things, bear him many sons, and see you keep the peace in this household."

Again the Minor Star bowed low before the first wife, and Shui Ching turning to the maid bade her inform the master that the "new one" had arrived. When Ma came into the room his wife said simply: "This is the new slave. Take her to bear you sons. I trust she will start no quarrelling under our roof."

"Fear not wife," Ma answered quickly, "this girl shall always treat you with respect. Am I not master in my own house and you the first wife here?"

A sad little smile softened Shui Ching's stiff dignity. It seemed to hint that women knew one another best. But she only said:

"Her old mistress tells me she is in good health, and of a quiet temper. All that I ask is that she makes no mischief and gives you children."

Listening meekly to the first wife's words the Minor Star bowed to the Master and murmured the conventional expression of respect. "I will obey."

Ma who had now recovered from his embarrassment looked closely at Lilac Blossom. With pleased surprise he saw that she was not at all the usual heavy peasant type but small and slenderly built, a graceful little thing no older than sixteen, with drooping shoulders and soft well-shaped hands. Her face was narrow and pointed like a squirrel's. Her skin had the milky texture of white lilacs. Her eyes were the colour of sunlight on brown leaves. Indeed her whole appearance was not at all that of the average slave girl. Her little feet, too, astonished Ma. "How can it be?" he questioned her kindly, "that you, a slave, have feet bound small like this?"

"My mother bound them," the girl answered with downcast eyes. "Even though I was sold so young this service she did for me."

But when he inquired further about her parents and her home she would say no more, but stood silent hanging her head while tears rolled softly down her cheeks. Later the merchant and his wife learned that she came of decent folk who had too many mouths to feed, and when, one famine winter, the buyers of girls knocked on their door and offered money that would purchase grain to save the lives of many for the price of one, they sold their eldest girl to feed their male children.

Seeing her face wet as with bitter rain, Ma soothed the little slave and bade her be happy in her new home. Her trembling lips seemed to say so much without forming words that he looked at her with new interest. She seemed so helpless—like a dainty flower that Fate had stamped upon too heavily. But he noted that she had thrust fragrant jasmine blossoms with a certain grace into the shining knot of hair coiled smoothly on her sleek head, and that her gown of flowered cotton was carefully made, and her high collar neatly buttoned at the throat despite the heat.

"If a man must take a second wife to bear him sons," he thought contentedly, "he might do worse than this,—much worse." But he neither felt nor pretended any romantic passion for Lilac Blossom. In fact there was something dignified and decorous, almost fatherly in his attitude towards her which did not escape Shui Ching's notice. Presently, after a long silence when all three actors in this little domestic scene judged one another while pretending each to ignore the others' presence, Shui Ching said:

"Let us bid the maid serve the Welcoming Feast," and turning to the open doorway called loudly in the direction of the kitchen — "Come!"—When the little maid appeared she told her to bring the dishes that had been prepared, and the two pots of fragrant wine. But Ma was the only one who relished the food when it was served. Timid and shy the Minor Star ate but little, and Shui Ching felt no appetite at all. She took only a morsel from one bowl and a spoonful from the next. Somehow she found it difficult to swallow and was thankful when the meal ended and she might go back to her own rooms, leaving Ma and the girl together.

There Shui Ching sat alone worrying over many things. Suppose the new one lacked discretion—suppose she was given to retailing the small tales that disturb the harmony of a household — Suppose... Even Amah Wu did not come in to comfort her mistress as usual for she was busy chatting with the new maid about the new woman. For she too was eager to hear what the Minor Star was like in taste and temper. So much depended in the women's quarters on whether a newcomer was lao shih— easy to live with—or, as some girls were, possessed of the Devil of Ill Temper or the Imp of Interference.

Down the street at the inn there was gossiping going on also. Sentiment was against the taking of a Minor Star. City men did such things, but not decent hard working country folk.

"The new one is young and pretty too they tell me," said the coffin-maker with a leer. "If that be true I'll wager her eyes will soon be cast upon some likely looking youth—and we shall see her slipping out of her courtyard at dawn when the master, exhausted, sleeps."

"Yes, Ma will probably find his bed cold one morning if he wakes early enough!" put in old Six Hairs of the Chiao family so nicknamed because his thin hair grew in patches.

"Serve him right too!" said the blacksmith, "Why take a Minor Star into his household?—It is not our custom to have idle women hanging round a man's home. One woman in a house should not only be able to bear children, but work, in the fields too when we need help."

"But it is not purely for. his pleasure, neighbour, that he bought her. It is because Ma wants sons!" put in another man.

"Bah!—that's only an excuse, I believe!" snorted the blacksmith. "It would be better to take his chance with his wife as we all do!—and who knows but he himself can sow no .seed!"

Old Chi overhearing the last remark joined the gossipers and put in his word.

"No," he said tolerantly, "it is surely proper for him to take a second wife. I always think a man must try two women before we have the right to say the fault is his."

"All very well for you, elder brother," the blacksmith retorted, "to judge so kindly with two sons living and one already with two fine lads."

"That's so, that's so," put in the cake-maker, "but mark my words, Ma is preparing trouble for himself.—One woman in a house is quite enough for any man!"

His neighbours interrupted him with loud laughter. Who did not know how Liang's old vixen of a wife kept him in order ?— A second wife of the same temper and he would not be permitted to draw a breath.

Juliet Bredon

IX. The Red Thread of Tragedy

A Minor Star was rare enough in Hundred Altars. No wonder her arrival caused gossip in plenty. Indeed the talk did not die down until several months later a newer sensation rocked the village. Then Fate wove the red thread of tragedy into the serene blue-grey pattern of everyday life, and once more rudely broke the rhythm of its peaceful monotony.

As usual a trifle caused the sudden, social typhoon—only a passing peddler who tempted the women with his packs of "Flower Cards." First one bought, and then another for gambling was their national vice permitted at the New Year, but wisely frowned upon when there was work to do. But now the matrons of Hundred Altars took to playing cards regularly each morning while their menfolk were out in the fields ploughing the lately harvested land, and sowing the winter wheat.

One day two of the women sat on for an hour or more after the game, talking over their luck in the stuffy, untidy little guest room of the coffin-maker's house. It was a golden autumn day. Still the paper windows were rolled down and the door tight shut, for the old crones were much too interested in their gossiping to care whether there was fresh air to breathe. Nor did they notice that the floor was littered with cracked melon seeds.

Wu Nai Nai, the coffin-maker's wife, a fat, placid woman was a shiftless housekeeper at the best of times. The chickens might roost under the table for all she cared, and the pig eat his dinner from a broken bowl in the corner. But lately, since she had taken to gambling, despite her hard working husband's disapproval, she was more slipshod than ever. Now the noon millet gruel was boiled too hard or too soft, and the children's clothes left un-mended. Nor would she even trouble to show her fifteen year old daughter-in-law how to keep things in order.

"What do I care?" she answered her husband's grumblings. "If luck holds as it has today we shall be able to buy new clothes and get a slave girl who has been taught to do housework!"

"When a man gambles," he replied angrily, "it is bad enough, but it is worse for a woman who knows no moderation. Those who persist in playing always end by selling their sandals."

But Wu Nai Nai continued a lucky gambler. Every day she won a roll of coppers or even a silver piece to spend on the gewgaws her greedy soul craved. Besides she loved the excitement of the game for its own sake, and the praise of the other women when she made a clever play.

Liang Nai Nai, the cake-maker's wife enjoyed the game no less than Mother Wu, and was usually a lucky gambler also. But this morning she had lost heavily to her neighbour, as village standards go, and was commenting acidly on the play, so that it seemed as if her husband's words were coming true;—that all this gambling among the women-folk would lead to quarrels, and end by making enemies of men who had been good friends and neighbours all their days. Liang Nai Nai was well known for a difficult woman who found trouble wherever she looked,— a woman sharp of nature and sharp of feature too, thin as a dried stick, and with hands like claws that could pinch with unexpected strength.

"A lucky woman you were today, Wu Nai Nai," she said bitterly. "One might have thought that you secretly put paste upon your fingers so well the cards stuck to them!"

Wu Nai Nai flushed at the suggestion of trickery, feeling her temper rise hotly at being blamed for sheer good fortune. But she swallowed the angry words that rose to her lips, too wise to risk a quarrel with her neighbour. Liang Nai Nai's tongue was like a scorpion's tail. When she spoke no one dared answer her back, though folk laughed when her malicious wit bit into others.

Least of all did her husband dare cross her. He was a timid little man and long years of being henpecked by his "inside person" had made him even more timid than he was by nature. Yet he often thought to himself that except for the old woman's cross-grained disposition his home would be a happy one. He earned a good income as the village cake-maker doing a brisk trade in flour dumplings at the New Year,—cakes painted with the Moon Rabbit at the Autumn Festival, and three-cornered pasties wrapped in leaves at the Mid-summer Dragon Feast. Yes, his household was well-off as village households went, with money to spare for meat and white rice a dozen times a year. But alas, he could no more control his wife than a man can control a volcano in eruption— "Hot as a tiger's temper your mother's temper is," he would say helplessly to his son. "Truly she fears neither men nor demons. And now that she plays at Flower Cards..."

Being a "peace at any price" man he did not try to manage the unmanageable but only worked longer hours, partly against the day when her luck should turn sour, and partly for the sake of the calm which he found in his shop. And his son, a gentle soul like his father with the same quiet habits and the same dislike of tumults was no less eager to be early in the cake-shop and to leave it late.

But for the son's wife, Ling-erh, there was no such refuge from her mother-in-law's furies. Her life was one long torment, for the old woman complained at her the livelong day. Over the littlest things she scolded the girl unmercifully. Yet Ling-erh was the best and mildest daughter-in-law a woman ever had, working hard always, and asking nothing for herself. Nevertheless, early and late the old termagant shrieked at her:

"Useless slut,—get out of my house! You are no good to me but only a clumsy creature who can do nothing right! Get out— get out!"

Alas, the poor girl had no place to go, and well she knew it. No neighbour would dare to take her in, and her father's door was closed to her now that she had joined a new family to whom she "belonged" body and soul so long as she lived. No, from her mother-in-law there was no escape.

When Liang Nai Nai began to criticize Mother Wu's good luck, the latter knew they were on the edge of a quarrel whose ending might be bitter, and deftly turned the talk to the subject of daughters-in-law. Never did two old women get together at the stone washing trough, at the temple fair or indeed anywhere out of doors or under a roof, but this subject was eagerly discussed. And none enjoyed reviling her son's wife more than Liang Nai Nai.

"Don't mention Ling-erh!" she spluttered quite willing to turn her fury on to this helpless victim. "She is a useless gad-about, or would be if I did not bolt the gate on her!"—Her words were interrupted by the coffin-maker's daughter-in-law who came as her duty was to refill the tea-cups of the old women. No sooner had she left the room than the cake-maker's wife resumed her revilings, scratching the bald spot on her head across which a few hairs were tightly drawn into a scrawny little knot at the nape of her neck.

"Quite properly filled this cup," she said. "Now the stupid creature in my house either trickles in a few drops or wastefully pours the tea to overflowing. What a careless girl!—And idle!— I'll wager she's sitting doing nothing at this very moment instead of getting the noon meal ready.—My poor old stomach may cry out for food for all she cares, and surely, after an unlucky morning like this, I'll go home to find nothing ready, nothing done. But I'll go,—I'll go!" she said rising and her temper with her. "And if she has not prepared the food,—I'll—pinch her,— that's what I'll do!"

She took up her stick for her eyesight was not good—except to detect the faults of others,—and hobbled off down the street, her lean face working with anger. When she was well out of earshot Wu Nai Nai said to her daughter-in-law:

"You can be thankful that you are *my* son's wife and not hers! Few houses there are like this where a girl is never beaten, though few too, like hers, where it happens nearly every day!"

No sooner had Liang Nai Nai set foot within her own courtyard than the girl, watching with frightened eyes such as a dumb animal turns upon a cruel trainer, saw she was in a vile temper —a worse one than usual, which was not saying little. Yesterday she had been cross enough, ordering her son to beat his wife for some fancied slight to herself. And he had beaten her soundly too, even though she was carrying a child. Nor could the girl blame her husband for the blows, for he dared not disobey the old woman lest he be called an unfilial son. No man—not even when his hair was touched with silver—could take his wife's part against his parents however cruelly they treated her.

But today the old woman was furious because she had lost more than she could afford at her gaming,—twice angry in fact, once against Fate and once against herself.

"Go fetch my water-pipe," she bawled at the girl, "and set a bench outside in the courtyard near the gate where the sun is,— I feel a chill in my old bones. Be quick about it too, for today I have small patience with slowness and stupidity!"

"I will do as you say, mother," Ling-erh answered meekly, lifting the heavy bench with difficulty and staggering with it through the door. No sooner was she outside than Mother Liang went softly into the sleeping room, noiselessly opened the cupboard where the bedquilts were stored and felt beneath them for the cracked jar in which, as the whole family knew, her son kept the silver he earned by cooking for the village birthday and funeral feasts. Quickly she clutched the coins and, furtively looking over her shoulder to see that the girl was still out of sight, tucked them inside her coat.—Then she screamed loudly:

"Gone, gone!—our silver is gone! Here I look for a wadded cover to warm me of a chill and I find the jar empty. Stolen that silver must have been. And who do you suppose stole it? We all know that no outside thief has entered this house.—Who, then, could have taken it?"

When Ling-erh hearing her frantic cries hurried back to the room, Mother Liang seized her by the shoulder and shook her.— "Who took that silver?—Answer me!" she screamed.—But the girl only stood dumb and trembling knowing it useless to answer one determined to lay the blame on her.

Perhaps had Ling-erh been less meek, she might have been less abused. But it was the girl's nature to be so, and she accepted her fate without complaining, thinking to herself it was thus evil, maybe, because of a sin committed in a former life. Besides she was no match for the old shrew at the best of times. But at night when her helpless young husband slept heavily beside her she could weep softly. By day she dare not cry, for if she did her mother-in-law would shout at her: "Crying, crying when there is work to be done! Lazy creature! I'll give you something to cry about,"—and pinch her wrists or scratch her face till the blood streamed down her cheeks. Six long months the girl had endured this cruelty and injustice, well knowing that nothing she did could ever be right. Six long months Mother Liang tormented her, relying on the weakness of her husband and son to protect herself.

Now finally things had come to such a pass that the whole hamlet knew how these two women were "eating vinegar." Neighbours whispered among themselves that Mother Liang was too hard on the girl, especially since a child was soon to be born to her.

But no one dared to openly take Ling-erh's part for fear some tragedy might happen, and she be caught in it, and none guessed how near tragedy really was.

For when the old woman accused her of being a thief, jeering at her, and repeating again as she gobbled her noon meal, "A thief for a daughter-in-law,—a thief!—A thief for the mother of my son's son—that's a pretty tale to tell the village!" the younger woman turned upon her in anger. It broke out of her violently,—unexpectedly.—Kindly, patient, long-suffering these peasants are until the moment of their sudden passions. Then, as the placid surface of a lake is lashed to fury by a typhoon wind, they change instantly from gentleness to rage, from forbearing meekness to wild revenge. Now for the first time Ling-erh looked her tormentor in the face:

"You lie!" she cried passionately. "You know I did not steal that money. You know too what has become of it, for you yourself took it for your gambling! But I am weary of your tormentings, and today I shall do what I have long wished to do!— Today I shall hang myself,—for surely I will be better dead. I have learned from you that life can be far harder than death."

Had the old woman been wise she would have feared the force of this long-gathered misery, and still more feared Ling-erh's threat of suicide, which meant serious trouble if she should carry it out. But her own anger made her careless of consequences.

"Aha, my girl! So you dare to answer back,—unfilial wretch! Get out of my sight. And set to work washing the food bowls, for idle hands mean an empty mouth. What is the meaning of this foolish talk,—slut and daughter of a slut! How should a coward like you ever dare to force the White Gate of Death— you who have only a chicken's heart in you to cringe and whine!"

So saying she left the house still in a fury, cursing and wiping her rheumy eyes on the same soiled cloth in which she had wrapped the silver coins. Three steps beyond the gate and she had forgotten her daughter-in-law's threat—so sure she was that fear would restrain a girl with such contemptible lack of spirit.

But Ling-erh was truly goaded beyond fear. Besides she had been trained in the oriental belief that suicide is the accepted way out of a situation too painful to be borne. Many a village girl before her had thus escaped forever from an intolerable mother-in-law, and revenged herself, besides as an unhappy haunting ghost bringing ill-fortune to those who had tormented her.

"Yes, I will hang myself," she muttered, "I will do so. Rather the Shadowy World than this life which I can bear no longer. And when I am dead and the silver is not found among my things but in her secret hiding place, all the neighbours will know that the old mother lied, and that she and not I was the thief. And the village will judge rightly concerning her wicked heart."

So the poor girl made ready decently for death. She combed her hair neatly, and placed her wedding hair-pins in it, put on the red coat of the six-months' bride over her bruised body, and hung her wedding earrings in her ears, thinking all the while of that day when her parents had decided, to marry her, and of how her mother had told her not to be afraid for the matchmaker, a poor aunt of theirs, promised that she was going to a good home where no one would ill-treat her. Well, the woman had lied for the sake of a bit of silver from her parents, and a bigger bit from Mother Liang whose temper was so well-known that she could get no girl from her own village to marry her son. —Ling-erh had never made complaint for when a thing is done it is done. What use to cause her mother grief for one that had "gone out of the door" of her own home, and entered another?

When she was ready and washed clean she set the room in order lest anyone might say she had not done her duty to the last, and put away the basket already half full of little garments that she was sewing for her unborn child. Then she went into the inner room, unwound her girdle, twisted it about her throat and set a bench under the centre roof beam.

An hour later a neighbour woman, knowing that the cake-maker's house was usually noisy with quarrelling in the afternoons, grew frightened at the silence. "Something is wrong there," she said to herself. "It cannot be those two women are at peace!"

So she left her work and went into the quiet house next door, and called and called again. But no one answered. The living room was empty and the kitchen too. But the door of the inner room was shut. Hastily she forced the wooden bolt with the meat chopper and saw with horror the girl hanging from the roof-beam by her girdle twisted tightly about her neck. Her breathless body seemed to greet the woman with a little mocking bow. Her bride's earrings tinkled gently in the breeze from the open door, and there was a strange steadfast look in her protruding, wide-open eyes.

The woman, seeing how death had come, screamed and rushed out into the street where the first person she met was Greybeard, the old man with basket and scoop who collected droppings from passing animals for fertilizer. A good simple old man he was following an honourable and respected calling.

"Where is Mother Liang?" the woman shrieked at him, "Have you seen her?"

"Yes, she has gone to Wu Nai Nai's house,—what now? Is anything wrong?" he asked, his mouth agape and showing all his toothless gums, so great was his surprise at seeing one thus distracted suddenly appear in that quiet street.

"Enough and plenty," she screamed, and did not stop to tell him more, but ran on as fast as she could with her cramped feet, shrieking for Liang Nai Nai. So loud were her cries that first one and then another neighbour came to her gate to listen. When a good crowd had gathered, she gasped out:

"Ling-erh is dead!—She has hanged herself in her red bride's robe. I have seen her with my own eyes!"

Shocked though she was, the woman felt fully conscious of the dramatic part she played as bearer of such news, and told her tale with a certain pride, weeping aloud and tearing her clothes to heighten its effect. Not often did such a tragic interlude rouse the whole village from everyday prosaics. Even the Blacksmith left his anvil and the hot horse-shoe he was shaping.

"This was bound to happen," he said gloomily, "surely it is the fault of Liang Nai Nai. Her tongue is like a flight of steps leading to calamity, and now she will be accursed of 'harrying' her daughter-in-law to death!"

Mother Liang who was gossiping again with Wu Nai Nai heard the noise outside the gate, and she too hobbled out to listen, her companion close after her. News is news after all in a village where for months on end nothing happens except weather, and no one can afford to miss any excitement. At the sight of the cake-maker's wife, the neighbour woman shrieked the louder,—"Ling-erh is dead—by her own hand. She hanged herself!"

But Liang Nai Nai quickly gathering her wits shouted back:

"It is not true. I will never believe such a thing. This woman spreads evil rumours to injure me!"

"Go see for yourself then," answered the neighbour.

And the old woman knew by her face that the tale was true though she started home with her head held high like one who goes to prove a lie.—It was natural enough for all the neighbours to follow her since the happenings in one house concerned the whole community. And as. they walked behind her they muttered to each other— "Now the old woman had best be careful. It is a dangerous thing to drive a girl to suicide."

Someone had already gone to warn the cake-maker and the dead girl's husband of what had happened, and the latter threw himself down in the inner room half crazed with grief. But the cake-maker himself stood helplessly in the courtyard where the neighbours came crowding in, half out of sympathy, and still more out of curiosity. Elder Chi, as spokesman for the rest, inquired politely:

"What is our brother's trouble?"

Of course he knew, but still it was proper to ask, and Liang in duty bound to explain:

"It is my daughter-in-law—she is dead by her own hand, and her unborn child with her.—What shall we do when her kinsfolk arrive?"

First one and then another neighbour tried to offer him comfort, though all agreed— "The blame is on your 'inside person' for Ling-erh was a good and gentle maid. Now there is nothing for it but to wait and see what comes."

Nor had they long to wait. The very next day the relations of the dead girl were at the cake-maker's door, for someone who had felt the venom of Liang Nai Nai's tongue had quickly warned the injured clan, and her father and elder brother came hurrying from their village. Without ceremony they strode into the Liang house as was their right. Alive their daughter must be left to the mercy of her mother-in-law and they had by law and custom no right to interfere. But, once driven to death they could avenge her—and it was plain they meant to do so thoroughly.

"What is this we hear that our daughter has hanged herself because of ill-treatment from the old woman in this house?" the father roared.—He was a big man, and with his big strong son beside him, he stood over the trembling little cake-maker menacingly.

"No, no," the latter answered softly hoping to cool the anger he so greatly feared.—"It is not true!"

Then let us see her, for like as not you lie since word has come to us that she is dead!"

"Evil gossip meant to harm us!—There was a quarrel—a quarrel only. The girl was unfilial and her mother-in-law rightly punished her," the little man faltered.

"Unfilial!—a daughter of our house?—May such lies choke you!—If there was trouble, it was the old woman's fault. Bring our girl here that I may know the truth from her own lips!"

As no one moved to do his bidding the father himself rushed into the inner room. There was Ling-erh lying in a thin pine-wood coffin. At the sight of her poor bruised cheeks and the marks of pinching on her wrists, he was half crazed with grief and fury. The look on his heavy spade-shaped face was terrible to see as he strode back to Liang who stood waiting with chattering teeth. But that two neighbours caught the big farmer by the arms he might have killed Liang.

'It is your old woman who drove Ling-erh to death—just as I knew!" he shouted, struggling to free himself.

"She died of a fever," stammered the cake-maker.

But the girl's father more than ever angry now he knew the girl was dead cried out:

"Do you neighbours here present bear witness that my daughter was cruelly ill-used. You, elder brother, and you, and you, and you," he added pointing first at one and then another, "shall testify for me before the magistrate to this foul play. It is a double murder too, since they killed her when she was near to bear a child,—doubtless a son to burn incense at his mother's grave! Now who can do that?—Who can appease her homeless ghost?—I ask you all!"

And the man beat his own breast strongly, blaming himself most bitterly for letting his child go to the home of a shrew like Liang Nai Nai.

Meanwhile the old woman, terrified at what she had done, hid in an outhouse. But she could hear the father's words and well she knew their inner meaning. Under the old law the fault of one member of a family must be paid by all, and in those days even babes in arms were beheaded for a murder committed by their father. It was plain that those determined kinsmen of the dead girl were set on seeing justice done. Such justice might demand Liang Nai Nai's life, and the life of her husband and son.

Or, if they sold their lands and bribed the magistrate for pardon, it would surely cost them all they had. Beggared and homeless they would be driven out of Hundred Altars to wander from place to place in bitter poverty. Thus all the world would know how they had treated Ling-erh, daughter of the house of Liu, who had borne her troubles meekly and without complaint.

Even the sentiment of her own village was against Liang Nai Nai. Of that she was well aware. The neighbours blamed her one and all, and none would raise a hand in her defence.—Yet among these neighbours Elder Chi did speak words that helped though not for her own sake. He spoke because he feared to see the law interfering in village affairs, and because he desired to protect the good name of Hundred Altars.—"When one family has trouble," as the saying goes, "none of its four neighbours can live in peace," and public opinion is a very real force when it can be roused.

"Now," said the Elder calmly and fearlessly as only an old man dares to speak in the face of angry men, "the maid is dead and neither the law nor your just anger can bring her back to life. Let peace talkers take this affair in hand and judge it wisely, for whatever happens this household will be heavily punished by the girl's revengeful ghost."

"No, no," shouted the Liu kinsmen with one voice. "It is not enough!—We will put out that evil old woman's eyes! She shall be blinded for her sins, and driven out by the law to wander homeless."

But again and again the Elder spoke his gentle words. And little by little the Lius let themselves be calmed somewhat. Three days later their fury had worn down enough to admit "peace talkers" to bargain over their revenge.

"The coffin in which they have put my sister," said the brother as both parties sat together discussing the affair, "is a disgrace. We demand one of catalpa wood, three inches thick and well- lacquered."

Hundred Altars

"And we will not have her buried in cotton clothes," added the father. "Let the old woman herself make a decent robe of purest silk and sew it well. As for the funeral—we want the finest ever seen in Hundred Altars. Not less than five hundred silver dollars must be spent on it!"

"Surely three hundred dollars would be enough," suggested the neighbour who spoke on the Liang's behalf. But this reduction was indignantly refused.—Four hundred, however, was the amount finally agreed upon.

"We did the best we could," the neighbour told Liang afterwards.

"I know, I know," the latter assented sadly. "Yet despite everything you could do the millstone of debt will hang round our necks all our lives. By the time I have settled with the priests and the carriers and paid the hire of embroidered banners and funeral drums, not much will remain for us. Yet all this show we must have not only to satisfy these angry men, but to placate the ghost—if that be possible!—And certainly the Liu family might have asked for more but for your kind bargaining. They might have demanded a theatrical performance. It is a usual thing in such a case—"

"Well, there was talk of that," the man admitted, "but the neighbours were against it. They said that, though drama is always welcome, they feared if their relations heard about a play being given in the village they might take the excuse to come and visit us. Guests are expensive—and the New Year settling day is not far off. Besides once a year at fair time is quite enough to feed uncles and aunts and cousins and all their children."

So it was agreed that a fine funeral should content all parties, and fine enough it was to leave the villagers agape. Twenty stout bearers dressed in flowered robes were hired to bear the coffin, and a paper house and a paper chair were bought for burning at the grave.

Until the date fixed by the diviner for the grand procession, Liang Nai Nai sat sewing on the silk shrouds, though, weak-sighted as she was, sewing was difficult work for her. But the dead girl's kinsmen insisted that she and no other woman should put in every stitch, and one of them came daily to the house to see their wishes were carried out. And as the old woman sewed the bitter scalding tears poured from her tired eyes. Now that it was too late she sorely missed the girl who had meekly done for her what henceforth she must do for herself. A strong young woman in the house was useful and necessary to one who was growing old and feeble, and though she had always despised her daughter-in-law, now she knew she missed her.

Tears and more tears the old crone shed. Yet no one came to comfort her. Even her timid husband, ruined by her fault, kept well away, and her son for once forgot his filial piety. Yes, life was bitter for her now, as bitter as once she had made poor Ling-erh's. Every day the sound of her weeping was heard in the street, and hearing it the neighbours said,— "So she should weep! —she has brought this trouble on herself."

Little pity they felt for her. But even less moved to forgiveness were Ling-erh's kinsfolk as they watched her following the coffin to the grave where she must knock her forehead on the ground before it for her sin's sake.

"Look lad," said Liu the father to his son, "now we are revenged at last!—See how the old crone stumbles even on familiar paths!—-See how she taps her staff in front of her. She cannot see!—Did I not tell you we should put out her eyes to satisfy our poor girl's ghost?"

X. Crossing the Year

The Liang family had good reason to thank their peace talkers. These neighbours had served the cake-maker and his household well,—not only saved them from legal punishment by keeping the Magistrate from being called to settle their dispute with Ling-erh's clan,—but also saved them from the fury of their fellow-villagers, and possible banishment from Hundred Altars. One thing, however, these wily bargainers could not do,— save their New Year joy. No family in mourning—and mourning could not be broken even for a day—was permitted to join in the festivities that marked the "Crossing of the Year" lest their grief bring ill-luck to those who rejoiced. So the cake-maker and his wife and their widowed son must remain at home,—alone, wearing coarse hempen garments and eating coarse food. The sound of the meat chopper preparing the festival dumplings could not be heard in their kitchen nor could joyous red luck papers be pasted on their gates. Sorrow is twice sorrow when it means missing the one great holiday of the twelvemonth, the official birthday of every man and woman in China, and the birthday of Mother Earth also.

Winter came early that year. The bitter silent cold crept down from the north through the passes of the Great Wall, moving stealthily like a beast of prey, devouring green growing things. The tiny spears of winter wheat no bigger than a mouse's ear scarcely dared show themselves above the hard grey earth, and the stark trees laced the frosty skies with an iron grill of frozen arms.

According to the old Chinese Moon Calendar, the first day of the new year was fixed to fall on a different calendar date each year for sixty years till the slow cycle of the planets was completed. But the farmers never needed to consult the Almanac. They knew instinctively, as the days grew a cock's stride longer, when the old year was due to die and the new one to be born. For them Nature herself set the day of the Earth's rebirth just as she set the day when the wild geese must fly northward and the swallows begin their nesting.

Juliet Bredon

While the land rested, men too could rest. They had the right to idleness during the short season when the Wind of Wide Spread Inaction, of General Powerlessness, was due to blow. During these "five coat" days the farmers piled wadded garments one above another, hid their hands inside their sleeves for warmth, and drowsed away their days on the heated *k'ang*. While the yang, the male principle of the universe rested, the yin, the female principle, was at its full strength. As with the earth so also in the homes where for two weeks before the New Year dawned the women ruled in a flurry of happy holiday preparations.

Clever Needle hurrying from one task to another said teasingly to her husband as he lazed in comfort: "Now you idler!—see how I must work for you! You want new clothes for the festival and I must sit up sewing half the night.—You want fine food and I must stand all day long in the kitchen to make 'happy congratulations *chu po po*' to satisfy your appetite!"

"Yes," he retorted lazily, "but in summer you sit idle under a tree fanning yourself while I bake my back under the hot sun!"

If the truth be told Clever Needle enjoyed the winter season when she reigned supreme, when the peace and warmth and contentment of the home counted for more than the outside world where men had full authority. She was ready and glad to work her fingers to the bone to make a happy New Year for her family, especially this year knowing what she knew and meant to tell her husband that very evening. When the old fortune teller had foretold "increase" for her she had not grasped his meaning. — It was six years since she had borne a child.

Luck indeed smiled upon the house of Chi with its three generations, devoted and undivided. "A cat in a strange house, a fish thrown upon land, a bird with a broken wing, are not more miserable than those who must be separated from their kith and kin when the new year dawns." But Clever Needle had her old father-in-law, her husband and her children close about her, and to feast in common, to worship the same gods and the same ancestors under the family roof fulfills the ideal of happiness of her race. And now to complete the circle of her New Year joy she felt another child stirring within her. Yes, she loved the holiday season with its new clothes, good food and visiting, loved even the extra work it made.

Hundred Altars

"You might go to Ma's shop and get what we need for the feast," she coaxed in her most wheedling voice. "You know what we want, but don't forget we already have sesamon stalks and pine branches to spread in the courtyard and crackle beneath the feet of any lurking devils!"

Grumbling that never a man could have a moment's peace, Chi went out wrapping his great sheepskin coat around him, secretly glad of the excuse to go. Ma's shop just at this time was likely to be full of neighbours on similar errands. A cup of wine in company, never came amiss, and it would be amusing to see the gaudy festival trimmings laid out for sale, and enjoy the heat of the tall brass braziers with their dancing blue flames. Colour and warmth and company,—Chi liked all these things, and the taste of the hot amber wine;—liked them the more since he could so seldom enjoy them all together.

Pushing open the heavy felt curtain that stretched across the door, Chi was greeted by a dozen neighbours; "Ah, so your 'inside person' sent you also! Come drink a cup with us unless she bade you hurry back!"—The quip passed harmlessly over Chi's head. He was known to be master in his own house. But it reminded Wu the coffin-maker that if he lingered longer a good sound scolding would greet him, and he arose swaying. He had in truth drunk very little, but his weak head made him sufficiently unsteady so that at one moment he seemed to be walking towards Peking and at the next towards Pei Yang Ho, which produced a comical effect that like most comical effects would not, when he reached home, turn out to be so comic after all.

The other neighbours chatted together for a while, discussing village affairs. A farmer remarked: "After the new year the Elders say we must clean out our wells and then wrap up big packages of medicine in lotus leaves to put down them, so that we may have no stomach sickness next summer." "It is wise," agreed one man. Another rose to go. "Must you leave?"—"Yes, I must— I must," he hiccupped happily and went off.—Chi at last well-warmed, quitted the group to make his purchases;—red candles carved with dragons and fairies for the home altar, portraits of the gods stamped in bright colours, red paper luck charms for doors and windows, incense, spirit money, lanterns shaped like bees and butterflies and bulgy-eyed fish, "religion fruit" better to look at than to eat, packets of firecrackers to scare away evil spirits. Like many a careful spender, Chi at New Year time burst willingly into extravagance. There were also the twenty ingredients for the special *La Pa Chow* porridge prepared in honour of Kwanyin which Clever Needle sent as gifts some days before the New Year to all the family friends. Chi's basket was brimming with packages;—five different kinds of grain, beans, lily and melon seeds, peanuts, chestnuts, walnuts, dried apricots, peach and pine seeds, dates, green plums and sugar. "Such a load!" Chien taxed his friend as Chi left the shop. "You should hire a donkey to carry it!"

"Yah!" the farmer retorted gaily, "and shall I send a pig to you eat your share of our *La Pa Chow* when it is heavy with all these delicacies?"

At home Clever Needle was still deep in house-cleaning. The day being marked in the calendar for "sweeping the ground," she was hard at work, her head wrapped in a cloth, handling her brooms with diligence and respect since the broom was a member of the family and when it fell must be picked up again like a child.

The following day when all was clean and tidy the old luck posters were torn off the doors and window sills. Their power to protect lasted only a year. It was time now to replace them with new ones,—squares of red paper on which fortunate phrases were written in bold black characters. Even the plough and the well-bucket and the mules' pack-saddles must have these luck labels pasted on them, not to mention the baskets for storing grain and the cupboards. Finally new pictures of the Gate Gods must be put on the double panels of the street gate,—portraits of fierce warriors in shining armour with spears pointing in opposite directions ready to attack evil from whichever side it might appear.

A few days later the Kitchen God departed for Heaven to make his report on the family entrusted to his charge. He had watched everyone in every house in the village from his bamboo shrine over each stove. He knew who had wasted water and who had spilled food—and he told tales... unless he was bribed not to. So each family with the sins of the past year in mind, gave him a good send off and provided every comfort for his journey. Before his picture was placed in the paper sedan chair his lips were smeared with honey so that his words up yonder might be sweet. Then folk bowed as they showed off the "honoured guest" and firecrackers popped to announce his departure. Many a housekeeper heaved a sigh of relief as she watched the Family Spy go heavenward in the flames. During his absence she could do as she pleased in her own kitchen and relax from the strain of being always polite before him. Yet all agreed it was most necessary to be courteous to the Kitchen God. He and his were noted for good manners and appreciated them in others.—His horse drank only water offered to him, never be-fouling what was drawn for household use. His hundred dogs were so polite to one another that if even one was late for a meal all the others waited for him.

On New Year's Eve Clever Needle was glad to finish up her cooking. She had been practically a prisoner in her kitchen for the last three days, breathing air thick with the strong smell of vinegar and spices. What with preparing food for the family, offerings for the ancestors, food gifts for friends, and refreshments for those who would come to pay New Year calls, she was worn out. But now work was over. Tomorrow she could rest for after midnight no knife must be used lest the luck of the incoming year be wounded. Nothing could be cooked either, though tea and cakes might be warmed over. Only a few last minute errands remained. The children were pleased to carry the gifts to neighbours.—Each housewife usually had one dish that she prided herself on cooking better than anyone else, and Clever Needle knew that her dumplings with sweet-sour gravy were second to none.

"Now do not spill the sauce," she cautioned her small sons, "and remember to thank the wife of Ma for the flowering trees she sent us!"

It was great fun to go to Ma's house where small boys were sure of getting presents—coppers wrapped in red paper. "For your New Year gambling!" Shui Ching said as she slipped her gifts into their chubby hands, for even babies were allowed to play for stakes at this holiday season. As she patted their little round heads and said: "Don't thank—don't thank! Get up my dears—you need not bother to bow to me—" just as they were making ready to ko-tow before her, her eyes were moist. Little sons, precious little sons,—of another happier woman!—But she choked back her tears and bade them run and find the master. "He must still be busy in the shop—and I think you might wish him joy there!" she told them knowing well he would fill their arms with toys.

Ma was in his shop and busy. This was the last day for paying debts and receiving moneys due until the next settling day in midsummer, though men might be dunned for what they owed and creditors go about "demanding" debts all night and even after sunrise provided they carried a lighted lantern.—The artificial light proved by a polite fiction that the New Year's first day had not yet dawned and debts might still be claimed.—But in Hundred Altars such sharp city practises were not the rule, and no man sat on his neighbour's doorstep spoiling his face because of money owed. In fact, Ma, from whom some of the poorer farmers had borrowed to carry them "across" the year until new crops would bring new credit, willingly let their debts run over to the summer settlement. It was bad policy to be hard on neighbours. Moreover this year he begrudged nothing to anyone, for Shui Ching had lately brought him news that his little wife was expecting a child.

So when Chi's two boys entered the shop Ma closed his account books and himself took them to choose the toys that pleased them. It was ask and have with him this year. But he even gave the children more than, in politeness, they dared to ask. And to his apprentices who feasted at his expense, he gave extra presents—money and cloth so that none of them needed to stint themselves in their pleasures or wear an old coat,—and bade them close the shutters early and make merry. This they did the whole night long with music and the beatings of gongs and the click of Mah jong tiles, and the firing of crackers by the hundred so that next morning the courtyard was littered with burst wrappers of the spent crackers.

Shui Ching too profited by her husband's good humour, for to her as to Lilac Blossom he gave gifts in money in plenty, and whatever she asked besides that she might have, even rich trimmings for her altars dressed in honour of the goddesses who were answering her prayer,—alas not in her way, but in their own.

When Ma left his shop he came back to find his home gay with New Year decorations. Pridefully he looked over his reception room, beamed with dark rafters, and filled with heavy blackwood furniture polished like mirrors to reflect the lantern light. The tables and chairs were covered with heirloom silks woven with phantom dragons sporting amid sea waves, or birds undulating in slow flight through trailing clouds. One altar for the gods was gay with lacey characters in gold paper, and dwarf cherry trees forced into early blossom in dainty porcelain pots, and platters of food, including a live carp chained to the dish with paper fetters. On a second table prepared for the ancestors stood the usual row of five simple wooden tablets surrounded by offerings of cakes and fruit and wine, and in front of these a fine old pewter altar set and on the wall behind hung the scroll on which the names of the remoter ancestors were inscribed.

"Everything is done just as it should be," said Ma to himself proudly. And in every house in the village whether people could afford to spend much or little on their altars, the master, overlooking all, repeated the identical words. Indeed in every house the self-same routine, prescribed by custom to its smallest details, was followed. The men retired to an inner room to bathe and the barber went the rounds shaving them, dressing their queues and cleaning their ears with his ear pick. Then all dressed in new clothes, for it seemed right that when the earth put off her winter garments they also should discard their old ones. True, Ma's robe was of heavy dark plum coloured silk, and Chi's of cotton, and poor Chang had only new patches on his old coat, which did not matter because the underlying idea was the same.

Meanwhile the women in their quarters were also dressing in their best and brightest, rouging their cheeks and painting their eyebrows in the shape of the willow leaf, the first leaf to bud after the new year.

As for the children, they were like bright butterflies in gay red coats and purple trousers and little caps with gilt figures of the gods and tiger-faced shoes with whiskers. It was the children's flight looked forward to for many weeks—the night when they need not go to bed, but could sit up as long as the grown ups did, the night when no harsh words might be spoken to them and none might be corrected for fear of spoiling his New Year luck. No wonder they were full of mischief. "That child!" exclaimed Clever Needle using a local idiom half tender half contemptuous, as she seized Little Silver for the third time and attempted to get both his arms into his coat sleeves,—"Will he ever be properly dressed!"—But he and his brother were far too excited to stand still. Carelessly leaving doors open, they broke away and ran in and out of the room to watch a neighbour's fireworks from the courtyard as the golden sparks splashed against the sky in starry sprays.

Clever Needle called after them: "Be still now my sons!—Your grandfather likes not that you should romp and play so roughly." She heaved a sigh of relief when the Elder and her husband appeared and the little lads were awed into good behaviour.

As they watched their seniors preparing for the home ceremonies the two boys suddenly became solemn as graven images, and their mother, slyly scanning their tense faces, said to herself:

"Can those be my same sons?"

These ceremonies twice repeated, once before midnight, in farewell to the old year the gods and the ancestors, and again before dawn in greeting to them in the new, symbolized all that is most dear in the Chinese cult of the home. They were the essential rites, ancient as the race itself, expressing the inmost feelings of the everlasting people towards this world and the next.

The Elder, as head of the family and high priest of his own house, led the way into the common room which had been turned into a shrine. Pictures of the Hundred Heavenly Ones stood on the gods' table, the ancestral tablets on theirs. Both altars were draped with red satin embroideries lighted by red candles and spread with offerings, while kneeling cushions were placed before them.

The old man knelt first at the gods' altar worshipping, in the joint names of his kinsfolk, Heaven and Earth, the household deities, and the familiar gods. But the ancestors, though they too were in a sense divine, received separate reverence apart. At their shrines Chi the Second and his sons placed themselves behind the Elder. As reeds bend before a wind, they bowed when he bowed and rose when he rose in the nine-fold homage of the ko-tow. Last of all and alone, because she was the only woman the house, Clever Needle bowed also.

The tablets signified the actual viewless presence of the dead and the family greetings were not in a true sense worship but the expression of loving veneration such as is given by children to their elders. Only these invisible members of the clan were older than any living ancestor and now that they dwelt elsewhere and had kindly come to visit their living kinsfolk, they were due a more ceremonious greeting when they returned home than those who were always together. Chi and his sons now ko-towed to the Elder, and the two little boys to their father and mother, generation greeting generation. Then they all sat down together at a round table to the feast of reunion.

During the long meal the two small boys over-excited, over-tired, were often near to quarrelling. One was bent on sitting in the other's place, one was eager to snatch from the other's bowl. But it did not matter. The rites were finished, now they might enjoy themselves at ease, and Clever Needle had taken her precautions against any naughty words bringing bad luck by rubbing their lips with rough paper, and pasting a warning on the wall that children's words do not count. Thus the evil spirits could not be angry whatever they said. Grown-ups might be trusted to speak only of pleasant things, indeed to speak but little since all were busy and happy over the luscious dishes she had prepared—their faces exceedingly grave with the dignity of the occasion, and their fingers exceedingly greasy.

Whenever the Elder nodded over his bowl someone nudged his elbow. To fall asleep on this "Watch Night" was ill-omened. But just after midnight, he went back to his duties at the altars of the gods and the ancestors. Besides the Kitchen God must be welcomed home again, and firecrackers boomed and banged in his honour. Thus in feasting and worshipping and courteous greetings to the New Year and to one another the long night passed.

At dawn the front gate, closed before midnight, was opened to let the luck of the New Year in, and then barred again for now their duties were done. the family retired to rest. The two men dropped exhausted on the warm k'ang, and Clever Needle having wrapped her drowsy children in a quilt lay down beside them tired and heavy, her feet swollen in her shoes from much Standing-

Next day not a soul, not a cart, not a donkey, passed down the village street. Every door was tight shut. Even the innkeeper refused to answer the hungry traveller's knock. He and his men were gambling together in the kitchen.—Why should they stop their game? He shouted through closed shutters, "This is no time to be on the road. Business is business, but pleasure is pleasure,—and above

83

Juliet Bredon

all it is New Year and you can be no proper person to be abroad at this time!"

It. was not until the following day that folk began to pay their calls. The head man of each house made a tour of the village bowing to the elders of every family. As it was well-known who was coming to see who, and when, neighbours were at home waiting for guests. Respect is paid by younger generations to older generations, and so it sometimes happened what with the intricate ramifications of a family tree, early or late marriages and adoptions, a man of sixty might well be the grandson or grand-nephew of a little boy and must perforce bend the knee to him. Chin the innkeeper who had the ill-luck to belong to a late generation was a case in point, and used to remark wryly after he had paid his calls:—"It seems I have to ko-tow to every child in the village two feet long.—I shall be lame in the knees for a full week or two!"—Yet each visit meant a good time after all, for at each food was served, and feast food at that.

Then on the third day Ma being a merchant held a home service to the God of Wealth whose favours are so dear to a tradesman's heart. Piety and prudence bade him keep in the good graces of this powerful and well-beloved God, and Ma invited his neighbours to join with him in a fine feast in his honour. Extra dainties had been sent for from Peking—sugared ginger, sweetened lotus roots and little candied crabapples such as the children loved. There was a grand picture of the God of Wealth seated beneath the money tree hung with golden fruit and dripping with the silver dew of coins set up in a new shrine, and everyone who entered made a deep bow to him, since without his help they could not hope to prosper.

Ma greeted his guests with a beaming smile, and gave a hint here and there, that, he was expecting a new mouth to be born to his Minor Star in this fortunate new year. It was a special pleasure to tell Chi this news—the Chis were always so fortunate, always acquiring face by their filial piety. When Chi smiling answered: "We too are expecting another child!" Ma felt for a moment as if the festival had turned sour for him.

This was the last feast held before the holidays were broken and life resumed its normal course. Three days later smoke rose from Ma's distillery again, and the farmers went out to look over their fields and decide where they would plant what, for they had an instinctive knowledge of the rotation of crops. Then they sharpened their ploughshares and made ready for the spring work. Even the children whittled sticks to dig for adventurous young dandelion shoots as soon as they should appear above the ground.

Juliet Bredon

XI. What the Gods Send

All through the spring Ma was comforted by the knowledge that a child would be born into his house. Whatever he did this happy thought was uppermost in his mind, and this hope changed his whole outlook on life. It gave him face before the ancestors and before his neighbours. It justified him for taking a "little wife." As the days went slowly by he longed impatiently for the moment when he could hold his manchild in his arms and his one desire was for the birth to come soon and make an end of his waiting.

But it was not until two days after the Midsummer Feast at the Dragon Boat Festival,—when all the world goes riverward to launch lighted boats upon the waters, searching for the soul of the great poet who drowned himself in the olden time and whose body the jealous Water God took to himself and nevermore gave back to a sorrowing people,—that smoke rose suddenly from Ma's chimney at two o'clock of a peaceful afternoon.

"That is indeed a wasteful household! Look at the kitchen fire being lighted at this hour when there is no cooking to be done!" a farmer said to his son as they lifted their heads from their hoeing and wiped the sweat from their brows.—"But I suppose the hour has come for the birth of a child to Ma's little wife. They say she is not strong therefore much hot water will be needed."

"Paugh! child-birth is normal and healthy—what is the use of weak and extravagant women?" objected the younger man. "The wife of neighbour Chi expects a child also, but I'll warrant hers will arrive when the fire is already made up for a meal, for she is a strong and thrifty person who bears easily as every woman should."

"Still, you cannot wonder that in Ma's house where there is so much longing for a son, there is also much careful preparation."

"Are they so sure a great joy, a boy, will be born?"

"The midwife pretends to know.—She says that if the mother carries her child facing inwards it will certainly be a boy. But if the baby faces outward it will be only a small joy—a girl."

"That seems reasonable since girls go out of the family to other homes, while boys remain within."

"Yah," grunted a passing farmer who joined in the conversation, "these midwives pretend to know everything, but what the gods send, the gods send."

It was the hottest day of the height of summer. Ma playing Mah jong with some cronies from the city had stripped off his short cotton jacket and sat naked to the waist, drinking innumerable cups of tea. In the inner room where his Minor Star lay writhing with pain the women of the family and several neighbours' wives were gathered. They crowded about her breathing the air she needed, and the small room was suffocatingly hot and close with the door shut, and every window tightly rolled down. Maddened by the heat, a furious bee stumbled against the paper window, unwisely a prisoner. "Open, open," groaned Lilac Blossom, but no one dared for fear wind might enter the sick woman and harm the child. Though air and cleanliness were lacking, charms against evil guarded the sickbed—two sets of holy pictures, one of Buddhist and the other of Taoist goddesses, and, in addition, a long sharp knife was placed beside the suffering girl to frighten away evil spirits who fear iron.

During the hours of waiting Ma sent a servant many times to inquire if there was good news. But as often as he went to the women's quarters he returned saying: "The child is not yet in sight. The door is narrow. The midwife says it will be a long hard birth;"—And so it was.

Again and again great pains swept over Lilac Blossom. Sometimes deep down within her she felt as if a fish moved its tail. At others, it seemed as if the whole earth swayed round her, and her eyes looked far away and strange. The midwife—a big gaunt woman whose fingernails were always black,—waited with her pile of dirty cloths beside her while Lilac Blossom lay gasping and panting like a weary horse. Yet she did not grudge her suffering—a son, a son for the master—and the crown of motherhood to establish her safely and forever in his house.

When it seemed she could stand no more and felt herself drifting off into oblivion, there was a thin wail from the child at last, —a cry proving that perhaps it is as painful for a spirit to enter a mortal body as to leave it.

At that very moment Ma at the Mah jong table completed a rare hand. "Ha!"—he exclaimed gaily, "The Thirteen Impossibles!—

What luck, what a fortunate omen!" But scarcely were the words out of his mouth than the midwife appeared at the door wiping her hands.

"Well?" he asked half rising from his chair, then hurriedly seating himself again.—To show much eagerness would be unseemly. The woman answered him sourly:—"It is only a small joy, after all, not worth mentioning."

Ma felt as if a knife had been thrust into his vitals. The shock of disappointment taxed his self-control to the limit, yet by a concentration of will he smiled feebly. A girl—a miserable girl, — was causing all this trouble in his house!—All this expense.

His friends were scarcely less uncomfortable than he. They had no congratulations to offer, nothing to say but the usual,— "What a pity,—what a pity!"—and as soon as the game was over they took their departure.

Left alone Ma cursed roundly, using the good coarse epithets of his race. He had always been a man who could say the worst of things when he was in a rage.

"Devils defile the woman for producing a girl!" he growled when Shui Ching called him to come and look on the face of the small new creature.—"A daughter with all the virtues cannot equal a splay-footed son!" He refused point blank to go— "Let her be—she is useless!"

Shui Ching sighed, and returned to the women's quarters. "Perhaps it is best that the master should not see the 'little wife' or the child until his anger cools," she thought. Yet disappointed herself, sad that her sacrifices had been useless, she listened patiently to her husband's complaining, and stood by silent while he emptied his sorrow into words.—A woman with a smaller mind would have felt pleasure in the Minor Star's failure. Not so Shui Ching. And at last she said, bowing humbly, "Master, the fault is mine. I am deeply ashamed at my choice of your 'little wife.' " She made excuses with a good grace for Lilac Blossom, taking the fault upon herself because she feared that he might wish in his anger to turn the Minor Star out of his house, an act that would be unworthy of him—and cruel too. Nor did she venture to tell him that the midwife thought it most unlikely Lilac Blossom would ever bear again,—turned against her as he was at the moment.

For many days after the birth of his girl child Ma hung round the house in no pleasant mood. He was very bitter for a time and often sighed heavily or groaned inwardly. Though he was a man who loved company he could not bring himself to go near the inn, hating to show himself before the neighbours after this loss of face. Nor did Shui Ching come to comfort him again for she too was despondent and remained in her own room. What use to speak more words at such a time?—A curse was on their house and nothing she could say or do would lift it.

"Is there any news?" Ma asked Jung-erh one afternoon. The coolie had just returned from the teashop. Ma's tone was casual as if he was really indifferent. "Has another mouth been yet born in the Chi household?"

"Not yet," the lad answered in his slow deliberate way, "But folk do say that Chi's wife has dreamed of bears and grizzly bears, and the diviner believes such dreams foretell a son."

"Get out of my sight! Crow of ill-omen!" Ma growled at him, and Jung-erh departed quickly.

Now Clever Needle, as the farmers had remarked, was not a woman to make a great to-do over childbirth. It seemed so ordinary to her—the natural, honourable duty of woman. Therefore she had no fear of it, but bore her children in a practical fashion with as little fuss as possible. When her hour was near Chi suggested that he should call the midwife, but Clever Needle said, "No."—There was need for her. Midwives cost money. Were this her first child it might be worth while sending for one. But a third baby should know its own way into the world. Perhaps the help of a neighbour woman.... "Very well then," he agreed,—"Shall I call Mother Chang?—She is so poor a small present will content her!" "Yes, she will do. Call her,—and call her now. My legs already feel soft as gruel. I will lie down upon the k'ang until she comes."

Chi tightened his belt, seized his jacket, and slipped his feet into his shoes not waiting even to pull them up so that the heels flip-flopped as he walked. The long street of the village was deserted and dark. Only the dying moon hung in the midnight sky, giving so little light that he picked his way down the rutted road with difficulty. Scarcely had he knocked upon the Changs' barred gate than it was opened. The woman knew full well that Clever Needle was near her time. She asked at once:—"Is your wife going to give birth?"

"Yes," Chi answered, "and she needs you."

"I will come," she said, and turned at once towards the house to make ready. Five minutes later she was padding hurriedly along behind Chi looking, in her ill-cut cotton gown, like a pudding sewed up in a bag.

When the woman reached her Clever Needle was in such agony that she could neither sit nor lie, and she suffered heavily all night but without crying out. "Birth is a natural thing, not a disease," she whispered to Chang Nai Nai more than once between clenched teeth. "It would be shameful to make loud complaints."

"Yes, it is right and healthy to be fertile. Tears are for barren women, tears of shame for their dry useless bodies,—not for such as you!" the neighbour agreed.—And when the day broke she went to tell Chi that his wife had safely borne a child. "Again it is a Great Joy," she said smiling.

"What?—again a manchild!" Chi exclaimed incredulous that such good luck should come to him for the third time. Then he shouted to the Elder,—"Father,—here is another grandson for you,: the third boy!"

"Good!" said the Elder heartily. "There can never be too many males in a house. Your woman is an excellent wife who bears easily and often."

When Chi had finished his morning gruel he went into Clever Needle's room. She lay exhausted on the k'ang with the tiny creature, wrinkled and red as a pomegranate bud, beside her. As he stood staring at the child which opened its mouth in a feeble yawn as a puppy does, the mother said weakly smiling up at him: "The Dream has come true. How fortunate I am! Three sons in as many births!"

Then Chi lifted the baby swaddled in cloth wrappings and bore it in his arms to greet his father, bowing its tiny head with his horny hand. He did the same in front of the Kitchen God and again before the ancestral tablets. The Ancestors had a new grandson. He must not forget to let them know.

When he brought the child back to Clever Needle, she reminded him that the announcement eggs must be sent out.— "They are ready. I boiled them myself yesterday. The Chang woman need only colour them red, thus, without words, showing we have a boy.— Then she can send them."

When Ma received his at midday he could not touch his rice. Shui Ching too, ate without appetite. In the natural kindness of her heart she was glad that Lilac Blossom still kept her bed and would not see them. The Minor Star was still too weak to bear this further shock, for a shock it would be to hear that, where she had failed Clever Needle had succeeded— Indeed from the birth of that third son the Mas harboured a certain secret jealousy towards the Chis.

Meanwhile Clever Needle lay comfortably resting during the "three tranquil days" while Chang Nai Nai prepared the meals and cared for the two elder children. They were good children, well-trained, and easy to keep quiet. "They need cuffing now and then," she reported, "but they are not such little devils as most. At least they do not climb trees to look for fish."

How restful it was for the mother, who never rested at other times, to lie with her new baby beside her and listen to the drip of summer rain upon the roof, and be dreamily conscious that it was feeding their thirsty fields. But on the fourth day, though she was still kitten-weak, she bade Chang Nai Nai comb her hair neatly and put a clean gown about her shoulders. Now that the baby had "passed three mornings" it was time to give him his first bath. A few close women friends had been asked to come to witness this intimate ceremony called "The Bath Biscuit Feast" because special biscuits were served afterwards to the guests.

Clever Needle fidgeted and fussed. Everything must be in order to receive her neighbours. The chairs must stand at the proper angle. The rooms must be spick and span. "This must be done so!— Don't forget!" she querulously reminded the Chang woman. "The water for the bath must be neither hot nor cold, —and give the child the powder to make him sneeze. Remind the master to place the bowl of uncooked rice with the incense stick in it before the ancestral tablets."—"Don't forget,—don't forget!" were the words oftenest on the lips of one who never forgot anything herself, but never expected others to remember.

At the Hour of the Dragon—about eight in the morning—the brass basin for the baby's bath was brought to his mother's room, and the women entered with gifts and good wishes. Each in turn dropped some silver thing into the basin,—a ring or a bracelet or a small coin,—at the same time wishing the baby wealth, while Clever Needle smiled her pride and happiness, and Mother Chang, knowing that the gifts were part of her reward, looked greatly pleased. While the baby screamed lustily as a manchild should when he was laid in the bath, his mother invited the women to pour a spoonful of water over him—since each spoonful meant a year added to his life. An egg from the basket placed beside the basin was put into it also as a symbol of happiness and an unpeeled onion and a slice of ginger to charm away sickness.

The little ceremony was soon over and Clever Needle answered the congratulations of her friends modestly, pretending that, although it was six years since she had last given birth a third son was nothing very wonderful. She was not through with child-bearing yet by any means, and doubtless would be asking them to come next year again to wish her joy.

When they were gone she bade her husband roll up the paper window that she might see the image of the Goddess of Birth sent back to Heaven in a paper sedan chair.

"Add plenty of mock money to the bonfire," she begged weakly, tired with the excitement of the morning, "We owe her a generous thanks-gift, but we must not keep her any longer in the house since other mothers need her."—And she smiled happily as the flames translated the Goddess to the celestial sphere, and murmured: "The worshipper is grateful indeed!"

Meanwhile the baby was being dressed for the first time, for hitherto he had been wrapped in rags. A silver lock engraved with lucky symbols was opened and moved down his body from head to foot—thus firmly locking him to life. Five-fold offerings of cakes were then made to K'ang Kung and K'ang Mu,— Father Bed and Mother Bed.—"Watch over our son," Chi whispered, "and guard him from falling off your high brick platform where he sleeps." Carefully then he gathered the ash from the incense burned to them and, wrapping it in a paper, placed it beneath the baby's pillow to ward off nightmares.

Now the days passed, and Clever Needle scarcely noticed their passing so happy she was watching her new baby kicking his fat legs and wrinkling his chubby face. He was a comely child, by far the prettiest of her three. And much time she wasted, she who seldom wasted a moment, running in and out of her room to see whether he slept or woke. Indeed her husband had to remind her—and he did it with a chuckle for she so often reminded him of what he had forgotten—that it was almost a full round of the moon since her child had been born. "The neighbours are already asking," he teased her, "when we are to have the Full Month's Wine,—I had to tell them the young puppy was born at such and such a time, and they all said, 'We'll be present and bring our presents of vermicelli!'"

Again as at the Elder's feast people must ask to come with their good wishes. To invite them would look as if the Chis were touting for presents. Yet the parents could not fail to provide a feast in return for the gifts offered. Luckily it need not be so elaborate as the one given for the living Ancestor. But, even so, such family festivals, coming close on one another, were a great drain on the resources of any household.

"I suppose," said Chi grudgingly, "that we shall have to hire young Liang again to make the 'long life vermicelli'?"

"Well," retorted Clever Needle, "would you prefer to have the neighbours say—'your wife never gets vermicelli sent to her?'—a local phrase meaning—'there are never any births in your house.'"

The "full month day" dawned clear and bright and hot, and neighbours visited the Chis early bringing presents for the new born son. In one corner of the courtyard where a scarlet trumpet vine in full bloom draped the wall like a brocaded curtain, the village schoolmaster sat, noting down each gift and announcing the giver's name.—"A cap with silver gilt figures of the genii upon it, from Neighbour Wu!—From Neighbour Chiao—a suit of red flowered cotton seven tenths new!—A sleeveless waistcoat with fine white silk lining from Neighbour Chien, a roll of a hundred cash, a silver amulet box to hang about the child's neck,"—and so on and so on. When the gift was lavish his tone was unctuous as if to say—"What face for you, my friend, to be able to make such a fine gift!"—if the present was humble, he named it in a careless voice hinting it was hardly worth mentioning.—Still he had to admit to Chi afterwards that taken all together the gifts made a brave show, in their red paper wrappings on the outside of which he, as the village scholar, had written by request words of congratulation—"to the small person who has attained the age of one month."

Again, as on the Elder's birthday, the Mas came reluctantly. They were too wise to stay away lest their absence be remarked and give rise to more gossip. But when Ma saw the little boy on show beside the Altar in the guest hall, with its large scroll representing the Star of Longevity and the lighted candles before it, he wished with all his heart that the child was his. He wanted this boy for his own,— this beautiful lusty manchild,— wanted him, wanted him,—wanted him hopelessly.

According to custom all the women praised the mother and admired the baby. Not unnaturally Shui Ching's admiration was tinged with melancholy.—"Ah, the fair child," she said wistfully laying her fingers against the tiny cheek, and again she was thankful that Lilac Blossom, still weak and ill, had not come. It would have hurt her even more deeply to see that lovely child. She was glad too that no month feast need be given for a mere girl.

At the lucky hour fixed by the diviner the child was carried in the arms of his grandfather as the head of the house, into the room where the ancestral tablets were set out. They had been taken from the closed cupboard where they were usually kept and were now arranged on a long table in order of rank. The tablet of the ancestor of the fifth generation stood in the centre—the place of honour,—for in his person all ancestors older than he were worshipped. Those of the more lately dead stood to the right and left of the "founder." The little head of this latest descendant was bowed before each, and his tiny hand guided to light a bunch of incense sticks. Then the Elder seated on a bench with the child on his knees announced his milk name— Little Dragon,—a name for general use in childhood years, and in later life, only for his intimates.

And now the barber was called to shave the tiny head. Little Dragon strenuously objected, kicking and screaming so that his mother was ashamed. But the neighbours only laughed, saying: "Do not distress yourself—it is a sure sign that he will grow up a valiant man!" Grandfather Chi and Chi the Second joined in the laughter too.—"Excuse our foolish lad," they said. "He does not know today is a great day in his life—therefore we cannot expect him to behave like a sage!" And instead of scolding or trying to hush him, Chi patted the little shaven pate with one thick finger and said over and over again,—"Live for a hundred years, little man,—live for a hundred years!"—When the baby stopped sobbing, he replaced the cap with the many gods upon it lest the child catch cold.

After this head-shaving the baby was made to salute each of the guests in turn, and as he bowed protesting towards them, they said—"He's a fine youth—may he live to be a white-haired man! May he study the 'Four Books' deeply, may he become Senior Classic"—for though they themselves could scarcely read or write they held to the ideal of scholarship. The best wish they could wish the baby was a life of learning,—unlikely though it seemed for a village child who could hope for no better education than the primitive school in Hundred Altars might give.

Ma, looking at the child, remarked jocosely:

"See! He has a bulging forehead—that's a sign he is born to be a high official! Why it's as high as the God of Longevity's!—What promise for this boy,—what luck for you his parents!"

And Chi replied modestly. "You are making fun of me. I trust entirely to you neighbours for his future welfare."

So saying he led them all to the feast tables where even the new-born son had indigestible dainties stuffed into his mouth.

Finally, when parting from their host, the guests said jocularly:—"We have had the birth feast today,—may the wedding feast soon follow!"—But in the privacy of their inner chamber Chi remarked wryly to his wife:—"I hope we may gather a good harvest or two before we are called to give another feast!"

Next day Ma spoke seriously with Shui Ching concerning Lilac Blossom. It was six weeks and more since the birth of the girl child and still the Minor Star kept her bed, and not once in all that time had he been to see her. Indeed Lilac Blossom long lay grievously ill. All through those hot summer nights she shivered as with cold, and sleep did not touch her eyelids, but she lay watching the stars through the window—hot pin pricks in the sky, and listening to the frogs croaking in the rice fields near the spring. She thought they felt with her in her loneliness, so plaintive was their call.

Like a little white ghost of her former self, helpless, unable to feed or care for her child, she brooded upon her failure to provide an heir—brooded upon her loss of face. Yet she could not weep away her pain. Tears would not come. Sometimes Shui Ching who felt much sympathy for her since in their common childlessness they were knit together, said to the Minor Star:

"It is no good to let sad thoughts stay always, in your mind. Take heart and gather strength, it may well be that the midwife was wrong and you may yet give the master his heart's desire!"

But Lilac Blossom only smiled vaguely, and seemed to retire more and more into a world of dreams and visions. She scarcely ever spoke of what she saw, but presently she began to see into the future and soon the neighbours heard that she had the gift and could see what she would and learn what she pleased. For this power they respected her, and the women came and asked her about what troubled them. At times she answered them; at times she said no word. Nor did she even when her strength allowed her ever go out but remained in her own courtyards. It was as if she lived in some far country and nothing and no one could trouble her any more.

Ma was ill-pleased with these tales of visions that Shui Ching told him. He wanted one thing of his Minor Star, and one only, strength to bear sons. The midwife's opinion impressed him little. "She is an old fool and knows nothing!" he said positively. "I have scant patience with these old wives and their tales. There is a good man of medicine in Pei Yang Ho. Send for him, and let him give her a potion that shall make her well again and strong enough to bear."

But when the old herbalist came, though he pierced her wrists with hot needles and gave her nauseous brews of antelope's whiskers and ground tiger's teeth, he could hold out no hope of further child-bearing. "It is useless. The woman cannot bear," he said. Ma, disappointed beyond endurance, dismissed him in a fury, shouting after him: "What good are you?—I should be willing to give you a hundred pieces of silver if you could guarantee me a son!"—Still the man being honest shook his head, and repeated: "It is hopeless. The woman cannot bear again."

When the doctor had gone Lilac Blossom dragged herself to the merchant's room where he sat alone, and, throwing herself on the ground, painfully ko-towed before him:

"Master,—it seems that even that one miserable birth was too hard for me and I am unfit for further child-bearing. Now that I have failed in my duty—will you cast me out of your house? —I deserve indeed to be sent away since I have so ill-repaid your kindness!"

"No, that I will not do!" said Ma generously, for he was at heart a generous man.—"What! shall I count every copper cash like a farmer?—and throw away a hoe just because the handle is broken? No you shall remain and we will find another way to have an heir in this house!"

Lilac Blossom told his words to Shui Ching, and the latter gasped.—"Can our lord mean to take another Minor Star?"

But Ma did not tell his womenfolk what he meant to do until the time came when he intended to put his plan into action.

For the present he would wait. It might well be that both the doctor and the midwife were wrong, as now with the return of the cool bright autumn weather, Lilac Blossom seemed to regain strength. But meanwhile his only satisfaction was the thought that the Goddess of Birth should go without her robe. She had done nothing for him—he would do nothing for her.— Besides, after all, he had never believed in her anyway.

Juliet Bredon

XII. Dangerous Years

The year of Little Dragon's birth the "great heat" was fiercer than usual. There seemed to be no air stirring and damp mists crouched low on the mountains. For some unknown reason an unusual plague of flies appeared in the village and sickness was rife. Just after his Month Feast, Little Dragon, greatly to his mother's terror, began to whimper and grow thin. Often he cried for no reason, refusing to be comforted.

"The child frets," Clever Needle said to her husband anxiously, "but I can see no sickness in him."

"If he loses instead of gaining," Chi replied, "it must be that you yourself have not your full strength and cannot give him all the milk he needs. Remember male children, like men, have lusty appetites."

"True enough.—And this one seems forever hungry. What shall I do?—The heat seems to have sucked all the life from me."

"Perhaps it would be well to hire a woman who can nurse him at her breasts," the father suggested.

"Oh, no—no," Clever Needle protested, "It will be cooler in a few days and I shall be able to give the child his fill. I would be ashamed to call a stranger to feed one of my sons. I fed the others and I fed them well."

But this time she was unable to do what she had done before and the child grew weaker day by day. Frightened at last she put aside her mother's pride, and begged Chi fetch a good strong woman they knew of in the next village,—one who had lately lost her own child and being poor would gladly come.

The delay nearly cost Little Dragon his life. When Chi returned to Hundred Altars bringing the wet-nurse with him he heard as he neared the house his wife's voice raised in that eerie cry used only to call back a soul.—It told him plainer than any words that the child must be unconscious and the mother trying to wake him from the deep sleep so perilously near to death. If his spirit failed to hear her, if it had already gone beyond earshot on its journey towards the Shadowy Land, it would never return to the little body. "Come back soul!—Come back soul!" she wailed again and again. Between her cries he could hear the sound of knocking as she struck the rice paddle on the door since that too is a sound a spirit hears.

Bidding the woman hasten, Chi hurried along the street and pushed open the gate. Clever Needle was wandering through the courtyards dazed and with staring eyes like one who walks in sleep. Not ungently he led her back to the room where the child lay: stretched on the k'ang,—it was very dark, coming in as he did from the outer sunshine, and at first he could see nothing. But presently he distinguished the little figure. It looked so very small and grey with tiny white finger-nails and the sight was like a hot steel needle piercing his heart.

But Clever Needle bending over her baby smiled a faint smile:

"He hears!" she whispered, "He hears,—I think his spirit is returning!"—and as she spoke the baby eyelids fluttered.—A faint flush of pink, pale as the petal of a peach blossom, touched the bloodless lips. Consciousness was coming back.

"Give him to me," said the stranger woman, and straightway taking him in her arms with a motherly smile she opened her coat and coaxed him to suck with soft cooing words.—Watching her way with the child the mother too found comfort. "If it be true my strength is sapped, this woman seems well able to care for my son.—She is good, she is kind.—I like her."

The amah whose name was Niu,—appropriately meaning cow, —was indeed a woman to inspire confidence,—an elemental type, with a large gentle face, smooth and round as a melon, big flat feet, and good maternal ways. From the first the baby prospered at her well-filled breasts. He took to her at once, and she loved him like her own child. Whenever he asked for food she gave it, and when he desired to be carried she carried him, and if he chose to cry all night, she walked him to and fro endlessly without complaining. It seemed indeed as if her mind never strayed from her duty and all the interest of her life centred in this milk-son who replaced the child she had so lately lost.

Soon Clever Needle treated her as one of the family as a good servant is treated in China where people are still proud to serve those who know how to be served. The amah's advice was often asked and as often taken, and she, like all who lived under the roof, might make her prayers to the family gods. Often the two women sewed together, embroidering the little shoes with a cat's face on the toes and ears and whiskers upstanding, the maid sitting on a lower seat with due respect to her mistress. The latest manchild in the house was a common bond between them, and they attended upon him as if he were a little god.

Perhaps it was because of the sickness which so nearly snatched him from her that made this third son especially dear to his mother. Of all her children it seemed that he, in a way, stood closest to her heart. He had come late, too, when she scarcely expected him and from the first he seemed a little different from the older boys who held together always and ran for choice to play beside their father in the fields. There they would chase one another with screams and laughter, two naughty, healthy imps, tweaking the poor mule's tail, or catching dragonflies and tying them to a string—loving the little cruelties that children, unthinking, practice on animals.

Alas, love is a sharp sword pointed at the heart of whoever forges it. And the more Clever Needle loved this littlest son, the more she feared for him. "Strange," she would often, say musingly to Amah Niu, "I did not fear like this even when my first son was born!" She dared not tell her husband all her terrors dreading his laughter,— nor how many times she slipped off to the temple and burned a candle to Kwanyin begging her to protect this dearly loved child. But when the first hundred days of his life were safely passed and the weather grew cooler, she murmured to the amah with relief: "Now the worst danger time is gone,—As he grows his strength will grow also and the mischievous spirits will not be so easily able to snatch him from us." —They say every nation has a devil at its elbow, but Chinese women feel not one but a hundred thousand devils threaten the lives of precious babies.

"Don't say such things aloud!" the amah chided her,—"You are daring them to try their wicked spells!"—All the peasant woman's lore was at her finger tips, and she knew, none better— how to outwit the cunning of devils envious of the happiness of mortals and eager to snatch a healthy happy child to be a playmate for themselves. Had they not taken her own child?—her little dead son? It was a bitter lesson. But this child they should not take. She had learned ways to beat them at their own game —and now she would not neglect a single one. Since charms and amulets were good protectors, she hung them upon Little Dragon, tied them to his pillow and stitched them upon his clothing, saying as she did so: "Fly away evil spirits—fly far away!"

But best of all precautions to deceive the powers of evil was to pretend the child was a girl. She told Clever Needle to say, (for only his own mother could say it efficaciously)—"What a pity that my last born is a female and ugly too!" She herself called him by mean, vulgar, even coarse nicknames—Little Idiot, Bad Temper, Old Woman—for she sensed, without knowing the underlying reason, that all nicknames were originally meant to safeguard those beloved especially during the dangerous years of infancy when a child is too weak to protect himself.

When Little Dragon was still but a few months old Clever Needle decided he was a most intelligent child. He had a way of pouting his little mouth that had not yet settled into definite shape, and his lower lip thrust the top one upward when they closed together after he had sucked. It was a usual baby trick— but Clever Needle would have it that no other child was ever clever enough to do such a thing.—And as he cut each tooth it seemed to her as if a miracle had happened. Both she and the amah were hurt when the Elder jokingly said that he had heard children usually cut teeth, and that the miracle would be if they did not.—"Men cannot understand children," Clever Needle remarked in disgust to Niu Nai Nai as she caught her baby up into her arms. He was little, little, little still, her youngest, not too big to be nosed and fondled by his mother. She winked one eye at him. He did his best to wink back at her but try as he would both eyes would shut together. She laughed aloud hugging and squeezing her baby in her arms. "Indeed men know nothing mistress," the amah agreed indignantly, "But all the women envy us. this child.—There is none other like him in the village nor in twenty villages. He is a lusty one, ten parts complete, a perfect manlet already.—Ah, thou little meat dumpling!" she exclaimed taking him from his mother and putting her lips against his cheek until he crowed with delight at her petting.

Their endless praise, their endless bending to his strong will spoiled Little Dragon thoroughly. Whatever he wished to do he did,

Juliet Bredon

and whatever he wished to have he had—and quickly for the women could not bear to see him cry. As he grew older they laid aside their work to play with him, and when he was tired and wished to sleep the amah walked him to and fro until he slipped off into dreamland, for he hated to be laid directly on his bed. He did what he liked, when he liked, as he liked. Very soon he was a *t'ao ch'i* child—a little tyrant. If when he crawled about even his grandfather failed to do his bidding, the little rascal would lie on his back in the courtyard and kick and scream and literally raise the dust until the Elder bent to his baby will.

Little Dragon was scarcely a year old and fat as Maitreya—the large bellied Buddha of good fortune,—when he decided he was tired of sitting and crawling, and suddenly raised himself erect and tried to walk, taking his first unsteady steps holding tightly to his mother's finger. She was excited and pleased at the brave way he thrust forward one small foot and then, with a worried look, slowly brought the other up to it. Chin-tzu and Yin-tzu her two elder boys had been big top-heavy babies, and months older before they stood upright alone. They had howled loudly too when they fell. But Little Dragon, though angry and surprised, did not cry. He only frowned and tried again—"Little lion heart," his mother purred, "Come quickly, amah,—look at our courageous one!" The Elder was also called to admire the baby, and as soon as Chi the Second returned from field work he, too, was asked to watch the "first steps."—It was a proud moment not without a deep significance to the father, who went at once to the kitchen and came back with the meat chopper. As the child toddled unsteadily Chi following behind him made a stroke with the chopper between the little feet thus severing the cord of memory that bound the baby to his last existence. Now he belonged wholly to this world, forgetting whence he came, loosed from the ties of his last earthly life. Such is the custom—A soul re-born must be set free from the cord which bound his feet together as he lay dead in his coffin.

When he was a year old a little feast called the "circle of the year" or the "noisy revolution" was arranged for the baby. The Longevity Star was hung up again and the child made to bow to it and to the intimate friends who had come in to join the family. A number of symbolic objects in a large basket were put on a table and the child sat beside it so that he might choose among them.—The first thing he took in his little hand would show what he meant to be in after life. If he chose an abacus he would be a merchant, if a packet of seed a farmer, if a tool an artisan, if a pen or an inkstone—a scholar.

For a moment he blinked with surprise at the strange toys. Then gurgling and reaching forward his tiny hands he firmly grabbed a pen with one and the ink slab with the other. It was so heavy he could not move it with one hand, but clung to it determinedly while he waved the brush aloft crowing with joy.

"See, see what he clutches!" his father exclaimed delighted. "Writing brush and ink—the tokens of a scholar.—What luck!"

"What luck!" the guests exclaimed in chorus applauding loudly. No one was more pleased than the Elder, himself grandson of a famous scholar, and asking no greater glory than to be grandfather of one.

"Watch the child carefully," he said, and his words had the force of a command. "Should he achieve a literary degree he will be the pride of our house even as my grandfather was."

By this choice Little Dragon confirmed his tyranny over his family utterly. So much so that at last his father complained that the child was altogether too unruly and should be corrected. Yet still his mother smiled on his naughtiness and made excuses: "Do not be anxious, husband, when he is older the child shall be taught to obey, but in these first years I can refuse him nothing!"—Chi could not but laugh at her for it was she who suffered most from the tyrant.—"You never let the others have their own way in every thing. But I shall hope that this crooked tree when it is large will straighten itself."

Word of the child's birth had, of course, been sent to his maternal grandmother who lived in a village near Pei Yang Ho, and now she clamoured to see the baby as was her right, for she had sent gifts and congratulations when he was born. So when the rains were over and the first cool autumn breezes brought healthy weather again, Clever Needle prepared to take Little Dragon to visit her own family. It was a filial duty not to be neglected, and a pleasure too for the tie between mother and daughter, even though the latter had left the home, was still strong.

Juliet Bredon

Amah Niu dressed the child in his best gala red and painted his chubby face with vermilion,—one spot on his forehead and one on either cheek. She herself wore a new cotton gown for which her mistress had given her the stuff, and Clever Needle put on the silk coat that she had worn at the Elder's feast two years before. So all three looking their best set out well content with themselves. Chi watching the two women mount their donkeys and handing the baby to the amah wrapped in a red wadded silk cape, remarked jocosely to his wife:

"You look like an official's lady, and the boy a rich man's son!" Whereupon the amah promptly covered the boy's head with a cloth lest the gods be jealous, and Clever Needle bade Chi cease his boasting.

When they arrived her mother too had to be reminded to be cautious in her praise, for she too longed to say the child was as lovely as she thought him. She held the baby against her and smelled his little body with deep content as one might smell a perfumed flower. It was her way of expressing affection since kissing was unknown to her.—"Ah thou small precious," she said again and again as she dandled him on her knee. He was a good weight now and the little grandmother none too strong— the very picture of what her daughter would be in another twenty years,—thin and wiry, her hair held smoothly into place under a stiff black satin bandeau, with an artificial pearl in the centre, her short coat and trousers of silk neatly cut and worn. She had trained her children well, and loved them well, and most of her sons and daughters of whom she had had four, had inherited a little of her talent for efficient obscurity. They were all sober earnest quiet people, rather like birds who had taken on the colouring of their background. In her home as in her daughter's there was happiness, for she well-understood the harmony of human relations and ruled her brood wisely.

Suddenly looking closely at this new grandson she exclaimed:

"But how is this!—You warn me against my words but you yourself have done nothing to protect him!—Where is the earring that will prove to all the imps he is nothing but a small joy?"

"We did not think to put one on lest piercing his ear might make him cry," said Clever Needle apologetically, "Besides I have heard that is a device used only where there is but a single son!"

"Unfilial daughter!" exclaimed her mother with a smile belying her words and embracing mother and child with tenderness—"Do you teach me the old customs now—you who are but a child yourself!—" Like every mother the older woman felt that her daughter was a baby still and needed her advice.

And Clever Needle, understanding, submitted meekly when her mother searched out a tiny gilt earring of her own, yet her heart turned over as she watched her preparing to pierce the precious baby's ear. She held her peace however as a dutiful daughter should. Her mother chuckled:

"Foolish one,—would I hurt thy child!"—then neatly knotting a thread of red silk she looped the earring over his ear, and feeling it cool and tickling against his skin the baby crowed with joy.

Presently his grandfather, hearing that his daughter had arrived, hurried in to greet her. He would have much to boast of at the teashop concerning this fine grandson who had taken pen and ink slab into his hand. Clever Needle knelt before him and bobbed the baby's head and folded his tiny hands in the proper gesture of respect. "Such a manling!" the grandfather cried in delight as he took the child. "Come, bring sweetmeats for him and cakes too!" The child stuffed them in his mouth greedily, then ran away staggering hither and thither and his grandfather after him laughing and picking him up when he fell. Then tired out the old man took off one ankle band and made a girdle for the child and held him up as he tottered to and fro in his miniature jacket that rode up to his neck and his absurd trousers accommodatingly slit up the back.

Meanwhile mother and daughter, separated for two years, had much to say to one another. There were all the doings of their households, and all the news of their respective villages to talk over. Both had questions to ask which had long been burning their tongues;—who had married, and who had given birth, and who had died or gone away. Clever Needle must tell of Ling-erh's tragedy, and Ma's Minor Star, and the arrival of the small joy instead of the great joy he had expected so confidently, and all the gossip of Hundred Altars, and her mother of her neighbours' doings. Indeed they had said scarcely half they had to say before twilight fell and Clever Needle had to leave if she was to reach Hundred Altars before dark.

As they parted, the grandmother once more caressed Little Dragon peevish and sleepy now—"I am well pleased with thee daughter—watch over thy fine son,—and of thine own health take heed!"

Amah Niu as soon as they were out of earshot and beyond the village remarked: "Mistress, the child is not himself. The Honoured One, your father, has made him sick with cakes. Let us return home quickly and I will brew him a broth of crushed spiders."

But she was wrong, for there was nothing really the matter with the child, and long before they were home he was fast asleep in her arms.

XIII. Young Tiger

The midwife and the old herbalist proved right after all. Lilac Blossom grew stronger, but she did not have a second child. Ma wasted money on ginseng, the reviving tonic, and on the precious lion's milk that the female of the species exudes from her paws at dawn on the mountain tops. But neither had any effect. The little wife sank slowly into a twilight of mind and body, a listlessness that drugs could not dispel. Her frail nature seemed unable to recover from the shock of her disappointment.

Still for another year Ma waited with what patience he could muster, hoping against hope. It was hard for him to believe that what he wanted he could not have. Nor did it make it easier when he overheard Chi telling his friends how Little Dragon chose the pen on his first birthday and how promising a lad he was.

"That earth-stained farmer!" Ma grumbled to Shui Ching. "It's a shame he should have a son like that.—Whatever made him deserve such a fine boy?"—Perhaps,—the thought flashed across his mind,—seeing the two babies were born about the same time, Little Dragon had been really intended for his house and the girl Swallow, so named by her "official" mother Shui Ching after the birds that flew about her cradle, destined for Chi's. Could the Goddess of Birth have carelessly mixed the souls, he caught himself wondering. But no, surely not. These were women's fancies. Goddesses had no power in such matters. For generations there had been many males born in the Chi family, few in his own. That was the answer to his bitterness.

Having tried a Minor Star and failed to obtain his heir, Ma decided the only thing left to do was to adopt a son. But who? How? When?—He turned the idea over and over in his mind. There would be difficulties. Somehow he felt discouraged and in no hurry to face them. Indeed, in his present mood, he might have delayed carrying out his plans but for a chance meeting with Amah Niu holding Chi's fine third son in her arms.

One day a story teller came to the village, an old man and blind men of his profession often are. He took his stand under a shady tree near Ma's house with his tea-pot, his fan and his wooden clappers beside him. A little boy, sight of his sightless eyes beat on a small round drum calling people to listen and soon a crowd of men women and children gathered to hear the wandering minstrel.

In his thin old voice the singer began a chant of olden days, of gods and heroes and high romance, accompanying himself on his serpent bellied violin. Such legends everybody loved, and he could make them come alive. With a wave of his fan, with a click of his castanets, or a few plaintive modulations plucked from the strings of his *san hsien*, he created an atmosphere of glamour and charm. His gift of mimicry, too, was little short of marvellous.—A bold bad rebel, a female shrew, a hypocritical priest, a swashbuckling soldier, he brought each type to life by simple dramatic gestures or changing voice tones. Though he was only an unlettered fellow, he had the marvellous memory of his race, the imagination of the true artist, the rare power of casting spells over his listeners. As he sang he called up a world invisible and the shadowy figures of the dim past at his command crept round him on ghostly feet.

But every now and then, just in the midst of some thrilling scene as when the three heroes of the Peach Orchard were about to sign the pact of blood brotherhood, or the beautiful Yang Kuei Fei is on the point of yielding to her Imperial Lover, the singer would cease his song and bid the boy pass round the bowl for cash.

"A coin from everyone!" the old man pleaded in his natural voice, "a coin or I will tell no more!"—And he waited for the sound of cash dropping into the bowl before he would go on with his tale.

As he felt in his belt for a coin Ma was suddenly aware that Amah Niu with Little Dragon was trying to push past him so that the child might see better.—"Give him to me," said Ma, "and I will hold him on my shoulder above the heads of the crowd." —The little boy fascinated him, had done so from his birth.

"He grows well," he remarked looking at the child tenderly.

"Oh, yes, your honour,"—the amah was proud of the merchant's notice. "He is a wolf cub now for strength. He begins to talk like a young prince commanding his kingdom. And his appetite! You should see him eat.—Already he pushes my breasts from him and demands solid food. But I will not wean him yet, no I will not.— Let him suck for his full three years, I say."

Hundred Altars

The child cuddled comfortably down on Ma's shoulder and the old story teller went on with his tale.—"The heir is the pride of his house, the first fruit of his father's flesh. He shall rule the land. He shall confound his enemies!"—But the merchant no longer listened to the tale. The touch of child's hands clinging around his neck stirred him too deeply. Ma made up his mind. It was wholly clear to him now that he must adopt a son, at once. Handing the baby back to his nurse with a mumbled excuse that he had business to attend to, Ma threw a silver piece to the story teller and strode home.

That same evening after they had eaten he told Shui Ching that devils might trust in women; so far as he was concerned he never would again. The failure of the Minor Star had utterly disgusted him. Now he meant to *adopt* a son.—No one could say anything to that. It was a common practice in sonless homes. There was hardly a family where there had not been at one time or another a "crossing over." Of course it often proved a ticklish business, the cause of more lawsuits than any other custom, for blood heirs were always eager to push aside a stranger. But, having no male kinsmen with a claim on him, Ma knew he was safe enough. He could do just as he pleased. Shui Ching, with peasant caution demurred: "When a man past middle life takes a little wife to bear him sons, there is often disappointment, —but when a man without nephews or any near of kin takes an outsider into his house there is danger!"

"Don't I know that?" he snapped back, his chin set like a rock. "If only I had a relation of the right sort the 'crossing over' would be easy enough—but when there is no one within the clan one must go outside."

"Ah, if only your uncle in Tientsin had a boy to lend. But he is childless too!" she said gloomily.

"If only,—if only,—what is the use of such words?"

"Well, you know as I do that it is seldom a man ventures to pick up a mere stranger. There are so many chances he may turn out ill, or be a puling child with some hidden disease.— Otherwise his parents would never let him go!"

"Don't talk nonsense!" Ma retorted sharply. "If there is good meat at one end of a boar, there are sharp tusks at the other. Besides, what choice have I when my two women refuse to bear me children?

Juliet Bredon

One would think to hear you talk that my whims controlled my actions!"

Ma was strong enough and ruthless enough to take his own way and create his own precedents in this as in the matter of the Little Wife. Even if village sentiment was against his adopting the son of a stranger, even if the neighbours would be inclined to taunt one who was "picked up," and nickname him "soil of a caterpillar" because he. relied on sustenance from a strange nest, Ma felt he could live down the prejudice for himself and for the lad also. How such a boy might turn out he could not, admittedly, foresee,—but he could make sure of getting a healthy child.

The easiest way to solve his problem, would be to find a lad in Hundred Altars whose parents might be willing to give him lip. But this proved impossible. The farmers needed their sons to help in the fields. None could be persuaded to part with one of his boys. "Why not take a lad from the city?" Chien suggested—But Ma shook his head thoughtfully.—"No, town-folk have town ways. He would not fit here as he grew older. The blood of city bred folk is thin and the tastes that might come to him through his forefathers are not our tastes."

At last the merchant bethought himself of one of the cameldrivers whose caravan sometimes brought him supplies from Peking. He remembered that he had heard this man had several sons, and, if no bettered offered... one of them might do. Ma knew well enough the hours and days when the caravan was due to pass through Hundred Altars. Next morning before the village was astir the merchant went out beyond the houses to meet it. The rising sun showed like the rim of a golden gong above the fields as the leading camel appeared in the distance, walking with stately dignity, his great furry head held high, his big flat cushioned feet expanding and contracting like sponges as he set them slowly on the ground and lifted them again. When Old Hundred approached Ma stepped well to one side,—the red rag tied to the beast's forehead proved him to be vicious, and camels, quick to resent the smell of strangers, often give a sudden twisted bite which is deadly or a kick strong enough to upset a cart.

Ma shouted to the driver: "Hi, there! stop for a moment! I wish to speak a word with you!"

Throwing the nose-rope of the lead camel to the boy beside him, the man crossed the road to where the merchant stood.—"Perhaps," he thought, "there may be some profitable business doing. It is strange that a rich merchant should come out himself to call to me!" He greeted Ma respectfully as became his wealth.

"Is trading good?" Ma inquired amiably.

"Not good this year," the man responded. "With our five sons it is difficult to 'pass the day'!"

"Would you be willing to part with one of those five sons?" asked Ma abruptly.

The camel-driver stared uncomprehending.—Ma repeated his question, and then the man said: "What does your honour mean?—Ah, one of my sons?—Do you want him to enter your house?—and which one would it be?"

"That I cannot tell you now," Ma answered, "What man would take a boy without first casting an eye on him? Maybe I'll come some day and look them over!"

The camel-driver was silent, partly to gain time for thinking. The proposal was so sudden, and sudden things troubled his slow mind. He could not say "yes" like this offhand. He must first talk to his wife about it. Suppose she refused and he was obliged to force her will?—In the end she would have to give in if he ordered her to do so, but she was not the kind of a woman who, having yielded, would forget and be finished with a quarrel. Every time he came home she would remind him how sorrowful and lonely she was, for she was the passionate type of mother, and never could have too many children round her. Personally he felt that one lad could easily be spared seeing how many sons he had. Besides Ma often gave him carrying trade and he could ill-afford to refuse the merchant's request.

"But your honour,—" he stammered presently, tapping the stem of his long pipe on the ground. "Our home is twenty li from here and it is a miserable poor house not fit for your honour's visit."

"No matter," said Ma, "I will come.—Yes, I will come tomorrow." Now that his mind was fixed why delay?

True to his word Ma went next day and found the camel-driver squatting on his haunches beside a tumble-down doorway waiting to receive his guest. He led the merchant across a courtyard

Juliet Bredon

littered with piles of refuse and spattered with the droppings of poultry to the crumbling mud house of a single room used for every domestic purpose. Obviously these people lived on the edge of destitution.

"Please be seated," he said to Ma as he cleared the torn felt mat off a corner of the %ang. Then he bade the old grandmother and the child, huddled half-asleep in one corner with a grey goat-kid clasped in its arms, get out of the room. "Begone!" he said roughly, and then in a smoother tone to Ma,—"Sir, I am ashamed that you should come to this poor house. It is hot in here and it smells. But we have no better place."

His wife brought boiling water instead of tea, and the man made further excuses.—"It is the best we can offer you," he said apologetically. "We cannot afford to buy tea-leaves these days."

Meanwhile the children played noisily in the courtyard, and Ma watched them through the open door as he sipped his hot water.

"Which boy does your honour fancy?" the father said presently though he could guess well enough.—The eldest was crooked in the knees, spindly and ill-nourished. Plainly no rich merchant would want him. Besides even a poor man cannot give away his first born son. The fourth and third were under-sized too, and not attractive. The fifth was a small baby with symptoms of eye disease, but too young to be judged yet. But the second was a bright looking little rogue of four years, a well-fleshed, chunky, rather clumsy little boy. He seemed strong and healthy though unkempt and uncared for. His jacket was ragged and his trousers too long and too loose. But he had a queer brave little manner, impudent and amusing.

"Perhaps you would take Number Five, the baby,—he is so young that he will be easy to train," the Camel-driver suggested slyly.

"No," said Ma firmly. "I am now acquainted with your family,—Number Two is the child I want."

The man sighed.—Much will ever have more and the best. Nevertheless, he called out to his wife pretending he had said nothing to her previously, "Wife here is good news.—Merchant Ma is ready to adopt our boy!"

"Which boy?" she shouted from the courtyard in a joyless voice.

"Number two!"

"That one he cannot have!—I am his mother and refuse consent!"

"He is the one my wife likes best," whispered the camel-driver.. "I do not think she will agree easily to let him go—"

"Well, think it over," said Ma rising from the k'ang. "Tell your 'inside person' that in my house your son will be fed full and he will always wear shoes and even stockings."

"Ai!—shoes are dear!" the man exclaimed appreciatively, "My children have never worn shoes in their lives. I'll talk with her again and give you the answer when I return from the 'Four Nine' market at Frog Village."

"Stop at Hundred Altars on your way back after sunset then. And remember that many a poor man in these hard times would be glad of a home for one of his sons. Remember too," (Ma hinted and his tone said plainer than any words,—no son, no trade!) "that I have often done you favours, and that yours is not the only caravan which passes Hundred Altars. With four boys still in your house, what matter if Number Two goes ?—No one will miss his presence!"

"Except his mother!" the camel-driver muttered to himself, though aloud he said meekly:—"Yes, your honour.—I will come."

When Ma had gone the father talked again with his wife. Though in many ways he was head of his family, and might run it arbitrarily, in all that had to do with her children the mother had strong rights too, because she was the centre of domestic life, and now he found her like a tigress in an angry sullen mood, ready to defend her cubs.

"Can you be sure the gods will send you another son if you so easily cast this one away?—Or are you rich enough to take a little wife to bear more children if I should prove too old!" she taunted him bitterly.

Then he told her patiently, moved by her grief though angered by her unreasonableness, that it was poverty and need which made him ask such a sacrifice. But for a long time the mother would not listen.

"To you it may mean nothing if the child goes," she sobbed, "but he is my heart's loved and the best of them all.—Now if the merchant had asked for Number Four—." —It was the custom thus to refer to sons by numbers that all the world might know how many a person had and be envious.

"What use are such words?" her husband asked crossly. "Number Two is his honour's choice. It is Number Two and no other. With five mouths to feed besides the old grandmother and ourselves, we cannot afford to spit in the face of luck!"—After he had told her over and over again that by parting with one she could do better by the others, she gave up her determination in the end.—When the stomach is empty pride is not strong, and even love cannot stand against hunger. At least, she thought, comforting herself as best she could, the child would be sure of a good home and much to eat.

Then on a day that the camels rested the camel-driver according to his word, took the child, in his little tattered coat which the. mother had mended carefully, to Ma's house. And when he saw the white rice prepared for himself and the boy, and the heaps of wadded quilts to cover him, he was content to part with his son,— unselfishly content. With scarcely a regret he set his grimy thumb mark to the paper which Ma had prepared to make the adoption legal, for ignorant as he was the camel-driver could not write a single character not even his own name.

As for the child, he was pleased with such a great house as he had never seen before. When Ma took him to Shui Ching, saying— "Here is the child that I have chosen, a fine strong little lad!—Let us hope that he will prove a good son to us!" the child bowed clumsily, for in his rough home no one had time to teach him manners.

But Shui Ching, ever kind, did not judge harshly. "He looks likely enough," she said pleasantly, "or will do when I have sewed him a new coat."—She could not help but think to herself that this coming of a son to her husband's house was not as she had hoped. If only the boy had been her own, what joy she would have felt, unshadowed joy!—But this little stranger,— who could tell what manner of man he might grow up to be? —And her heart felt sad thinking of the sadness of the "own mother" who had given him up. She could picture the poor woman's nights spent in weeping and her days spent in watching for his impossible return, her dress carelessly unbuttoned, her hair loose and uncombed, her face swollen with weeping.

Had she a son herself nothing on earth could make her give him up.—Yes, one thing might—hunger—his hunger. To think that there were homes with too many clutching baby fingers, too many mouths to feed! The injustice of Fate! Shui Ching felt she could never understand that.—"The only way," she said to herself, "is to cease asking those questions to which only the gods know the answers."

Juliet Bredon

XIV. The Dragon's Mark

For a few short years Little Dragon was allowed to play about the village as he pleased with no more responsibilities than a puppy or a kitten. In summer he went naked as his mother bore him save for a red string about his neck with a lucky cash blessed in the sight of Kwanyin attached to it. In winter Amah Niu dressed him in wadded clothes, one suit on top of another, so that if he tumbled down he lay like a beetle on its back, unable to get up again. Chin-tzu and Yin-tzu were ten and eleven years when he was only four, and ordinary boisterous boys. Their natural high spirits often took them into mischief and out again. But Little Dragon was from the first a quiet dreamy child and sometimes annoyed his elder brothers by refusing to enter into their rough games. Even as a tiny mite he preferred to amuse himself by tracing characters in the dust with his chubby finger. But when the three Chi children did happen to trot about together passersby would whisper, pointing at Little Dragon,—"That's the best one,—no doubt about it! He is finer boned than the others as if there might be something in him of different blood!"

Usually Chin-tzu and Yin-tzu kept to themselves, however, seeming to feel instinctively that they had little in common with their brother. Together they stooped over the spring fishing for tiny shrimps, together they collected stones and dammed the stream, or built miniature houses; together they caught fireflies,—the younger following the elder everywhere just like a little dog. Only when all other games failed these two would sometimes urge Little Dragon to play "farmers" with them. Hoes and rakes were their favourite toys. But their father, if he happened to cross the courtyard, always noticed how awkwardly his third son handled such implements. "Not like that, Little Dragon," he would say, "How clumsy you are!—Hold it like this!" and he would change the grip of the little hand and place the fingers where they should be. But it seemed as if as often as he corrected so often the lad went wrong again.

"That child!" Chi muttered to himself, "shows no taste for farmwork like the others.—If he cannot and will not do his share, I fear there will be bad blood between him and his brothers when he grows to manhood—unless, unhandy with the plough he turn out handy with his books."

One day he said to Clever Needle, "Seeing that Little Dragon is content to play all day long drawing characters, even though he knows not their meaning, it might be well to send him to school early and try to make a scholar out of him. His two brothers can work the farm. They are built for it,—big-framed boys who love the land as I do, and ask nothing better than to till the fields. A little knowledge will suffice for them, just enough writing to make up accounts and enough reading to check the grain receipts. But I do believe our third son has the dragon's mark of the scholar on his forehead.—The diviner says so too, and his opinion bears out the lad's choice at his first year feast. If that be true there is no telling how high he will rise.—All doors open to the key of learning!"

Clever Needle feared his boasting. "It is not well," she warned, "to expect too much lest Heaven become envious."—Then in a loud voice for all the evil spirits to hear she added:—"Our toad is a very small toad, nothing to be proud of!"

Chi smiled.—Women were always so,—misty minded, ever fearful.—But he answered kindly:

"Well then, we will not look so far ahead if it frightens you, wife. Let the child first learn to be useful for a few years. He cannot help much yet, but it will be good for him to get the feel of the sun on his back and the loose earth under his feet. When he is older it will be time enough to send him to school."

Presently Clever Needle called the child to her and told him that now he was near to be a little man and must begin to be useful. There was so much to be done that even children must do their share. Big sisters carried little sisters on their backs. Big brothers helped their fathers in the fields, and after four little boys were given tasks as much as possible like play.

"Look," she said to their youngest son, "the ground is covered with wild spinach—dandelion leaves.—Go get a sharp stick and a basket and dig a good lot for our dinner!"—and the child ran off pleased, for it was fun to reach down into the roots of things and get food that cost nothing and was fresh and damp with dew.—Or again she would send him out to pick up the dry branches that fell from the trees for fuel. Not a twig, not a branch, not a leaf was wasted since anything helped to keep water boiling for the tea drunk all day long.

At times he would wander up and down the dry river beds, where long strings of laden pack mules and donkeys picked their way among the stones, to gather lumps of coal dropped from their paniers. And when such light tasks were done he would just sit idle in the fields watching the great black crows feeding or the dragon flies flashing by like jewels, or listening to a meadow lark winging skyward, and trilling his octaves until the heavens seemed full of flutes. He made a curious picture, this little peasant lad, as he sat there clad in rough cotton, his clothes fitting clumsily and hiding the lithe beauty of his slender body. Often he fell into a reverie, his clear cut chin resting on his hand, his dark eyes gazing on the distant mountains until a passing goatherd, singing to himself for company, roused him to a more boyish mood.

Then suddenly, when he was eight years old his life was broken sharply, and he said goodbye to dreamy babyhood. Now the time had come for him to go to school. Chi ordered a bench and chair for him from the carpenter. His mother made him a new long gown like a grown man's to wear. His father bought the "four precious things" that every scholar must have,—the ink slab, with its little well for water, the ink-cake, the writing brush, and paper. The only book he needed was the "Three Character Classic"—the Chinese child's guide to knowledge, composed eight centuries ago. Perhaps no book has ever been ground so deeply into the memory of so many millions of the human race as this, and still suffices for the need of village scholars.—Ma kept a stock of these primers, and when he met his neighbour buying a copy, he remarked: "I see you are getting ready to send a son to school."

"Yes," Chi answered proudly, "the youngest, Little Dragon. He has a taste for learning which the others lack. A few years' schooling sufficed for them, and they will soon be 'staring blind men' anyway, so seldom they use their book knowledge. They prefer farm work, and have no heart for anything else.—It is that or nothing for them."

"Well," Ma replied, "To do is easy, to know is difficult. Young Tiger shows no love of learning either. But I do not mean to let him be spendthrift or idle. He shall have but a few years' schooling, just long enough to learn to read and write and use the abacus. Even a snail, the teacher says, can learn to fly through space if it attaches itself to a dragon's tail. But I don't expect Young Tiger to fly far. I plan to take him, as soon as possible into my business."

The new term opened after the September Full Moon Feast. It was necessary to wait until that was over for not until then was the harvest in, and during the harvest even little boys were useful helpers, and field work of necessity took precedence over lessons. But as soon as all the grain was garnered school began, and Chi walking ahead, for it was not correct for father and son to walk side by side like equals, took Little Dragon to Hsu Hsien Sheng, the teacher.

The school occupied but a single room in a little abandoned temple at one end of the main street,—a small stuffy place airless; in summer, and unheated in winter save for a flaming bundle of dried grass or twigs set alight on the stone floor, and giving a false warmth for a few minutes.

Chi, entering, bowed low to Hsü Hsien Sheng, and addressed him most politely and with the exaggerated humility that was his due—

"Venerable teacher,—I am only a common unlettered farmer and to my shame I can scarcely read or write. But I have brought my stupid son to you. Pray try to drive learning into his head that he may be a credit to his ancestors."—Then he offered the presents he had brought, a pair of red candles, baskets of fruit and cakes,' and also a gift of money, while Little Dragon, following his father's example, likewise bowed stiffly.

Hsü Hsien Sheng rose from his chair and returned Chi's bows with great dignity and a certain elegance.

"I will assist your son to lift his darkness and borrow light," he answered pompously. "He shall study the Classics and learn by heart the twenty four examples of filial piety. He shall be taught to respect Heaven and Earth and his ancestors, since such knowledge is the foundation of a virtuous life."

Chi bowed again. He was quite satisfied. Education to his mind must follow tradition and be based on the wisdom of the ancients. The moral side mattered more than the practical. In his day men preferred the sons should acquire a stock of apt classical quotations rather than be able to write a simple letter free from mistakes. They were content that the study of history should end with the Ming dynasty, which collapsed three hundred years ago when the reigning Manchus supplanted it. How, these ultra conservatives argued, could anything that happened since be considered impartially—yet? Geography began and ended, vaguely enough, with China. Arithmetic was regarded with contempt. The abacus sufficed. Science was despised. Astronomy was left to the Imperial astronomers.

So Chi bowed himself out with the sure and certain hope that his third son would acquire the wisdom of a magistrate by learning the "progressive nature of numbers,, the names of the heavenly bodies, the three relations between sovereign and minister, father and son, man and wife, the four seasons, the five elements, the five cardinal virtues, the six kinds of grain, the six domestic animals, the seven passions, the eight kinds of music, the nine degrees of relationship and the ten moral duties."

Hsü Hsien Sheng, though scarcely appearing to notice what Chi had brought, slyly appraised his gifts. It was all very well to be a school-master. No profession was more respected and a teacher need never do manual work. Indeed custom forbade him to plough or reap or harness an animal or drive a cart, fetch water or move a bench, as undignified and unsuitable to his learning. Rewards in honour he reaped in plenty, but rewards in cash were scarce. The families of his pupils gave him food and fuel,—each in turn supporting him for a few days, though meagrely enough. True, at the great festivals they made him cash presents. Sometimes, too, he earned silver by tracing good luck characters on the New Year posters in his fine scholar's hand, or again he served as public letter writer, writing for those who could not write themselves. Such services procured him his one luxury, a few pipes of opium. Then new thoughts floated through his dull brain, and the weariness of the day's routine slipped from him. Then he was happy despite his poverty, then he was king of his dreams, and lived over again the days of his youth when full of ambition he had gone up for the Imperial examinations—and failed.

Since a new pupil meant added income to him, Hsü Hsien Sheng bade Little Dragon take his place among the other boys with an ingratiating smile. And Little Dragon did as he was told shyly,—

a. frightened small boy in his well-starched blue gown with his cap set at a decorous angle above his serious little face, and his eyes fixed upon the ground in deep humility. Venerable Teacher filled the child with awe.—His way of swinging his robes as he walked, and planting his feet outward as scholars do when he sat, of pushing back his long sleeves with an exaggerated gesture when he opened his book, of turning polished walnuts between his long fingers to keep them supple, all added to the dignity of his appearance.

There were no separate classes in the school. All the boys learned the same thing at the same time and learned aloud. That first day when the teacher read over a line from his book Little Dragon understood not a word of the classical phrases. —"Now repeat what I have said," the master commanded his pupils, and the frightened lad tried like a parrot to say the words and was corrected and tried again.

The boys studied all together, shouting in chorus at the top of their voices,—otherwise, if they kept silence, how, the teacher argued, could he be sure that they were learning?—Yet somehow in that babel of noise the old man's ears were sharp enough to detect an error in a word or even in a tone. When the dullest-witted boy could repeat the whole of the task without the slightest mispronunciation the little scholars were called up one by one to the master's table. There each was bidden to lay down his book, and turning his back to Hsü Hsien Sheng, expected to rattle off his lesson without the support of his fellow pupils. Memory and nothing else— none of the boys knew what he recited was about or cared.

So long as he could manage to keep awake old Hsü Hsien Sheng was quick to detect a fault. But now and then he would doze off after the noon meal, and then the boys turned mischievous. Queues were pulled, shoes snatched off, and the big lads teased the little ones until the teacher suddenly awoke and scolded them roundly.

Young Tiger was usually the ring-leader in whatever mischief was afoot, talking, whispering, idling, so often that Hsü Hsien Sheng gave him many a good crack on the head with his folded fan, remarking sarcastically as he listened to the hollow sound,— "Wooden drum—nothing but an empty wooden drum!"

Young Tiger hated school. Unlike most Chinese children he could not bear sitting still and the long hours of study unbroken by cheerful recesses were agony to him. He had no reverence for the written character and would never understand that it is a crime to tear up papers covered with brush strokes or throw them on the. floor. Such things should be burned reverently in a temple brazier. "Can't you learn?" Venerable Teacher would demand despairingly again and again, "Whoever rescues a thousand characters from being trodden under foot or otherwise insulted adds a year to his life!"

As for books, Young Tiger thought them good only to be used as a pillow, the better to snore on. Every morning when it came time to go to school he begged Shui Ching for just one more hour's sleep, and every morning she shook him in disgust, exclaiming: "Shame on you, lazy lout! Your father pays the school-master to teach you! It is your duty to learn. If you refuse people will say, and with reason, that you are wild!"—Ma too reproached him sternly. "Do you want to be like the boy who would not learn but preferred to walk the roads with a pitchfork and a manure basket gathering dung?—Must I like his father put you in a basket and have you carried slung on a pole to school as a pig is carried to market?"

Ma told Hsü Hsien Sheng privately not to spare correction.— A teacher like a father has full right to punish any boy under his care, and the more severe he was the more respect he had from parents. So often Young Tiger was forced to kneel on the stone floor in front of all the boys for the time required to burn three incense sticks. Again he had his hands rapped with the ruler, and sometimes the exasperated Venerable Teacher made himself a judge and solemnly condemned the lad to be thrashed by the other pupils.—But the more he was punished, the more rebellious Young Tiger became. He played truant as often as he could, and learned to take his beating for it philosophically. Someday, he said to himself, they would give up trying to beat knowledge into his head. He looked with envy at the passing caravan men, free to tread the open road. He would so much rather have been a camel-driver like his blood father than a second Confucius.

Little Dragon was cast in a different mould. Even in appearance the two boys contrasted strongly. Little Dragon was a comely lad, bright with charm,—an exceptional boy not only physically but mentally in that community of earth-grimed toilers,—whereas Young Tiger was the typical peasant, loutish, ungainly, all joints and knuckles, good tempered at bottom, but lazy and mischievous, and often a blusterer or what folk called a "paper tiger" by nature. Sturdy and muscular he could excel in all sorts of outdoor games whereas Little Dragon, though no less brave-spirited, was an indoor lad with a pale skin that sun and wind had no power to bronze.

After the first few frightened days he loved school. He was never happier than when he set out shortly after sunrise with the other boys in single, file, their books wrapped in blue kerchief under their arms—as solemn as grown-up scholars. He learned because he liked to learn, well and easily, and soon he could repeat his lessons better than any boy in the class, better indeed than those who like Young Tiger had been studying far longer than he. Hsü Hsien Sheng not unnaturally felt pride and pleasure in this promising pupil. He was an old man and not ambitious, content to drone away his life, still even he tired sometimes of teaching clumsy hands to write characters and unnimble tongues to repeat words especially as few of his students stayed with him long, and few came regularly, for in the poorer families, there were times when boys must be kept out of school to help with farmwork.

"That third son of yours," he said to Chi one day, "will be a degree man one day. Have you ever thought of preparing him for the examinations?"

Chi hid his pride as best he could, saying:—"I fear you flatter me! The boy is really stupid. Anything he has learned he owes entirely to you!"—But he could hardly wait until he got home to tell the Elder what Hsü had said. The Elder who was still hale and hearty despite his great age took a keen interest in his grandsons, particularly in Little Dragon. He thought for a moment over the Venerable Teacher's words, and then advised his son that he would do well to pay extra to the school-master. "There are times to save, but there are also times to spend," he said.

Chi agreed. Thereafter he paid Hsü Hsien Sheng twice the usual fee of two silver dollars a year in addition to food supplies. So while the two dollar pupils got two dollars worth of reading and reciting aloud, Little Dragon was given extra instruction until soon

Juliet Bredon

he could read, and in a measure understand what he read with a very little help.

But Little Dragon despite the teacher's praise still kept the gentle modesty which distinguished him all his life long and remained unspoiled despite a favouritism which might so easily have turned him into a little prig. For some strange reason a strong friendship grew up between him and Young Tiger, though their tastes and characters were so different. Little Dragon felt a sneaking respect for the brute strength of Young Tiger, and Young Tiger for the quick brain of Little Dragon. Perhaps it was natural, for even grown men admire in others the qualities they lack themselves and therefore secretly envy.

Diligent scholar though he was, Little Dragon often joined Young Tiger in his games even though he did not care for his wilder pranks like fruit stealing. He was proud to play foot shuttle-cock with the older boy and prouder still when Young Tiger would say: "Come along, we want, you for 'cat and mouse!' "—Some of the other boys were a little jealous and might have tried to leave him out but the leadership of Young Tiger in their games was undisputed and if he wanted his friend, Little Dragon must come. How happy he was, this timid but friendly little boy, to join in the ring. To please his comrade he would always play mouse and stay inside the circle, leaving Young Tiger to be the cat prowling and growling outside. "Is brother mouse home?" he hissed in classical cat language. "Oh wait a moment," squeaked the mouse tying up his queue and tightening his girdle the better to elude his, pursuer when the chase began at the word "Ready!" In and out of the ring the boys ducked and dodged, but it was a rule of the game that the cat could use only mouse-holes through which his prey tried to escape. Finally when the little mouse was tired out, the cat pounced on him and ate him, growling and shaking him the while, and finally with a great gulp, pretending to swallow him whole.

This was but one of many games they played. These children had vivid imaginations fired by passing story tellers, and the actors at the temple festival.—A few wooden spears and cardboard faces with horse-hair beards turned them into a band of warriors.—A tiger mask sufficed to start them on a mighty hunting expedition. A cave near the dragon spring made an ideal bandits lair. They attacked it and defended it by the hour to the great terror of the wild pigeons nesting there. Having few toys, and those few so fragile that they never lasted long, the village lads developed a gift for make believe, and even in childhood they extracted from their lives the double enjoyment that comes to those with the dramatic instinct. "Now I am doing this, now I am doing that,"—-they told themselves as they were doing it, looking on while they participated.

    Thus their school years passed happily enough broken by few holidays save at the New Year, varied by few excitements except those they created themselves. Soon, too soon, work would be hot on their heels, and life flow on in a smooth unending rhythm of labour. But for these few short years of childhood they were alternately solemn little scholars, plaguing the patience of Venerable Teacher, and—once they had escaped from his classroom—carefree urchins, dirt-streaked, sunburned, and otherwise defaced by the bumps, bites, and scratches that are the common lot of farm children, whose mothers have neither the time to wash them nor to worry over them once they have safely passed a devil haunted babyhood.

Juliet Bredon

XV. White Business

Not till his ninetieth year did Elder Chi begin to fail. Up till that time he had been a vigorous old man taking an active interest in village affairs though for many years already his son, with filial care, had dissuaded him from working in the fields lest he tire himself. This Chi the Second did so tactfully that his father, standing by watching the labour of others, still had the pleasant illusion that he was active and indispensable. It would have hurt him to think the farm and the family could get on without him.

Then, quite suddenly, he seemed to enter the twilight of old age and his body began to wither. He became simply a living mummy, his body brown and sapless as a winter branch, his face yellow as bone, and the lids and corners of his eyes pale and bloodless. He lifted his feet slowly and more slowly and put them down carefully so that he looked like an old tree walking. Even on warm days he used a windhood to protect himself against mild spring breezes, and that last year he wore a wadded coat well into the summer. Towards the end of his life he carried a stick. It was his right to do so. Such aids were forbidden to the young, but a man after sixty might use one in his own village,—after seventy in his own province, after eighty even at court.—All through the last summer of his life the old man sat and gazed pridefully over the fields which his son, with his sons beside him, tilled well and carefully as he had taught him years ago. But sometimes he would sit dreaming over his pipe and looking straight in front of him just at nothing, his thin shoulders bowed under his loose robe,—forgetting the world and letting it flow past him as quiet water flows past a familiar landscape.

Clever Needle, as genuinely fond of the old man as he was of her, coddled him and treated him as a beloved patriarch. Now and then she called him "The Immortal" and teased him tenderly about his discovery of the Elixir of Life. He liked it, for till the last the old man loved a joke. He liked too to have his favourite dishes prepared for him, and to find his grandsons devoted listeners to his long stories.

Occasionally, on days when he felt strong, the Elder allowed Little Dragon to bring the neighbours' children to hear his tales, and they would gather round him, awed and thrilled as he talked to them of the long ago, for whatever was past was still clear to him though whatever was present or might be ahead was misty and confused. "Yah," he would say with a wise smile, "it is fitting that the old should tell the young what they remember!" —In time they came to know his tales by heart, but loved them no less for that. Sometimes there were surprises when suddenly in the midst of one story he would remember another and ramble off into it, confusing both.— The man of action had long since passed away, but the philosopher lived long enough to teach the children of the village wisdom they would remember all their lives long and later pass on to *their* grandchildren.—Only a few years at the beginning and end of life were the peasants permitted to be idle. While the fathers worked in the fields and the mothers were busy with their never-ending household tasks, grandfathers and grandmothers taught the youngest generation history and legend,—local lore and custom,—from the living store-house of their memories. Thinking of his grandfather long afterwards, Little Dragon wondered if the Elder had not been secretly over-burdened somehow by all his wisdom and experience.

It seemed as if that year summer was loath to bid farewell. Day followed day, calm and sunny. But old Chi could feel a change coming. He had lived so long with the seasons.

"We shall have frost," he said at last, "if not tonight, then soon. It is close to October, time the leaves turned red and yellow. Soon the earth will fall asleep and I too am near to rest. Make haste to get the harvest in. The corn is ripe and ready to cut."

Strange how these Chinese peasants, like peasants the world over feel by some sixth occult sense when Death is near. They hear his stealthy footfalls long before he comes, but they do not fear him. Ever acquiescent with life they yield peacefully and unresistingly to death.

"I doubt if the Ancestor will last much longer," Clever Needle said to her husband, and they looked at one another sadly.—Yes, the corn was ripe and ready to cut. But the old man lingered, after all till the crops were safely on the threshing floors. When Chi the Second would have carried him out to look over the golden grain the old man refused:—

"No, my son,—I have no desire to be moved about. I will lie here until I die, and I will die decently within the house and on the k'ang where I have slept these many years."

And when Clever Needle would have fetched the herbalist, his answer was the same: "Why trouble me, why trouble me? I tell you my time has come. Not all the medicines in the world can change the hour of a man's fate, and only a fool fears that which is inevitable.—My life is done and I am content with it.— A wise man looks upon the grave as a cool soft bed wherein he may rest after the struggle of the day."

Chi asked him if he desired to see his other son who had left the home years ago and gone to another province. But again the old man answered—no.—That son had been no comfort to him in life. He had cut himself off from the family by his own wish. The old man could forgive him now for his unfilial ways, but he had no desire to see him.—But his neighbours,—friends of a lifetime,—who came constantly to visit him as he lay dying, he was glad to have about him. They were in and out of his sickroom all day long, urging him to eat, inquiring how he felt, talking freely of the funeral arrangements in his presence—good words that the dying man was glad to hear, proving how anxious they were to know, like himself, that all was prepared for his face-sake, and his soul's comfort.

"Do not be anxious, neighbours," Chi the Second assured them, "the grave clothes are ready and the coffin is ready also.— It is a fine thick coffin—a 'five, six, seven' one in fact, the bottom five inches thick, the sides six inches thick, and the top seven inches, and on the panel at the head is a gilded Long Life character.—More than ten years my father's 'longevity boards' have lain waiting in the temple."

"There will be a fine procession for the funeral too," said Chien speaking as a friend who enjoyed the family's confidence. — He was a quiet man, ever unwilling to talk unless forced to it and broke silence now only to comfort his old friend. "We shall all be there to weep for you, and our wives and sons with us.— We have already rented mourning clothes, and I will take charge of everything so that your son shall not be distracted in his grief."

"They tell me," said another neighbour, "that priests are waiting to chant your soul to the Western Heaven,—Buddhist priests

Hundred Altars

and Taoist priests also,—so your spirit cannot possibly miss the road!"—"And I hear the paper workers are busy making the things you will need yonder," put in a third neighbour.—Life in heaven was after all a counterpart of life on earth and there as here a man wanted the home he knew, the books he loved, the old coat he had worn into comfort, and his favourite pipe.

Hearing these things the Elder was not shocked—but greatly pleased and cheered, and he talked contentedly with all who came, and thanked them for their friendship.—"My son is a good son, and you, my neighbours, good neighbours," he said that last day as he lay dying, "and I am glad indeed to know that all is ready and I shall lie peacefully beside my ancestors. I do not wish to outlive my time. My son will take my place among you, ready to serve you if you so choose."

The next morning at the hour of the hare just as the day was breaking Chi and Clever Needle, seeing the end was near, propped the old man up on the k'ang, folding wadded quilts behind him, in order that his soul might leave his body easily. And so he died after a hard drawn breath or two, scarcely knowing the moment when life went out of him.

Clever Needle, feeling there was no more warmth in the old body, broke into loud wailing, the high falsetto wailing for the dead. "It is done,—He is gone!" said the neighbours as the wild cries echoed through the waiting village.

Hearing, they knew it was time now to send "help"—gifts of money folded in white envelopes with a yellow band.—A curious superstition made them careful to send these without delay. If they arrived late the body might already have left the home and the gifts, should they be accepted, presage a second death. Naturally the recipients must return them at once. Yet the sender if he took back his own present in its funeral wrapping also risked bringing death into his house. To avoid this there was but one thing to do—tear the envelope open and send the money again as a gift without any special significance or intention. This social strategem insured that a family in mourning might know in good time what financial assistance could be counted upon. The custom had its cynical side too, as it outwitted the stingy giver who might otherwise be willing to take back what he had deliberately offered too late and only to save his face.

Meanwhile in the Chi house there was much to be done. The diviner must be called to choose a lucky day for the burial, and the body must be prepared for its long journey according to the rites. Seven times Chi and Clever Needle washed the front of the body themselves with loving care, eight times they washed the back since all services done for the dead must be in odd numbers. Then they dressed the Elder in his grave clothes—the three long robes which Clever Needle had stitched herself, and all made without buttons or button-holes, but tied with ribbons,— and laid him in his coffin with his head resting on a pillow shaped like an ingot of silver, and tucked silk wadded quilts softly around him. And by his side they laid what he would need for his journey,—his pipe and an extra coat, and in his hands they placed silver money that the ghostly company might know he was a man of substance and not a beggar, and welcome him among them accordingly.

A spirit tablet also was prepared for him—a strip of lacquered wood like a miniature tomb-stone, in which one of his three souls was solemnly invited to dwell. After the funeral it would be placed with the other ancestral tablets and revered as a thing alive. But now Chi the Second set it in front of the coffin which had been carried into the main room and raised on two stools.

All being ready the funeral drums at the outer gate were beaten and the great gilded trumpets blown to announce that friends might come and make their farewells to the dead Elder. As the neighbours entered they ko-towed three times before the coffin and the tablet. Each time they bowed the family bowed with them. The mourners stood in two groups robed in white sackcloth—white, white,—everything white, for death is a white business. On the east side of the coffin, the place of honour at the left , shoulder of the deceased were Chi and his sons and his male cousins who had come from a neighbouring village to attend the funeral. Clever Needle with the women relatives were opposite to them on the right. They keened loudly as the proprieties demanded. Clever Needle sobbed hysterically and throwing herself upon the ground beside the coffin appeared so broken with grief that the women exclaimed: "How filial a daughter-in-law she is to mourn like this!" and raised her by the elbows, begging her not to make herself ill with such weeping.— Chi too, with his three sons also cried aloud and the men friends of the family comforted them in the same way.

It was a weird impressive farewell to Elder Chi, with sobbing and wailing and the group of priests at the coffinhead chanting prayers to open the way to heaven for the spirit,—and the guttering white candles on the altar table, and the neighbours bowing deeply and offering incense. Men like Chien, a life-long friend of the dead man's, presented a complete feast, and to leave his spirit free to enjoy his old neighbour's hospitality as well as to make space for all his dishes, the family removed their own,— excepting only the baked clay water dish with the hole in the bottom that must stand before the coffin so long as it remains in the house, and be broken on the ground when the corpse is carried out.

Just a week after the Elder's death the diviner consulting his Almanac as usual in such cases, found a suitable day for the burial. Chien, as he promised took complete charge leaving the family free to indulge their grief and attend to the mourning rites. But while they wailed someone they could trust must attend to practical details. Everything needed had to be ordered from the "Hell Clothes" shop in Pei Yang Ho since there was no funeral shop in Hundred Altars; bearers;—banners, and all the elaborate paraphernalia for the procession. A check had to be kept, even in times of mourning not only on all these people but also on the innkeeper and his helpers who provided the feast for the neighbours, a list made of presents given and moneys spent— Accounts must be kept carefully for at times like these squeeze was rampant. Cooks and carriers were prone to take advantage of a distracted household. So the Chis felt themselves lucky indeed to have a reliable friend like Chien to control expenses that already taxed their resources to the utmost.

On the day appointed for the burial the gates of the home were opened wide and the coffin was carried out and placed in the catafalque. Then the procession formed, a grand procession worthy of the Elder. A double line of men and boys, dressed in long green cotton coats with longevity characters woven in them and black felt hats with a long red feather standing straight up in the middle, carried embroidered banners and umbrellas, lions and deer made of evergreen branches, the paper figures of servants, a house, a cart, furniture—even paper washbasins and towels. Chi as chief mourner walked in front of the coffin carrying the soul manner on which the old man's death name was written, and after him came his sons and the other men of the family, and then the coffin borne by sixteen bearers.—The women and a whole crowd of neighbours followed behind.

The leader of the bearers acting as master of ceremonies, shrieked out at intervals, "Friends, it is time to weep!" and the mourners obediently wailed. Now and again he gave an order for a shower of white paper cash to be thrown into the air,— "buying the road money," it was called,—spent to bribe the evil spirits who might choose to block the street.

Though the procession had cost thousands and thousands of cash it presented that queer mixture of show and shabbiness usual in a Chinese funeral as it straggled through the village. Ordered—yet without order, dingy yet colourful with the priests in saffron robes, the peasants in stained white mourning, the gay banners, the tatterdemalion bearers with the black grease marks of their queues down the backs of their showy green and white patterned robes.

When it reached the grave the coffin was lowered into the earth on creaking horse-hair robes. The diviner called loudly: "Let those who mourn bear witness that all is right!" The head bearer summoned relatives and friends to form a circle round the open grave, marking time with his wooden clappers as each came forward, bowed and threw a handful of earth upon the coffin of their old friend, and retired. Strange, weird music,—gongs, horns, drums, bells, cymbals, and flutes, sounded all the while and crackers exploded loud as bombs. Then the priests sent the paper effigies for the soul's comfort by fire to the other world.— One moment a lighted house was a furnace of bright flames, the next a flimsy heap of ashes.—Now all was over save for one final wail—a last sorrowful farewell.

Then the long procession disbanded. The bearers slipped off their coats and tucked them under their arms; the musicians covered their drums with odd bits of cloth, neighbours returned to their homes in knots of fours and fives.

Chi and Clever Needle were the last to leave after the grave was covered and smoothed. They too left silently.—There was no need to wail loudly now, the crowd was gone, but quiet tears filled their eyes as they turned away leaving the Elder alone in the earth he loved.

The family home seemed strangely empty without him—strangely still now that all the bustle and commotion of the past Week with people coming and going was over. Yet there were still certain observances to be carried out; still certain things to do for the spirit of the old man,—things which comforted and soothed the soul and held his memory and living presence close.

That very evening Chi prepared a brass tray covered thickly with incense ash and placed it in the room where the Ancestor had slept. It was left untouched until the third day afterwards when he and his wife anxiously inspected it to see what impress if any there was to be found on the sensitive surface. Then they would know which of the six paths of rebirth the Elder's spirit had chosen. Chi stooping thoughtfully over the tray sighed contentedly—surely there was the trace of a human foot!—Clever Needle said with satisfaction:

"It is well. —well indeed.—Our father will be born again as a man, not as an animal or a bird!—Let us rest our hearts for his life here was good and the next will be good also!"

Yes, it was a relief to know that already the Ancestor had chosen the path to a fortunate re-birth.

And so with comfortable minds they continued the proper sacrifices, offering food and burning money on the appointed days, when a family must in decency go to a grave, and go at such hours when there were people about to see how filial they were—and not only then but at other quiet times, secretly, when their hearts were sad and lonely. On the sixtieth day after his death when their deep mourning ended, they burned a boat of paper and two paper bridges in order that his soul on its journey through the Shadowy Land might cross the river of gold and of silver—which were small and for which the bridges sufficed,— and the great river of Life across which the little boat might carry his spirit to the further shore.

After a decent interval Chien gave Chi the expense account. The farmer read it with pride. Certainly that alone would prove what a filial son he had been to a father who, as everyone in the countryside knew, deserved a filial son. Though a great funeral like this drank deeply from his reserve of silver it was worth it. The account would be kept in the family archives for face sake as well as for future reference. He read it several times with deep approval. Yes, a child might be buried for a few dollars, three or four,—just rolled up in a mat and laid anywhere,—but a man of the Elder's years,— that was very different, and Chi knew he had spent a proper sum. The "helps," though, cut the expenses somewhat. People had been extraordinarily generous, but that under the circumstances was but natural, and they would be repaid when they in their turn had a funeral or a wedding in their homes,—cash for cash, dollar for dollar. Chien had noted everything carefully. Before he put the accounts away Chi read them aloud to Clever Needle :

"White cloth for family mourning clothes	$15.
"buy the road money" of white paper	$1.
Ancestral tablet	.620 cash
Box for tablet	900 cash
Tip to bearer – for directing the wailing	300 cash
Incense	520 cash
Priests	$ 4.
Rent for mat pavilion and extra tables and chairs for the feast	$ 2.600 cash
special bread offered before the coffin	700 cash
clay dish for the bread	500 cash
diviner's fee	$ 1.
Hell Clothes shop in Pei Yang Ho for musicians, coffin-bearers, effigies, rent of catafalque etc.	$80.
wine for feast	$ 5.
tips, wages, for cooks & servants	$20.
feast food—	$80.

"If we reckoned the cost of the coffin which was two hundred dollars, and the grave clothes which we bought some time ago," Chi said proudly, "the funeral must have cost over five hundred dollars."

"A great sum!" she exclaimed, "But necessary, —one cannot bury a man as old as the Elder properly for much less."

"True, true, woman," Chi agreed, "and now since we must stay in mourning for so long we will have at least a chance of saving money. There can be no excuse for feasts and spending for a long time to come, not even at the New Year. —Little joy will it be for us to eat the 'feast of reunion' then without our father. —Well, wife, so it is, death comes for us all, for Emperor and beggar alike!"

"Aiyah!—Aiyah!" she echoed. "It will be sad indeed!"

All the time they were in full mourning the Chis wore their white hempen robes and white shoes. Chi and his sons did not shave, nor wash their feet, nor join in any village ceremonies, nor could Chi take up the post of village elder which the people offered him in his father's place till some time later. Clever Needle put aside her bracelets and wore white thread in her ears instead of earrings, and a white bone hair pin replaced her silver washed pin with the jade tip. Yet when the days of full mourning were ended and they might put off their white garments and wear blue or grey with a white mourning belt, they did so reluctantly for it seemed to separate them further from the old father they had loved and cared for all their lives.

Indeed when Old Chi died a generation died with him, and to the villagers his passing was a bitter loss. He had lived among them so long that they had come to believe he would live forever. So many years he had been their leader. They looked up to him as their example of the just man who in the words of their beloved Classics:

"Avoided the six offences, remained beside his parents as long as they lived and provided them with grandsons, forbore to tread on benevolent insects, safeguarded all printed paper, refused to consume the meat of the industrious ox, and was charitable towards the needs of the hungry and homeless ghosts."

For Little Dragon especially the memory of his grandfather was very dear. He never doubted his debt to the old man, who, loving him best of his grandsons, had taught him the wisdom of the sages. The spell of his fine personality, the tales he told the boy, his natural intelligence so superior to the clumsy wits of many of the peasants, and above all the reverence in which he held his scholar grandfather, impressed his grandchild deeply. Long after the Elder's death the boy drew inspiration from the remarkable old man, and indeed even after times had changed his neighbours judged the new standards by his judgments. Thus being dead yet he still lived and by a queer kind of earthly immortality still guided Hundred Altars.

Juliet Bredon

XVI. Scandal

It was a year after Elder Chi's death had cast a gloom over Hundred Alters and again autumn like a tawny tiger was prowling around the village. Crisp air allied with brilliant sunshine tempted fold out of doors. No one wanted to stay under a roof, least of all Young Tiger. School, never pleasant to him, was unbearable at this season of ripening persimmons, —so easy to steal, so luscious to eat. He would run away from his lessons one day in seven.

Young Tiger had grown by this time to be a strong lad, almost man-size, and ugly too with a flat face like a bean-cake, and an absence of eyelashes that gave him the unblinking expression of a lizard. The bigger he grew, the bolder the youth became. He was proud of his nickname of the village bully, and proud of his skill in "fist and foot" practices. "I can strike such a blow as will knock out a brick from a wall a foot thick!" he boasted. Nothing delighted him more than to show his skill in balancing the pole with a round millstone at either end before an admiring circle of younger boys. He lifted the heavy weight with ease and swung the pole with, a grand gesture above his head as he had seen the actors do. However, he was not really a bad boy, but simple an incorrigible young scapegrace.

Shui Ching tried to soften him by kindness, and Ma by beatings and scoldings. But it seemed that the more he was corrected the worse he grew, until Ma was at his wits' end to know what to do with him, and how to make his future sure. Nor was his unrestful spirit entirely the boy's fault. Born for an outdoor life, he had never somehow fitted in to the merchant's home, never really fitted into the family life. It seemed as though he was a guest in Hundred Altars, a passerby, only waiting for the time to come when he should go on his way or back to the home whence he had come. There is no truer adage than "Phoenix gives birth to phoenix, and the son of a beggar is born to use a stick."

Unfortunately Young Tiger's taste for stealing persimmons nearly led him into serious trouble. It was fatally easy, this form of petty thieving in a countryside where a man's fields and orchards were separated from each other by a neighbour's property. When a farmer was working in one grove of fruit trees he could not be watching another. So Young Tiger merely waited his chance to slip into an empty orchard. He did this once, he did it twice successfully. But the third time the owner hid behind a grave-mound and caught the lad in the very act of picking his fruit.

"Hey!" he shouted menacingly. "What are you doing,—you wind blown seed of a camel-driver?—Are you by any chance stealing my persimmons?"

"Oh, persimmons, yes, yes, persimmons!—Are they really yours? I thought they belonged to the tree!" Young Tiger retorted impudently.

"You impertinent son of a dark turtle!" the farmer shouted advancing on him angrily, hoe in hand.

But Young Tiger was too quick to be caught and scurried off across the fields biting into a ripe fruit as he ran.

Not unnaturally the farmer made a complaint to the merchant.

"I am not the only one to suffer from that boy of yours," he said angrily, "I warn you to stop his stealing.—Remember how Lame Leg was hamstrung for thieving from the threshing floors! Your Young Tiger risks the same fate if you cannot control him."

Ma understood well enough how serious a crime it was in a hardworking farming community to take advantage of the labour of others. The crushing grinding poverty of the majority makes men cruel in an over-crowded land. Hard earned property must be protected at any cost and fear put into thieves. Ma knew, too, that the moral resentment of the village was not always a hot resentment. People might bide their time to punish, but they neither forgave nor forgot. He worried greatly over the matter, applied the bamboo once or twice, and Young Tiger gave up stealing persimmons, but only because, as the season advanced, there were no more persimmons to steal.

Unfortunately he took to another form of mischief which ended by leading him into even more serious trouble.

The lad was a born gambler with no idea of moderation. This vice he kept well-hidden from his adopted father. Had the merchant guessed his son's proclivities he would have been angry indeed for no wild gambler makes a reliable merchant. Such a man cannot be trusted in money dealings.

Juliet Bredon

Young Tiger could, of course, indulge his love for gaming only in a. small way for he had no regular pocket-money. But now and then he scraped together a few strings of cash by hook or crook and slunk off to the teashop in a nearby village, where word of his doings was not likely to reach his father's ears, to play at dominoes with the crowd of idlers, who, like himself, would rather gamble than work. Excitement gripped him, and holding tightly to his queue at the roots of his hair with one hand, he nervously announced his stake, and tremblingly awaited the fiat of the stake-holder as he lifted the lid of the pot containing the dominoes.—Usually after an hour or so Young Tiger's money found its way to the loin-purse of a more lucky neighbour, and then the lad perforce had to leave the game and stand outside the circle watching the fortunes of the luckier players. No gambler likes to lose, but Young Tiger was to find to his cost that to win is not always an unmixed blessing.

One day his cash returned to him time after time as silver coins, and even these turned somehow miraculously into large round silver dollars. It was the first time the lad had ever had real money in his belt, and he felt like a man, and a man whose desire is to spend. Followed by a sour smile from the stake-holder, and the noisy congratulations of his new-found friends, he left the game, deciding that on his way home he would stop at the shop of a trinket seller.— A sudden impulse had come over him, an impulse understandable enough in a youth of his temperament, to buy an ornament and give it to Lilac Blossom.

For some months he had begun to be conscious of woman's beauty. He was growing to manhood now and already the soft net of desire was closing over his heart. A new feeling stirred within him,— something indefinable yet warming, something that he had never before experienced, an enemy of reason and common sense. And whenever he saw Lilac Blossom, the very last woman in the world whom in decency he should ever have cast eyes upon, he felt imperative desires awakening. True, he saw her but seldom, since a grown lad is kept away from the women's quarters where his father's wives live. But when he did he realised that she was different from the village women.—

She, who unlike them did no field work, had time to wash herself and comb her hair neatly, and keep her hands, unroughened by housework, soft and white. Sometimes just to look at her and see her smile her sweet vague smile thrilled him like the sudden intoxication of strong wine. The peasant girls with their chapped skin and dusty hair never aroused his interest. Yes,—now he was a man grown and had silver to spend like a young lord, he would buy Lilac Blossom a trinket—because she was beautiful, because she pleased him.

"Show some gold washed earrings," he said to the shopkeeper clinking two dollars suggestively in his half-closed hand.

The man looked at him suspiciously. "What can a boy like you want with such things? Is your father so proud of you that he desires to dress you as a girl and cheat the gods?"

"Am I not old enough to desire a woman and give her gifts?" asked Young Tiger grandly, straightening himself to look his tallest. "Besides, my silver is as good as another's!"

"Oh, certainly, certainly, young master!" the man hastened to apologize as he caught the clink of the coins, "And why not add a pair of bracelets while you are about it?—Here are some of like design to the earrings!"

"Yes. I will see bracelets also," Young Tiger agreed. The thought struck him how they would make a soft sound as Lilac Blossom moved through the courtyards,—two and they tinkle together, one and there is silence. "What is the price of these?" he asked fingering a pair of silver bracelets engraved with a pattern of happy bats.

"Very reasonable, very reasonable!—The price is two dollars only for the four things!"

"Now that is too much!" said Young Tiger, eager to show his skill at bargaining. "I will give you one dollar and sixty cash only—not one cash more!"

"Wait!" said the man hastily, "I will weigh them and see how much silver they contain!"—He put them on his little brass scales.—"One dollar and forty cash the value of the metal is, and forty cash more for the working.—I cannot sell for less."

Finally the lad after haggling a little longer with grave dignity agreed, and when the shopkeeper had wrapped the trinkets in paper he put them, carefully in his belt and went home—very pleased with himself.

But it was one thing to buy such gifts, quite another to present them. Openly he dared not do such a thing, and for several days he hung about Lilac Blossom's gate in the short autumn twilight waiting for a chance. But she did not leave her rooms. The air was crisp with the first frost and she would never venture out in the cold unless she must.

Unfortunately Ma spied Young Tiger prowling about and noticed that the lad wore a new coat and had smoothed his hair neatly and washed his hands cleaner than usual—sure signs that a youth is beginning to look longingly after women.

"That son of ours," he said to Shui Ching, "is ripe for manhood. I caught him yonder near the new house, sighing and skulking in the shadows. If he looks lusting after little Swallow—(for it never entered his head that Young Tiger could possibly be interested in his own Minor Star)—trouble will follow. When the right time comes we will arrange for his betrothal to a suitable maid."

"It would be well," she answered, "to consider the matter soon. I too have thought for sometime this youth has a head hot with desire.... He seems to me to be afflicted with lovesickness and you know as well as I that falling in love is like slipping on a peach skin!"

Ma scratched his chin thoughtfully.—"May be so, may be so,— do you see that he and Swallow are kept apart and I will ask the herbalist to prepare us medicine to cure this ailment."

Such love was considered as dread a sickness as the smallpox, —dangerous and greatly to be feared. It upset family life. It was an element of confusion in the village world, driving young men and women to unreason, blinding their eyes to the plans of their elders. It must be treated in the early stages, and treated with expensive medicines. The herbalist was not surprised when Ma applied to him for a remedy. He had known other cases.

"A viper's broth each morning instead of tea, and a dose of powdered unicorn's horn at midday!" the old man prescribed, adding gloomily as he peered and searched among his jars and boxes for the drugs, "Woe to the youth who gets his feet entangled in a woman's hair!"—A cure was never certain.

And alas, his potions failed in their effect. Young Tiger grew no better. He was restless and ever more restless in a continual mood of high excitement until one day, when no one was about to see, he managed to give his gifts to Lilac Blossom. "I have bought these for you," he stammered. "Take them. They are yours!"—And before she could recover from her surprise he was gone again beyond her gate. When she unwrapped the things and saw what pretty trinkets he had pressed into her hand, it was too late to give them back.—And yet she dared not keep them—though they were dainty enough and pleased her. And being a woman she felt pleased too at this tribute from the boy— for he was young and he liked her just with liking, not for any other reason. But at the same time she was afraid to keep the jewellery, knowing too well trouble would come if it was found about her house.—Ma would not fail to ask:—"Whose gifts are these? They are not mine!"—And Shui Ching too would wonder and question. And even if she did not happen to notice, amahs were hawk-eyed in such matters and told tales. So she looked at the pretty gewgaws a little while as they lay shining in her hand, and then sighed and wrapped them up again.

"I must take them to the mistress, myself," she murmured, "It is best to tell her the whole truth of how I came by them and beg forgiveness for Young Tiger—he is only a foolish boy."

But Shui Ching was not inclined to treat Young Tiger's indiscretion as lightly as the Minor Star. The latter who lived out of touch with village life judged things more leniently than those still in the thick of it. The foul mouth of gossip might speak, but she was beyond earshot.—As for Ma, when Shui Ching told him' about his son, his astonishment and rage were dreadful to see—A son philandering with his father's women,—what could be more shameful than that? He was literally aghast that such a thing could happen in his house.

Young Tiger had indeed created an impossible family situation. The little wife ought, when she had time to consider, feel that she had lost her self-respect and should .not easily recover from her sense of humiliation. Shui Ching must know herself at fault for permitting such things to happen in the home under her. care. Friends and neighbours would explode with ribald laughter and make Ma's life a burden to him. He could not lift his head again if this tale got around the village, as get round it would, one way or another.

"It is your fault woman!" Ma shouted at Shui Ching. "You should have known, you should have seen. Are you blindfolded like the mules who grind the grain?"

"Oh, master, it was but a whim of youth—nothing to matter, nothing I could foresee," she said excusing herself.

"Tell me no lies!" Ma thundered, "but send that lad to me!"

Shui Ching went off to do so, not a little relieved to escape from her husband, and not sorry either to know the master would take out his boiling resentment on one whom she felt richly deserved it.

"Son," Ma said sternly when the boy stood before him, frightened now as he saw by his father's face that he had been found out. "Your ways will bring disgrace upon us. You have been talking alone with my little wife and given her presents such as only those who are betrothed may give.—What does this mean?"

The boy hung his head and mumbled in excuse:

"I sought to speak to her only!"

"It may be so, but whoever heard of a filial youth who chatted idly with his father's women under his father's own roof?"

Young Tiger dropped on his knees and knocked his forehead on the ground in contrition. Trying to save himself from punishment he muttered:—"Sir, if you but knew,—she is not only your little wife, but the mistress of the garden coolie;—The other night I heard her talk with him.—I heard their whispered plans and followed them in the darkness. They lay together in the fields sheltered by the tall millet, and I saw him fondling her, I did with my own eyes."

"You—mangy-hided dog!" shouted the merchant furiously, seizing a long bamboo that stood temptingly at hand. "You scoundrel!—You low lusting youth! Have you no respect for your father's house that you can tell such lies to cover your own sins. Evidently your bones ache for a thrashing!"

Then with his stout bamboo he laid on the kneeling boy—thwack,—thwack,—thwack,—many times until his anger was exhausted, then hade him get out of his sight—and stay out.

Ma himself had always been a man of strict morals with regard to women. It seemed doubly hard therefore that scandal of this kind should come to his house, and through his own son. "Alas!" he said to himself as he turned in sleepless misery on his bed, "He is the child of low people and acts as it is natural for them to act. As for the woman, if there is any fault of hers in it, that is to be expected also. She was a slave and such women always consort with servants.—Faithfulness one cannot buy."

But Shui Ching assured him when he was fit to listen that Lilac Blossom was in no way to blame, and that she herself believed Young Tiger's story was a tissue of revengeful lies to coyer his own foolish act.

Meanwhile, Young Tiger, sore from his beating, went and hid himself in the grass hut of the night watchman now snoring like a pig on a pile of straw in a corner. "Beast!" said the boy, referring to his father in this most unfilial manner while spittle like a snake's venom, spurted from the corner of his lips. His bones ached and his flesh burned. Turning this matter of his punishment over in his mind a bright idea came to him. He knew a way to avenge himself on his father for that horrible beating.

When dusk fell he crept out of the hut, and down to the well where the village boys were playing at that hour. He espied Little Dragon tracing characters as usual a little apart from the others on a patch of dry earth. Little Dragon was his heart's friend. Together they had gone to school. Together they had flown kites. Together they had gathered wild dates. He would understand and sympathize. They were like two apples on one tree.

"Hi, there!" he called softly, "Come here. I have news."

Little Dragon left the character he was tracing unfinished, and came.

"I have been beaten," Young Tiger whispered, "There is a fire in my vitals."—And then he told the whole story of what had happened in Ma's house, not forgetting to make himself the hero and blacken the rest of the family.

Little Dragon rubbed his hands together with pleasure.

"Eh,—how amusing!" he said, "What a beautiful scandal!"—and he sympathized with his companion's misery. "There is no need to hide yourself and brood. When people hear about this they will all be on your side."

"But who will hear?" asked Young Tiger bitterly, hiding the cunning gleam in his eyes.

"Well,—I shall tell my father and mother, and perhaps they will tell others," answered Little Dragon understanding perfectly what was in Young Tiger's mind.

"No one can blame me if people talk," the older boy remarked. So saying he slouched home again, pleased with himself though his back was bent from soreness.

When Little Dragon told the story to his father Chi the Second laughed greatly amused. "It will be a pretty tale to tell the village!" he said, and his eyes sparkled with malice.—Not that he wished ill to his friend Ma, but between the farmer and the merchant there had always been a slight feeling of envy,— just a shadow. "Serve the rice quickly," Chi said to his wife after he had told her the gossip. "The scandal has made me hungry. I will go down to the inn after our meal. This juicy bit of gossip will assure me a great welcome."

Ma voiced the same thought in the same words, though his tone was very different. "How the teashop will enjoy *this* tale!" he said bitterly to Shui Ching. To him the scandal brought loss of appetite. For two days he would not take up his chop-sticks, and for two days Lilac Blossom (who though she had been told that she was considered blameless in the matter) wept.

Hearing her sobbing, he bade Shui Ching reprimand her.

"Who doesn't know she is a good woman?" he said sarcastically. "Tell her under no circumstance to think of suicide, and you, too, refrain from jumping down the well. Suicide is the rightful protest of virtuous females to slander, but in this case it might look as though lies were truth."

He could not but choose to accept Shui Ching's explanation that Young Tiger was telling lies about his household. Whether in his inmost heart he believed her or not, he must pretend for face-sake to think that Lilac Blossom was innocent. Otherwise not only would he confirm what people were saying, but he would have to take a cruel decision, Innocent Lilac Blossom might remain under his roof, guilty, she would have to go, and the wretched woman had no place to take shelter and no strength any longer to earn her living. Moreover, he would have to dismiss the garden coolie also, and he was loath to part with such an excellent man. Ma thought of the succulent young onions that this gardener coaxed to their full growth weeks before they appeared elsewhere. He thought of his melons, the juiciest in the village, and he made up his mind to give everybody the benefit of the doubt. After all he had no proof beyond the word of his scapegrace son.

But of what to do with Young Tiger he must take thought.

Juliet Bredon

XVII.   Revenge

Chin, the innkeeper, that little stout brown jug of a man from whose loose mouth gossip poured out as easily as it poured into his wide ears, retailed the scandal at the merchant's to each new arrival and added with gusto, "Ma would indeed seem to have picked a frail blossom for his Minor Star!"

Most people agreed with him though others could not quite make up their minds where to lay the blame. One said sarcastically: "A kingdom is easy to rule, a household hard to regulate." Another declared Ma was foolish to adopt the son of a camel-driver, a third excused the lad saying that it may well have been that he meant nothing, a fourth reviled the garden coolie, and a fifth said gloomily that he had always expected a scandal in the Ma household and was only surprised that it had not happened before.

All felt, however, that a slur had been cast on the whole village where virtue in women was so highly prized that carters were forbidden to sing ribald songs when passing down the street. Indeed it was the proud boast of Hundred Altars that no widow had ever remarried there, no prostitute had ever been permitted to corrupt youth, and adultery was unknown.

It hurt Ma's pride that his household affairs should be common talk, that if he came unexpectedly upon a group of neighbours they would fall silent or begin to chat with eagerness on indifferent matters, making it clear they had changed the subject on his arrival. He tried to pay no heed to this. What, after all, did he care for their gossip? He had always held himself apart and above such foolishness.—Realities, affairs of actual moment, were the only ones that interested him. Let men wag their tongues if they chose. The talk would die down in time. But it was not pleasant all the same to be so cheaply judged. Even his own friends no longer met his gaze frankly, no longer laughed heartily at his jests, and in the distillery his orders were not received and obeyed with the same willing alacrity as before,—if any task called for special effort there was not the same eager haste to help. It seemed as if he was being left to struggle by himself,—he and his ostracised,—objects of curiosity as to how they would manage alone.

The thing Ma most wanted to discover at the moment was who started the story of the scandal. He could not rest until he knew, and finally he found out, when Shui Ching's amah had occasion to borrow a sieve from the Chi household, that it was the Elder who told the news at the inn. How Chi happened to hear it Ma neither knew nor cared. What angered him was that Chi had been the one to broadcast the scandal,—Chi, the neighbour who seemed to stick in his crop on every occasion with his smug "face," his fine sons, his position of Elder. Yet how could the merchant prove his backstairs knowledge?—If he accused Chi, the latter would loudly assert his innocence.

Ma, in his fury, longed to curse aloud and revile Chi in the hearing of all Hundred Altars. But if he did so he would only be laughed at again. No, better wait an opportunity for a more subtle revenge. So he waited with the patience characteristic of his race, planning how to return evil with greater evil until suddenly Fate put an unexpected weapon in his hand wherewith to strike his neighbour.

Twice a month a man known as a *pao shan ti*—one who runs over the- hills—came to Hundred Altars. This private messenger, paid like the village watchman by the community, carried letters and parcels from the nearest postoffice at Hai-tien—a little town half way between the village and Peking and close to the Emperor's Summer Palace. Hai-tien was a centre of gossip because of the couriers going constantly to and fro between the Capital and the Court. Everything that happened all over the Empire leaked out with more or less truth via its inns and tea- shops and the *pao shan ti* retailed what he heard throughout the countryside. He was a walking newspaper for those who could not read, and his news of the great world was coloured by a vivid imagination and as often spiced with fancy as seasoned with fact.

Now the messenger was due again in Hundred Altars and Ma for some strange reason felt prompted to go out and meet him. The merchant was in fact the only man in the village with leisure at the moment to chat with a passerby. It was harvest time and the crops ready for cutting. heavy work, absorbing work to the thrifty farmers to whom the produce of every little field no bigger than a wrapping cloth meant an extra bowl of millet.—Men rose daily at four to begin their reaping and worked long hours, straightening their numb backs for a moment's respite now and then as they swung their scythes down the close set rows of grain, or wiped the sweat from nose and forehead with a quick duck of the head in the crook of a bent arm, without freeing their hands from their work.

In the fields, and in the village too, every soul was busy. As soon as the grain was cut it was loaded upon donkeys and carried to the threshing floors of beaten earth—centres of life and gossip Ma picking his way along the street stopped at each as he passed to exchange comments on the harvest, but the farmers did not halt in their tasks even for a moment and the blind-folded mules still dragged the small stone rollers, no bigger than a lady's muff, round and round in a circle husking the grain with monotonous patience. Here a farmer stacked the *kao liang* stalks against the side of his house while his woman winnowed the grain with a palm leaf fan. Half-fledged chickens scratched hysterically among the chaff while old hens ran about helplessly looking for quiet corners to lay their eggs.—But there were no quiet corners. Even the littlest children pretended to help, stacking up sweet potatoes and laughing gleefully when their pyramids fell down. Girls set out the golden persimmons on the drying racks. Boys clambered, limber as monkeys, to the flat roofs and spread out the cobs of Indian corn that made bright patches of colour against the adobe. Any who could be spared from these tasks dug pits for storing winter vegetables—green cabbages and wine red turnips laid, out in rows waiting to be buried underground.

Beyond the village many of the fields were already bare and Ma standing on the high bank by the roadside, spied the *pao shan ti* while he was still afar off, shuffling along beside his little donkey with its collar of tinkling bells,—a strangely biblical figure in the wide horizoned landscape beneath the clear blue arc of the sky.—He was a queer looking fellow, his bony forehead pitted with pock-marks. His cheekbones were very high and on the right side of his face a conspicuous scar like a patch of purplish brown onion skin stretched from chin to ear. An air of mystery and secrecy—such as he imagined proper for a bearer of news and a companion of Imperial couriers,—albeit only in second rate inn kitchens—clung to him like a garment. His pay might be poor, but he never lost a sense of the dignity of his position which gave him the right to the title of "Walking Official."

When he came within earshot Ma hailed him by it,—a politeness often overlooked and, coming from a merchant of Ma's standing, very gratifying to his pride. He stopped and returned the greeting, straightening his stiff spare figure that somehow gave an impression of ungainly sprightliness. Then he climbed the bank and his donkey scrambled painfully up after him to make room for a dejected white pony harnessed to a battered cart. The animal had stopped wearily and stood with all four feet bunched together in a drooping pathetic attitude singularly suited to the decrepit vehicle. They seemed indeed indefinably united and of one mind in never wishing to move again.

"You must be tired, brother," Ma said to the *pao shan ti* noting the frayed soles of his shoes, and his head cloth grimed with sweat.

"Yes, I have done sixty li (twenty miles) today. The nights are cool, but the midday sun is still hot and my donkey is lame in one foot and cannot carry me without stumbling."

"Well, come home with me!" Ma said impulsively, "and I will give you a bowl of macaroni and you shall rest awhile!"—He did not know what prompted him to invite the man. He had never done so before. The messenger turned and looked at him surprised, and as he looked his eyes were slippery. About his mouth the muscles had slackened, marking a long slow process of disillusionment with his fellow men until now his lips hung wide and loose with one corner sliding down a trifle into a suspicious leer.—He wondered at the unusual invitation, but accepted eagerly. Ma's food would be better than he could get at the inn, and it would be free.

When they were seated at table they began-to talk of local happenings, of crops and prices and the weather. They talked until the meal was served and then both men fell to with good appetite, though try as he might Ma could not eat as much as his guest. "Walking the roads makes a man. hungry," the *pao shan ti* apologized, as he shovelled the macaroni into his mouth with loud gurglings and suckings that put a stop to conversation for a while.... Only after his bowl had been three times emptied and three times refilled and he sat back replete and wiped his face with a hot towel, did Ma venture to ask—"Have you any news to tell?"

"Oh, one hears things now and then,—they say a Grand Councillor has been dismissed. He was too rich to please the other officials. But when he came for his farewell audience at the Summer Palace, it cost him a matter of several thousand taels to thank the Sovereign for punishing him by depriving him of his post. First he had to fee the Keepers of the Gate heavily, then the guardians of the Throne Hall, and after that the Imperial Chamberlain, the Master of the Household, the Master of Ceremonies, the Introducer of Officials, the Chief Eunuch, and some others before he could reach the foot of the throne!"

"Well," said Ma absently, "I suppose the Court must live!"

"That is as may be. But such practices give rise to ugly rumours. These costly futilities are a sign of institutions already undermined which look most splendid outwardly when they are ripe for downfall."

"Well, and is there no other news?" Ma asked.—He cared little for official gossip. The government did not concern him though good or bad he had to bear it.

"They say there has been a tragedy in a village ten li from here. One of the farmers' wives, a cloudy-minded woman who has already lost three sons from the 'old sickness'—consumption —cut up the body of her last child.—The corpse was found in a cleft among rocks, face downward with the arms and legs severed and a meat chopper by it.—A wicked thing to. do, for now the child will lack these members in its next life!—-The magistrate was called, but when the neighbours told her she might be accused of killing her child, she only said:—'I did not kill him, but only cut the body up after he died to let the evil spirit out.—But if I had done murder—why should they punish me? This devil of disease that haunts our house must be destroyed to save the life of future sons!' Aye, she is a misty minded woman, and distracted, and there is no knowing now what the magistrate will decide about her. But the village is much distressed that he be sent for to mix in their affairs."

"A strange business, a strange business indeed," commented Ma absently, listening with one ear only. He was wondering whether the story of his own scandal had yet reached the *pao shan ti*.—It had of course. News of this kind leaps from village to village as flame leaps over rocks in a grass fire on the hills. But the man gave no hint that he had heard a word, and it seemed as if the stream of conversation that had begun to trickle from his lips was about to dry up again.—Still Ma persisted. In his subconscious mind he knew there was something he wanted to hear, and must press to hear it. "Any other news?" he asked.

The question seemed to create a difficulty for his guest.—A sly smile stole over the messenger's face, and he appeared to be trying to shake his head two ways at the same time, agreeing and denying.

"Oh, nothing much," he nodded, "but I heard the other day from one of the couriers who passed through Hai-tien that there has been famine in the North, in that very district where Chi's brother settled. The crops have failed and the people are starving."

"Is that possible?" Ma interrupted eagerly.—The messenger was quick to notice his interest. He scented intrigue, and intrigue was the breath of his nostrils.

"Well, in our vast land there is always famine somewhere with this uneven rainfall. There may be a drought one month, a flood the next," he remarked indifferently.

"So there may, so there may," said Ma trying to appear casual. "Now have another cup of wine," he added hastily, "and please take some more cakes. You must still be hungry after your long journey."

"Thanks, I will,—I was hollow as a wolf and thirsty too. A little more will not be too much."

"About that famine," Ma said again when the wine cups had been several times emptied and re-filled.

"Oh, you may believe what I have just told you. The second cousin of my wife's nephew who runs a cookshop where some of the couriers eat gave me the news. This man says, too, that Chi's relations are worse off than most. His brother, as you know, ever had the reputation for improvidence."

"Yes, I have heard he was that kind of a man," Ma agreed. "He had left Hundred Altars before I came, but people told me he was not contented here, and wanted a wider life. He thought to rise high in a new place."

"I knew him," said the *pao shan ti* smiling grimly as if he hugged a secret joke. "He was a restless spirit all his days and gave the Elder no peace until he got his share of the inheritance in silver and went off to establish himself separately. He scorned the villagers as 'rice-pot-keeping turtles'—'I have the courage to break away,' he used to boast. 'I would brave fortune with even an empty pocket, but with silver to start me within a few years I will return rich and prosperous/—And. indeed at first he did send messages telling what good times he had and how easy it was to make a living yonder. Then he married a wife without even consulting his father though he promised to bring her back some day and grandsons with her. For several years there was no news at all, and Elder Chi was uneasy and said to Chien: 'The salt can never be quite washed out of sea water, I fear my son "the galloping guest" fares no better, if as well, as we "rice-pot-keeping turtles." —And now," the *pao shan ti* added, "they tell me the man is dead,—leaving, a wife and three girl children behind him, and not a copper saved to feed them."

He fell silent after he had brought forth this news, motionless and staring, as he let his words sink in. And they sank like moisture into Ma's heart thirsty for revenge. Try as he would he could not hide his pleasure, though he answered with mock sympathy: .

"Ah, the beginnings of such men are many. But the end none can foresee. And this indeed is a pitiful end. Does Chi know that his relations starve?"

"Maybe he does," the *pao shan ti* answered, "though I doubt if he has yet heard. His sister-in-law is a shiftless woman, well-matched to her dead husband. I doubt if she would write to his family and ask for shelter, though of course she has a right to it."

"But *has* she the right?" asked Ma with acute interest.

"Maybe not by law," the man answered, "but, were it common knowledge that his relations were in want, Chi would lose face before the village if they asked to come into the home again and he turned them from the door."

"True," said Ma. A little malicious smile curving the corners of his lips, "but doubtless Chi does not desire any hungry mouths and useless hands under his roof!"

"Who does?" chortled the messenger, sensing amusing possibilities beneath the surface of the merchant's remark. He

Hundred Altars

possessed in a marked degree the faculty for seeing "underneath" words and was clever at putting two and two together and making five.

But Ma said no more. He was busy with his own thoughts. He saw a way, yes, a safe way to get even with Chi. The gods had delivered his friendly enemy into his hand!—Impatient to be alone, Ma raised his tea-cup. His gesture set a polite limit to the visit. It was a tactful unspoken way of telling his guest that it was time to leave. The *pao shan ti* understood. Emptying his own cup he rose to go, and Ma did not press him to linger.

Giving orders that he was not to be disturbed as he had private business to attend to, Ma sat down at his desk in his own room thinking heavily. Intrigue and plotting were second nature to him after long years of trying—though not dishonestly,—to get the best of a deal, and he enjoyed planning how to annoy Chi. With deep satisfaction he drew forward his ink block, poured water on it, moistened his brush, and thoughtfully began to write a letter, poking the tip of his tongue out of his mouth now and then like a parrot as if to steady his thoughts.

It took some time to get his phrases to his liking, but at last he read over what he had written in a low tone to himself:

"This letter is sent by a friend who has heard of your misfortunes and is pitiful. Know you that your relation, Chi the Second, Elder of Hundred Altars in place of his father dead these twelve moons, lives in a good home in ease and plenty."

"If that woman has an ounce of brains, I need say no more," Ma added aloud as he sealed the envelope and set the address upon it. The hint should suffice to bring the destitute family to take shelter in Chi's house. The plot must work as Ma foresaw. He could imagine how this widow would go secretly to the letter writer in her village and bid him write to her rich relation and say that she was coming back to her husband's home,— and Chi could not refuse her lest public opinion in Hundred Altars turn against him.

Ma said nothing of what he had done, not even to his wife, for, he argued that if a man cannot keep his own counsel no woman can do it for him. But late that evening, tucking the letter into the folds of his coat he strolled down to the inn where he knew he should find the *pao shan ti,* who would be leaving next morning for the city where he could post it. For in the city there were official offices where for a postal stamp a letter could be sent.

The evening was pure as the day had been. The sky throbbed with stars and the "Bamboo Grove" twinkled with unusual splendour. Half the village slept already. The silence was broken only by the occasional bark of a dog, and the rattle of the watchman's clappers as he made the round of the threshing floors. He was a half-wit brother of Wong the blacksmith, willing to exchange night for day. Instead of treading with cat-like steps in order to catch those who might come to steal, he walked noisily and clapped loudly to warn them he was watching and that they would be well advised to stay away. From his meagre wages he paid a pittance to the thieves guild so that many a night he might doze in peace. As he said to their chief: "I must ask you to accept this silver and keep your men away from here. If you don't avoid Hundred Altars I might be unable to frighten them off—then I should lose my livelihood and you your bribe." So except at harvest time he had a quiet life and a good rest at night.

As Ma hoped he found a lamp still burning in the inn and the *pao shan ti* still chatting with the innkeeper. He called the messenger aside and secretly handed him the letter and a piece of silver. "Take this to the city and give it to one of those new fashioned persons with bags upon their backs and bid him take it to the one whose name is written on it.—Here is money for the stamp and enough over to buy you a cup of wine."

The messenger, who was no fool, smelled strange doings. He took the letter, promised to do the errand and asked no questions. Ma hinted that there was no need for all the village to see the letter, and the *pao shan ti,* well paid to do so, kept his bargain so loyally that not a word leaked out in Hundred Altars to whom Ma had written, or that he had written a letter at all.

As he strolled home under the stars Ma muttered to himself:

"Trouble in my house Chi enjoyed—it is my turn to feel a little joy when trouble comes to his!"

XVIII. Chi's Relations Arrive

Although the *pao shan ti* agreed not to mention Ma's letter, he did not feel in honour bound not to tell the village of the famine in the North, nor that Chi's younger brother had lately died leaving his wife and children destitute. It suited Ma's plans admirably when this news spread through Hundred Altars and folk said to one another:

"Why don't these relations claim a home with Elder Chi and share his food since they have nothing of their own to eat? It is not right that some should prosper while others of the same root starve!"

"Doubtless Chi will bid them come," Chien, ever loyal to his friend, remarked when he heard the gossip.

Wu the coffin-maker winked slyly:

"For my part, I wonder if they will wait to be asked. Should they hear by any chance that Neighbour Chi has grain to spare they'll come anyway. If they can't pay mule hire, they'll walk. With such a goal in sight the tenderest feet are strong and willing and once they are here these women know as well as you or I that what they need Chi must provide."

Ma avoided joining in the talk. He kept his own counsel, only listening now and then and waiting for village opinion to help push events the way he wanted them to go.

Chi, on learning of his brother's death felt a certain sadness notwithstanding all the high words that had passed between them when careless of their sore hearts, he had insisted on leaving the home. Often these days Chi was far off in his memories. This brother of his was jolly and easy in his ways, eager after pleasure, longing for new faces, new places, and with no great taste for steady work; the kind of man ever hunting after easier living. So when people he met at the temple fair told him how quickly he could make a fortune yonder where they had been he went confidently, never doubting he would soon be a rich man, nor thinking to ask them why they themselves had returned from this land of opportunity.

Well, he had proved to be a man of evil destiny. Nothing had prospered for him. Luck and nature seemed to work against him. His fields were unfertile, his cabbages got worms in them. Insects ate his sweet potatoes. When he planted largely of maize hoping for early rains, the rains came late. And if the following year he counted on a damp summer, there was a drought. Still he had never whined to come back to his father's house. And now he was dead, miserably, half-starved, with none to burn the candles for him, leaving a wife—a stranger to his own kin,—and three girl children,'—just at a time when Chi had been put to great expense with the old Elder's funeral so lately in his house, and the marriage of his eldest son pressing as soon as the mourning should be over.

All things considered Chi decided he would offer no immediate help to his brother's widow. She might, after all, be able to help herself. Perhaps her neighbours would assist her.—Let Fate decide.—Unless she asked to come, and that was most unlikely, he would not invite her to share his home. Surely no one could blame him for that? Why saddle himself with other people's troubles just at a time when he could least afford to do so? If she asked, that would be different. To refuse then would be a loss of face. But he judged that the widow would have neither the wit to ask nor the courage to make the journey to Hundred Altars without first asking. And neither would she have dared do so but for Ma's encouraging letter.

That message spurred her to an effort which she could never have made otherwise, since she was a woman to whom all effort was painful. Besides she knew that her husband had proved un- filial to his house and had already taken his share of the property, and there was nothing more for her to expect by legal right from his family. So before deciding to start on her journey she went to the letter writer of her village and bade him write to Chi announcing her coming. It was a good cautious thing to do, and the letter a very proper letter full of respect and flattering words. Little else was said in it except that her husband was dead some months since, for their crops having failed they had had insufficient food and his strength was not enough to resist the first small sickness that came along. Therefore she craved a home with her brother-in-law, and the more so as she had heard from one of Chi's friends in Hundred Altars that his roof was whole and he had grain in plenty. Very cunningly she bade the scholar end the letter thus:

"We know that under the law we have no right to claim a share in your home, yet we feel sure that you will still admit the blood- relationship, since it would not look well before your neighbours if news got about that we are hungry while you and yours are fully fed. On the first auspicious day therefore we shall begin our journey, and bring your brother's body with us for it is only right that he should lie beside his ancestors in the family land."

The letter, dictated by herself, proved that Snow Peach—Chi the Third's widow,—might be fat and shiftless and her house all "sevens and eights," but that nevertheless she was no fool.

The *pao shan ti* brought her letter with him when next he came to Hundred Altars.

He arrived at the hour when the farmers were home from their fields and when he knocked loudly at the gate, Chi opened it himself. "Here is a written message for you," he said and watched the former closely as he took the letter, suspecting its contents might prove interesting.—Chi likewise knew that something unusual was afoot. He received so few letters, perhaps not more than one a year, if that. News mostly came by word of mouth. An envelope with a stamp upon it smacked of magic like the rare trains which to him were only a whistle in the far distance, and the fanciful legend of ships without sails that moved across the great seas.

"Now who would send me a written message?" —Chi inquired wonderingly, speaking half to himself.

"It is a peaceful family letter," suggested the *pao shan ti*, "probably from the widow of your brother who moved to the north province."—It was a wily guess and one that made Chi start.

He blinked and stared at the address then handed the *pao shan ti* some coppers, and turned the letter over and over in his hand as though pleased to have it. Then he shut the gate and returned indoors, disappointing the messenger who had hoped to hear its contents. Chi opened the letter and read it slowly, for he had no great skill or habit in reading characters.

"Here is a letter come, wife," he called to Clever Needle. "It is from my brother's widow!"

"What does she say?"

"She says that my brother being dead and she his widow and her three children destitute they are coming here to make their home with us, for they have heard that our fields are fruitful. While you have borne sons, she has borne daughters only who cannot help to till their land,—so we shall have to feed four useless 'mouths' and waste money to clothe them."

Chi read the letter over several times and each time he grew more angry. The colour surged under his dark skin and his hands hung limp at his sides,—large hands, strong to make their hold felt when something might be grasped, but weak in such a case as this where he was helpless. The tyranny of the family system had him in its toils and there was no escape. He looked sourly at Clever Needle and she at him. She understood also, and with a woman's intuition sensed the polite blackmail in the last phrases. Presently she said tartly:

"There are people who think of nothing but the meals they can get in other folk's kitchens—without doing their share to earn them."

And Chi responded grimly:

"Someone bade that woman to write thus, someone who wanted to see additional mouths claim a share in our household.—Now who could that be?"—He was to ask that question of himself many times. Ordinarily he slept like a log after his day's field work, but now for three nights he lay tossing wakefully asking it over and over. Then suddenly he guessed.—He knew as surely as if he had been told.

"I have the answer!" he told Clever Needle next morning. "I have the answer!" and a bitter smile came over his face as he spoke. "I see the trick now and who played, it. It was our friend, Ma the merchant! May donkeys defile his family graves!—Don't you see why? He has heard that I told the tale of the scandal in his house which shamed him before the village.—A man may forgive much but not such loss of face, and a man proud as the merchant is will do anything for revenge in such a case!"

As he talked Chi beat his knee with an impotent fist.

"What can we do?" he went on, "Nothing!—If only I could think of a way to stop the women coming! I hate feeding them all their lives worse than I hate feeding rats. But there is no way to forbid them. If we do not take them in we shall be ourselves shamed before the neighbours who know we have enough and to spare."

He thought of the sly looks and the whispered comments of the gossips, and dared not ignore the force of public opinion which is often as useful in enforcing the tyranny of custom. The cruellest part of the whole unlucky business was that he and Clever Needle must bury their anger in their hearts and smile and pretend how pleased they were to welcome their kinsfolk.

"Yes, I must hide my rage if I choke upon it," said Chi to himself,— "And so must I," said Clever Needle ruefully thinking of her doubled housework.

It was but a few days later that Snow Peach and her three girl children arrived in Hundred Altars bringing with them the coffin of the dead man with a white cock in a basket a-top of it.

Crowing morning and night the "soul chicken" had led the dead man's spirit back to its ancestral home. Though they felt no pleasure at the sight of all these females with their ragged grey mourning clothes, their dusty white shoes and their pinched faces roughened from exposure to wind and weather on their long journey, Chi and Clever Needle greeted them at the gate politely knowing how many eyes were fixed on the meeting. Both would have liked, as the saying goes, "to have eaten their flesh and slept on their skins."

Snow Peach herself felt none too sure of her welcome, but she asked properly concerning their health and the welfare of their children.

"Now do you take these women into the house and show them the east room that we have prepared for them," Chi bade Clever Needle, "while I direct the cart to the temple and arrange for storing my brother's coffin there until such time as we can bury it."— "Another expense!" he groaned to himself as he bade the muleteer drive down the street, "But that woman is no fool.—By bringing my dead kinsman with her she assures herself of the sympathy of the village."

When Chi had arranged with Trembling Sea about storing the coffin he paid the carter, collected the baggage and carried it into the house. Snow Peach had brought all the poor furniture she owned—a sign that she did not expect to go away again. Nevertheless now that she had arrived in this clean well-kept home she was uneasy and

159

abashed. Her own had always been mismanaged,. dirty and higgle-de-piggledy. But her first words to Clever Needle were full of tact: "If at one time our husbands disagreed, sister-in-law," she said as soon as Chi was out of earshot, "there is no reason why you and I should not get on well together."

And when Chi returned she said to him apologetically, "I hope, elder brother, we shall not be a burden upon you, but Fate has dealt us a cruel blow and we cannot help ourselves."

"Naturally, naturally," said Clever Needle smoothly. "We are happy to have you come."

Snow Peach understood. "Outwardly is, inwardly is not!" she thought, as with courteous words she thanked husband and wife, flatteringly referring to them as rich and charitable.

Chi corrected her quickly with velvet bitterness:

"We are not rich, not rich at all, I and my sons. If we have food it is because we bend our backs the livelong day and do not change from place to place in search of better things. True we have land, two acres of this, five acres of that, a dozen chickens, two mules, a few pigs,—but little or no silver stored away."

He could not help speaking sarcastically, but yet he looked at his sister-in-law with pity because she was the kind of a woman she was,—a slattern whose youth had left her early. One ankle band was half untied and a loose wisp of hair straggled down her neck. These little details he noticed as she stood there with her noisy quarrelsome children round her, herself a noisy heavy-handed person with a loud voice and brusque manner, slapping one child and bidding another mind its manners,—but good-humoured withal and, on the whole a kindly creature in her skin deep;—aware too that in this house she would have to change her ways. Here would not be a life to her liking for she far preferred good-humoured confusion. Chi with his solid prosperity was so different from her own happy-go-lucky husband always pretending to be better off than he was, and Clever Needle with her evident housewifely thrift was quite unlike her sloppy, easygoing self. Their domestic partnership was going to be a strain. They would be the proverbial ox and donkey hitched to the same plough.

Presently Clever Needle, feeling that something must be done to clear the uncomfortable atmosphere, exclaimed: "Well, have you yet eaten?"

"No," answered Snow Peach eagerly, "and there is a bitter gnawing in our stomachs. It is long indeed since we have had our fill for there was little food in our province, and on the journey it was expensive."

While the meal was being prepared the newcomers stood about hungrily, tonguing their lips, and as soon as food was ready they sat down to it so greedily that Clever Needle could well believe they had not eaten for many weeks. She was horrified at the way they helped themselves to all the dishes as fast as they appeared. Those children!—with their gangling elbows sprawled on the table, spilling food everywhere in their eagerness to eat the quicker. What an example for her own boys taught never to waste even a grain of rice!—But these naughty little girls ate until their eyes were glazed, and then patted their bellies, and grunted and yawned, and still their mother urged them to eat more as Chinese mothers often do. Chi watched them with disgust.

They were dull coarse girls, even at that young age for the eldest was only twelve. Their mouths were too large and their features flat, their hair a rough dusty brown instead of glossy black. Mei Li, the eldest, Chi thought was the best. He could see a trace of the Chi blood in her. The other two little ones, Instead-of-a-Brother and Enough Hawks, were even less attractive, near sighted, harsh voiced, pinched and drawn and sallow from poor feeding.

After the newcomers had finished stuffing themselves with the good food they talked awhile of family affairs. But not for long. Soon Snow Peach yawning heavily remarked: "Now I am ready to sleep, for we have had many wakeful nights on our journey."—So Clever Needle helped her to arrange the bedding on the k'ang in the east room and mother and children lay down under a single coverlet, stretched alternately heads to feet. Little though she wanted these house guests, Clever Needle could not but offer them an extra quilt.—"Oh, don't trouble!" Snow Peach thanked her with a loud giggle as she pulled the wadded cover up to her chin, "We are quite used to making one quilt do. We turn in shifts when I give the signal, all pulling the same way at the same time so no one is left uncovered.—Besides we are not cold for we still have all our clothes on!"

The Chis' clearest memory of those first few days their relations spent in the house was a perpetual hubbub and a ceaseless round of work. Clever Needle was daily up at five rousing the others to whom dressing was a swift shaking of their garments into place with no time wasted on such refinements as washing and hair combing. Food must be cooked before the farmer and his elder sons went off to the fields, and then Clever Needle had the house to clean not once but several times, and Snow Peach was more trouble than help. No sooner had Clever Needle or Amah Niu wiped a table than the little girls spilled tea on it, Or marked it with their greasy fingers—habits their mother seemed to find quite natural. When Clever Needle scolded them Snow Peach was liable to sudden squalls of irritation which only made matters worse. Chi understood his wife's harassed face and heavily swift feet never at rest.

He was glad to get away from these women and children, and driven by the thought of four extra mouths to feed, worked longer hours than usual. Every inch of land must be made to yield fits utmost. After work he went to the inn where there was a tranquility and peace now lost in his home. Here, soon enough, sooner than he wished, he met Ma who had heard of the arrival of the women. The merchant came and sat down near his neighbour and with a bland amiable smile remarked:

"I hear you have a full household now. And lucky you are to be able to give shelter to your poor relations. Such a chance to show filial piety! How pleasing to your ancestors!"

These unctuous phrases confirmed Chi's suspicion of the trick he suspected Ma had played on him. Still he refrained from taking offence openly, merely responding with a sorry little laugh:

"Very lucky indeed,—I should in fact condole with you that the gods have not given you equal opportunities! If only they had sent more women to your house!"

Knowing, understanding too, the reason for Ma's malice he could not resist this dig.—Ma flushed at the reference to his lack of sons. It made him wince, but he kept the bland expression on his face and answered smoothly:

"Fate decides such things.—Besides my business is uncertain while you have the land which is always fertile, and your elder boys, though scarcely able to tell the difference between one character and another in their books, are already good farmers, young as they are."

Thus the two men sparred politely, each knowing that the other knew of how he had tricked his neighbour, but feigning ignorance. To Clever Needle, though, Chi spoke his mind:

"He wrote the letter just as I guessed," he said, "Otherwise Snow Peach would have accepted her evil fate contentedly. Because of it I must spend good silver feeding and coddling her and her brats and put a good face on it to boot!"

Husband and wife were thinking meanwhile of ways and means to lessen their burden. Finally Clever Needle suggested:

"Perhaps we might betroth the eldest girl, Mei Li, though she is scarcely twelve, years old."

Chi scratched his head as if to wake up his brains.

"Now who will marry a girl like that?—The slatternly daughter of a slatternly mother?"

"Ah," said Clever Needle as a bright thought struck her, "I heard the other day that there is a certain Li Nai Nai in Red Temple Village who has a son scarcely of marriageable age either. But she herself is growing old and infirm and might be willing to take a young girl into the house as his betrothed. It means the household gets another pair of hands and a maid young enough to be trained easily in the ways of a new family. The wedding can take place when both are ripe for it. If we are able to arrange this "rearing marriage" then the girl could go at once to live with her mother-in-law,—and that would be one mouth less to feed!"

Chi stared at his wife admiringly:

"What unusually good advice for one of your ignorant sex!" he said with deep approval. "And if such an arrangement can be made not only would we spend nothing now for the dowry and the wedding, which is a consideration since our own first born will have to be married within the year, but the talk can be done directly and so we will save even the middleman's fees! —Tomorrow I will ride over to Red Temple Village and see this woman before she can hear of any girl to suit her better."

"Yes," rejoined Clever Needle gratified by his praise, "it would be wise not to delay. Alas!—a 'rearing marriage' such as this brings no great face!—Still it will be a comfort to have one more maid who bears our name safely provided for."

When Chi spoke of his plan to Snow Peach she was indignant, and flushed with disappointment.—A "rearing marriage" for one of her girls!—there was no honour in that! But when he asked if any of them were already spoken she had to say "no,"—how should she pay a matchmaker's fee in all her poverty?

"Well then," Chi answered shortly, "I have nine mouths to feed now, and my brother to bury. True he is but a 'moved body' and needs no funeral and no elaborate mourning rites, since he is dead so long. Still something must be spent to bury him. And I shall not be rich enough till after several harvests to give your girl a fine wedding. So there is no other way but to arrange this 'rearing marriage' if we can. Your daughter is twelve years old and fit for that though she is too young to bear children."

"It is unkind to force a child like this!" Snow Peach retorted angrily.

"Do you prefer then that she should run wild about the village for so many years that no youth will wish to marry her? Even now she is a bold girl who looks men full in the eyes and willingly joins my eldest sons in their rough play!"

"There is no harm in her, but she is strong and full of life."

"Well, we cannot risk a scandal in our house," Chi said firmly. "And what I have decided must be done."—Finally the mother, though she wept and wailed for an hour and more consented because she had no other choice. And Chi gave her no chance to brood and work herself up into a fury but went without delay to see the old woman.

Li Nai Nai lived in a small village hidden in a fold of the western range of hills. The low houses seemed to keep as close to the ground as possible like a flock of animals cowering before an approaching storm, and indeed the winds shrieked wildly down on the hamlet from the top of the pass above. Her humble house was clean and neat, and she herself proved to be a greyhaired woman, whose face had a certain worn sweetness of expression, a look of benevolent resignation. Chi found her sitting beside her door on a low stool, pushing a long needle in and out through a shoe sole made of many layers of cloth, but when she saw a man approaching, she laid her work aside surprised and eager to know what business this stranger could have with her. They greeted one another and presently when Chi explained his errand, she nodded her head slowly:

"It is true that I seek a wife for my son though he is still young, not yet fourteen. Meanwhile I wish a daughter to help me. My own girl I had to 'throw away' soon after my husband died as we could not afford to feed her then.—That was the time when we kept a small shop, but robbers raided it, and we were desperately poor for many years thereafter. But now we have paying land as land goes. We are out of debt and the crops promise well. If your girl is willing to work and of a peaceful nature I would be glad to take her. My son is a good lad. He works like a slave,—young as he is!"

"That seems the right kind of a man for my niece, and as you think that she will suit you," Chi said cheerfully, "we are ready to have the 'Red Papers' of betrothal exchanged. I will see that they are written and sent to you within a week, and the girl can follow a handful of days later. She will be twelve on her next birthday and is not uncomely."

"Very well, send the girl," the old woman said, "she will be safe here with me until my son grows older. Then when the right time comes you can have her again for a few days and send her back here in the red chair for her marriage!"

Chi was well-pleased to have got the girl off his hands so easily. He felt no anxiety about her for all the inquiries he made satisfied him that the old woman and her son were good people, honest and kindly natured. This knowledge eased his conscience. He would not have liked to send one of his relations, little as he enjoyed feeding her, to a mother-in-law such as that old hag Liang Nai Nai, the cake-maker's wife. A "rearing marriage" was a delicate affair at best. The girl who became a party to it was more often than not an orphan or the daughter of poor and helpless parents unable to ensure she was not treated as a servant or a drudge. One had to be careful of the kind of home to which a mere child was confided while she had all the duties of a daughter-in-law, and none of the rights of a wife.

Juliet Bredon

XIX. Ma Apprentices Young Tiger

In course of time the bitterness between the Mas and the Chis lost its edge. There remained only a lurking ill-feeling like the sediment in a bottle of old wine, and both the merchant and the farmer, who could ill-afford to be open enemies were, careful not to stir up the dregs of their anger.

The season gradually deepened into cold. Autumn passed in a procession of brilliant sunshiny days, each one a little chillier than the last. The sky grew a paler blue as the warmth went out of it. The hills turned brown with deep purple shadows. The ginko trees hung out their golden leaves and lost them again. Little dancing dust devils raised by the winds appeared from nowhere and whirled quickly across a field or down a winding lane. The Bitter Moon brought a flurry of snow flakes that refreshed the earth tired after the heavy harvest. The New Year dawned soon after this happy omen and folk ate, drank and made merry as usual.

Ma decided not to send Young Tiger back to school after the holidays. Either he could not or would not learn and his father was frankly tired of trying to "help a dead dog over a wall." Besides Young Tiger had made himself disliked in the village where the farmers could not forget his habit of fruit stealing and often cursed him loudly for all the mischief he had made. Sometimes a bitter tongued woman would call after him in the street:—"Son of a camel-driver, are you not ashamed to pilfer from folk who work as hard as we do?"

It would be best to get the lad away until he should outgrow the dangerous age when a boy is all spirit and no sense. It would be wiser too, to put him under a stricter discipline than he had at home. Shui Ching was in full agreement with her husband that the lad had best be sent elsewhere lest he annoy the village further and bring disgrace again on the family.

"Young Tiger is naturally idle and spendthrift," she said, "He needs the hardships of the life to which he was born to make a man of him. Look at Chi's elder sons.—They have no time for mischief;—up at dawn carrying out the plough, slaves all day long to the earth. If Young Tiger had to work as hard as that his wildness would soon be cured!"

"You're right," Ma agreed, "but what are we to do with him? He has no love for the earth, no patience with things that grow. He is not one to be set to the plough and we cannot let him become a cameldriver—though that would seem what he is best fitted for! No, a merchant's son should be a merchant. But it would seem useless to take Young Tiger into my shop seeing he is what he is, and a father is never a good teacher for his own son. Our life is too soft for him.— Now were he only like Chi's Little Dragon.... Ma sighed.—Always that boy, always that boy....

"Well, he is not!" Shui Ching's nerves snapped. She was weary of reproaches spoken and unspoken on that subject, and small wonder. "Write," she said with a firm decision unusual to her, "to your merchant friend Hu, in Peking, and ask him to take the lad. He has many men in his employ and he owes you many favours so he should be willing to receive Young Tiger as an apprentice!"

Ma did: write to Trader Hu after Shui Ching had tactfully convinced him the idea was his own in the first place, and he wrote frankly, hiding nothing of Young Tiger's character.

"It will be a venture," he said in his letter, "but my son must learn business and perhaps under strict discipline he may yet make a good merchant. So if you will accept him I will put up the usual guarantee."

"Let him come," his friend answered though he felt no great enthusiasm. He could not well refuse Ma's request. "Let him come, but of course his pay will be no more than his food and clothing while he is learning. After the first three years or so, if he deserves a wage, then he shall have it."

Ma, thankful to get the boy settled, replied at once:

"I will send the lad to you as soon as may be after the New Year. He is fifteen years old now, strong and healthy, and the harder you make him work the better I shall be pleased."

The exact term of Young Tiger's apprenticeship was not fixed. The future was left to take care of itself. But, if as Ma hoped, the Peking merchant succeeded in making the lad into a sharp business man and a steady character, he planned to take Young Tiger into his own shop in Hundred Altars later on.

In the plans for his future Young Tiger was not consulted, he learned of them only when they were completed. The servant sent to call him to his father found him as usual in winter lying on his k'ang, dead asleep as though drunk with wine. He had to be called not once but twice and came yawning out of the inner room, his clothes not properly buttoned about him, his trousers held up insecurely by his loosened girdle.

Ma by his first words waked him roughly to his senses:

"Prick up your ears!" he said sharply eyeing him with disgust "that what I have to say to you may penetrate your thick skull.—I have been ill-pleased with your conduct these last two years and I do not want you to end your days in disgrace and shame. Work is what you need,—regular work,—so I am sending you to my friend Hu in Peking who will train you in his business. I have already settled with him and paid your bond. Had you been more obedient you might have stayed here and learned trade with me, but you have made yourself a nuisance in the village, and so I think it best that you should go elsewhere."

Young Tiger listened eagerly. Like every boy he had a desire to see new things and new places, to know what lay past the next turn in the road, the next hill, the next village. Beyond them, outside in the great world he sensed that things were happening, things which he wanted to see and in which he wanted to play a part.

"I would have liked a better son than you to send," Ma went on but Young Tiger had ceased to listen and thought only of how wonderful it would be to see the great city. He was tired of treading a pendulum path between his home and the next hamlet and back again. These pleasant dreams were rudely shattered by his father's next remarks:

"You must obey the merchant in everything, and if you are diligent and obedient and win your master's approval your future is assured though your life may be hard for the next few years."

"Diligent!" "Win your master's approval,"—"the life will be hard for a few years!" Such words were like a bell tolling the doom of his high hopes. Evidently Hu's shop was to be just like the distillery where experience had taught him that the last apprentice must work the longest hours and eat the left-overs. He was everybody's drudge with scarcely a moment he could call his own. He was expected to eat and sleep with the business.

Only one thought consoled the lad. At least he would not have to work on the land or pore for hours at a time over books he loathed, and he might, if he were sharp, manage to get a squeeze from a customer now and then. Hope sprang up again in his heart, and with a tinge of interest in his voice: he asked:

"Honoured sir, when is it decided I should leave home?"

"The first of the new month is a good day to begin a new business, but the diviner says that the last day of this month is not a lucky day for starting on a journey. So you will make a false start on the previous evening. This date happens to be highly propitious, therefore you can sleep that night at Neighbour Chien's and then continue your trip next morning. Bent Neck who is to be trusted will take you to Peking and see you reach the merchant's house safely."

So on the fortunate date Young Tiger made his bows to the ancestral tablets and to his parents who replied with the usual parting platitude—"*I lu ping an!*"—"May your way be smooth and peaceful!" Young Tiger with his up and down nature was now in high spirits at the idea of escaping from the narrow life of his father's courtyards too narrow for his hot blood. He forgot the prospect of hard work. He refused to look beyond the present joy of going somewhere for the love of the road was strong in him. In this he was very different from the farmers who hated travel as a cat hates water and would rather sit and stare at the same fields day after day than go on a journey ten miles distant to see the Emperor on his golden throne.

But Young Tiger, having learned to hide his feelings lest he be scolded for having them, listened with feigned attention to his father's final counsels to work hard and avoid quarrels, and responded with formal politeness:

"I thank you for your plans for me. I know nothing of business, I am young and inexperienced, but I will do my best to please you."

So saying he bowed again respectfully and went to neighbour Chien's, with Bent Neck walking behind him, carrying a bundle containing his wadded bed quilts, extra clothes, and several boxes of cakes and melon seeds wrapped in flowered paper— presents for his fellow apprentices. He also took a pair of ceremonial red candles and a bundle of incense. At the beginning of every enterprise homage must be paid to the gods.

Early the following morning the young master and his servant mounted their donkeys and with their baggage tied on behind them took the road for Peking. The little grey beasts accustomed to close human companionship obeyed the directions of their drivers with almost human understanding. They started and stopped at the word of command and if there was a slippery place in the road heeded the warning "Hua! Hua!"—"Slippery, slippery!"—As a class, they were garrulous fellows, these donkey drivers, talking to their beasts constantly when they were not chatting to their riders.. Full of curiosity about the business of those who hired them, their questions enlivened the road this frosty morning when a thin film of rime covered the ground like a net work of sparkling diamonds and hung a tiny glittering tear on the tip of every twig. Why was Young Tiger going to town—for how long? Who was he to work for? How much wages would he receive? By the time all these inquiries had been satisfactorily answered and not without some boastful exaggerations by Young Tiger, the little caravan was already approaching the city and about to cross the "Sweet and Sour Water" Bridge just outside the walls.

Here they stopped at a road-side tea-house to refresh themselves, and it was Young Tiger's turn to ask questions now about his new surroundings. A barrow coolie with two big wooden water casks joined Bent Neck and the boy at the same table, there being no room elsewhere. They greeted one another as comrades of the road— Who are you?—and who are you?—they asked, and where are you going, and what is your business?

"I distribute water," the man told them, wiping the sweat off his furrowed brow for all it was a crisp day. "You know the local saying, 'Peking's running water runs around in carts.' "

"Are there no wells then inside the city?" Young Tiger asked with eager curiosity.

"There are," the man answered, "but they are bitter. Folk prefer the sweet water from the hill springs and rich men pay me a good sum to fetch it."

Hundred Altars

"But why," the boy persisted, "should the water inside the city be bitter, and the water outside sweet?"

"What?" exclaimed the man in amazement, "Have you not heard? It is an old story, and connected with this very bridge here!"

Young Tiger pricked up his ears at the thought of a story, and the water-carrier needed no urging to tell the tale.

"Several hundred years ago," he began,, "a saintly man with magic powers decided to punish a wicked emperor for his sins by cutting off the water supply of Peking. He filled two barrels, one with sweet, and one with bitter water from wells within the city and wheeled them outside the walls on a barrow. The Emperor heard of the wizard's plan and, much frightened, called for volunteers to frustrate it. A warrior, renowned for his courage came forward. He was ordered to pursue the wizard and pierce the barrel containing the sweet water with his spear, then gallop back to the city at full speed, but on no account to turn round lest evil befall him. The man obeyed, but no sooner had he pierced the barrel and began to dash towards safety than he heard a sound of mighty waters rushing behind him. Just before he reached the gate, the sight of a sheet of water rising above his horse's hoofs made him forget the caution that he must not turn his head. Recklessly he looked back and in an instant the waves swept over him and he was drowned on the spot where the Sweet and Bitter Water Bridge now stands.— Worse still the champion in his haste had pierced the wrong barrel, the one containing bitter water. Thus," the man ended with a dramatic gesture, "though water did come back to Peking, it has ever been bitter and hard!"

The weather was still too cold to sit long in a draughty room so when the water-carrier had finished his tale Young Tiger and Bent Neck started on again. As they approached the North West Gate they heard a low surging roar. The mouth of the gate was a narrow, dimly lighted passageway tunnelled through the thick masonry of the high city wall. Congested into this bottle neck was a struggling mass of squeaking carts, pack donkeys," an occasional mule litter or a sedan chair, and many people on foot all set on getting through at the same time. Once inside Bent Neck paid off their donkeys whose drivers were village men and would go no further. He hired a cart with a blue hood like a Quaker's bonnet to take them to the merchant's house.— There was much haggling, but even so the carter demanded twice the village price and Bent Neck's own squeeze was cut down to a minimum.

Though devoted to Ma's interests and serving him honestly the old retainer took a commission on all his transactions.—Why should he not? The governor paid a squeeze for his great office and the peddler paid a squeeze for a good place to set up his stall. It was the custom and natural enough when so many million people had but a handful of coppers a day to live on, and, taught by bitter centuries of want could not refrain from making a tiny profit on every deal.

The house of Merchant Hu was in the south quarter of Peking so Bent Neck and Young Tiger must cross the city. The lad was well pleased. The streets and strange sights thrilled him. He admired the big shops with their carved and gilded doorways and their signboards lettered in red and gold, the glimpses of yellow Imperial roofs splendid beyond anything he had ever imagined. As for the crowds they were a fascinating kaleidoscope of colour and movement;—Manchu women in long rainbow robes and flower decked head-dresses, the rich merchants in dark silk gowns so different from the dull everyday blue cotton coats of Hundred Altars, smart young blades riding by in velvet jackets with the beggars holding to their bronze stirrups and shivering in rags as they begged for alms. Even an occasional foreigner afoot mingled with the crowd. Young Tiger had never seen any of these pale barbarians before. Now he understood why they were called devils. They were so white arid their hair was so yellow and their blue eyes seemed to him like the eyes of dead fish.—Amid all these unfamiliar sights he laughed to see one that recalled the village;—a big black sow suckling twelve little balloon-like babies in the shelter of a gutter.

When they passed the great Central Gate and entered the narrow side streets the strangers felt more at home. The mule scuffled along over uneven pavement now. The cart wheels bumped in and out of ruts. They had to ask their way, after they blundered into a "dead" lane with one end closed, and had to back out again because there was no room to turn. But finally they reached the big red doors of the merchant's house, and the driver jumping down off the shafts shouted, "We have arrived!"

Not until he had made sure, and doubly sure, of who asked entrance would the gate-keeper open his heavy doors beyond a crack.

Hundred Altars

Through this narrow slit he stared at them awhile and then somewhat grudgingly let them in. "We are from Hundred Altars and expected," Bent Neck assured him humbly.

"Then follow me," the old man said and led the way across several courtyards connected with one another by doorways cut in the shape of a vase or a leaf or a half-opened fan. "Yonder are the master's living quarters," he explained, proud to impress the country bumpkins, "and beyond, to the east are his pleasure gardens, with patterned stone paths and rockeries and pavilions. His shop stands by itself in a separate compound a few doors down the street."

The boy was deeply impressed by all these evidences of good living and comfort so much greater than in Ma's household. But he was not allowed much time to look about him. The gatekeeper's shouts soon brought a man-servant with a glossy queue and a long smoothly ironed gown, not like the peasant's gowns which were never properly pressed but only stretched out to dry on the grass or hung up with poles stuck through their sleeves. This servant came and went and returned again. "The master will greet you," he said opening a door into a large, room divided into two parts by carved woodwork partitions with paintings on rice paper framed in them.

The floor was of black and white stone slabs uncarpeted and there was much heavy lacquered furniture, stiff sofas, high chairs and blackwood tables with inset marble tops arranged in geometrical patterns.—Soon the merchant appeared treading with heavy step. He was a large man and fatter than the common, fatter even than Ma. His small ears sank well into the flesh of his neck and his belly got in his way when sitting down at table. He had a single gold tooth that glittered when he smiled—a sound tooth, gold capped to give him face. Upon his thumb was a ring of fine green jade, and he wore a long fur- fined. gown of some foreign woollen stuff, dark grey with chiselled brass buttons,—for the room was unheated save for a charcoal brazier. Even the two walnuts which he held in his right hand and moved constantly between his fingers to keep them supple were beautifully carved.—

"Here," said Young Tiger to himself, "is a great merchant, head of a big business. It must be wonderful to be as rich as he! He does not look stern either." Indeed Hu, despite his dignity seemed to radiate good-humour from the soles of his heavy black velvet shoes to the red button on his shiny round black satin cap.

He greeted Young Tiger genially and ordered a supper for him and for the steward, which they were both ready to eat after their long journey. But meanwhile the slow forms of politeness were gone through and they talked gravely of this and that, of relations and the price of grain in the village, and whether the harvest had been good.—"And how did you leave your father, my friend Ma?" Hu asked the lad. "Does he eat his rice well?"

"The home father is fortunately in excellent health, and begged me to present his compliments to you, his honoured friend," Young Tiger replied politely.

As well as might be while keeping his eyes respectfully downcast the lad was watching his new employer—a kindly, easygoing man he appeared to him.—But the next day when Young Tiger met Hu again in his great shop he quickly changed his opinion. Hu greeting the son of his old friend Ma was one person, and Hu, the cool practical man of business handing over a young apprentice to his shop superintendent was quite another. In his guest hall he was a genial kindly host, but in his shop he was the serious trader, a man to be feared and respected.

"Obey the shop-manager," he instructed Young Tiger gravely. "You must always do what he bids you, and thus show your respect for your honoured father and for me. And be sure to treat the business you learn as confidential, and keep all you hear locked in your heart."

Young Tiger thanked the merchant nervously for the confidence reposed in him, and slyly observed his new master. The superintendent did not look promising, nor did he prove to be lenient to the young apprentice. He was a tall, thin old man, with a head like a bald eagle and an enormous Adam's apple. His face was shrunken and yellow with sunken eyes that yet were keen and sharp in making up accounts and watching the youngsters in his charge. There was no chance of a lazy comfortable existence under his rule Young Tiger was convinced the moment he set eyes on him, and never a hope of fooling him either.

Indeed the shop life proved hard enough. For more than twelve hours a day the clerks and apprentices were on duty, running errands, clicking the wooden balls up and down the abacus, writing up accounts, receiving moneys or paying them out, striking each silver dollar upon the next to prove it rang true, and woe betide the careless youth who accepted a false coin!

Yet though the work was constant and the hours long there was a certain leisureliness about it. The employees might stop once in a way and enjoy a few whiffs of tobacco, or a few sips of tea. But the manager knew well enough which boys were really lazy and punished them as he saw fit.

At the end of his first day Young Tiger was thoroughly tired and went willingly to his shelf bed beneath the counter. He had already decided that this was not the career for him, not even if he should become as rich as Hu himself by sticking to it. "No, no, and No!" he told himself over and over again. "I was born for the great world and for adventures,—and somehow I am going to get out of this!"—But the opportunity did not come, and day after day he worked and worked on in the same dull routine, hoping for an escape and finding none.

Meanwhile Ma in Hundred Altars heaved a sigh of relief now that Young Tiger was gone—-and settled. In the evenings the merchant loitered in the doorway of his house and dreamed dreams of a future when the hot headed lad should have been tamed into a serious man and build, with his help, a business as great as Hu's and greater.—Perhaps not in Hundred Altars,—no surely not. Already he was reaching out in his visions for a larger stage whereon to play a more dramatic part. Money like scholarship might one day mean power.

Juliet Bredon

XX. Red Festivities

Autumn was the marrying season in the villages of the plain. After the crops were cut and sold the farmers had money to spend and leisure to attend to family affairs.

It so happened that the year the mourning for the Elder ended the harvest was ten parts good. This was great luck for Chi who disposed of more surplus grain at better prices than usual. And he needed the silver badly since he could no longer delay marrying his eldest son. Even his second was of age to take a wife, but Chi could not afford "red festivities" for the two of them at the same time. Let him wait. The eldest, who carried the ancestral torch, must first take a woman to provide descendants.

Chin-tzu and Yin-tzu were grown men now,—solid, square, hard-headed farmers, alike and yet unlike. The second born was a phlegmatic type with some of the peasant virtues and some of their defects also. He was miserly and suspicious, but steel-strong and a powerful worker. He wanted money only to buy more land and more land because it assured more work. Chin-tzu on the contrary had a streak of emotion in him and a sly round-the-corner look in his slanting eyes as if he sought sideways for some ideal he scarcely hoped to find. He was a crafty bargainer like his father, and mistrusted strangers. Indeed his roots were so deeply planted in his own clan that he wasted no talk interest or energy on outsiders.

Chi sighed with relief now that the time had come when he could afford to establish this eldest son. The family tree lacked branches of the third generation. It was foolish to delay. Snow Peach and her two remaining girls had been eight months already under the roof,—"mouths without hands"—dead weights to carry, as Chi had guessed. So not only was there a pressing need for grandsons but it was important to have a reliable woman in the house to second Clever Needle and safeguard the future. She knew this as well as Chi himself and constantly pressed him to ensure against the future, constantly reminded him that a wife must be found for Chin-tzu,—a good sound woman, able to take her place when age or illness came upon her.

Chi preferred not to consult a professional matchmaker about his son's affairs. Such men were notoriously unreliable and many a dishonest go-between pushed a bad match simply to earn his fee. So he called on his friend Chien and said: "Do you know of any maid who would do for my eldest born's wife?—Someone easy-tempered, a good worker, and likely to bear sons ? She must be healthy and well trained to do housework. As for her dowry I will not ask too much provided she be a sound maid who is not wasteful of food and wears out no shoe-soles gadding."

"We will see what offers," Chien advised. "It is indeed high time we found a wife for that long lad of yours. Nineteen years old is he not?—and grown to manhood almost without my noticing it. But yesterday it seems he played a little naked boy in the street."

Chien, in his turn, consulted Trembling Sea who being often called to chant Sutras for the Dead in neighbouring villages, knew every family within a radius of ten miles and could make tactful inquiries concerning which girls were ripe to wed. Then Chien, deeming it his duty, saw each likely maid himself, and three weeks passed before he found a girl with all Chi's requirements, the daughter of farmers of good repute in Hsi Pei Wang.

"Her family and yours," he reported, "are quite suited to be tied together with a double rope. I am prepared to guarantee it. The girl is not a beauty, neither has she a great dowry. but her disposition is easy and she is well-trained in housewifery."

"Excellent!" exclaimed Chi rubbing his hands together. "I do not tare if she be plain of face.—Look at Ma's useless, beauty! Nor do I desire too rich a girl who will be forever sighing for the luxury of her father's house.—From what you say this maid seems just the kind, of daughter-in-law we want, and if you are satisfied I approve your choice. So please make the bargain in the name of our family if you think the girl's clan will agree."

"I have every reason to think they will," Chien was able to assure him. And he was right. They did. But before the affair could be definitely settled the diviner must be consulted concerning the omens. At Chien's request the old man wrote the "eight characters" giving the hour, the day, the month and the year in which the youth and maid were born on two sheets of red paper. These he thoughtfully compared and found favourable. "Chin-tzu," he explained wisely, "is

Juliet Bredon

born under the sign of the Bull and the maid Willow under the sign of the Rat which proves the union should be happy for the Bull is stronger than the Rat, and a man must rule his woman.—Yes, the stars are propitious. Let the 'red festivities' take place."

Once the horoscopes were cast the marriage passed from the hands of mortals into the realm of geomancy. Fate had decided the future,—Fate as revealed by the Almanac, and neither party to a marriage would dare to question the will of Fate.

As they worked side by side in the fields next day Chi informed his son of his coming marriage.

"It is high time you were wed," he told him, "you are already in your nineteenth year. I have found a suitable wife for you, a good honourable maid. She is well-born and well-bred, and her 'eight characters' harmonize perfectly with yours. I hope that you are pleased."

The youth straightened himself suddenly and slowly rubbed his hands on the seat of his trousers—a typical farmer's gesture.

Though he was a grown man now he flushed darkly at the thought of marriage. Where women were concerned he was still green wood and no spark of fire had yet set his heart alight.

With natural curiosity he asked:—"What does the girl look like?"

"You'll see that on your wedding day!" Chi answered sharply.

"Don't be so impatient."

"Yes, but I do hope she is pretty and such a wife as other men may envy," the young man persisted. "Have I ever seen her?"

"Chien is our go-between, and tells me she is what we want. She comes from a household in Hsi Pei Wang—it is possible you may have seen her at the temple fair. But why these foolish questions? One might think this wedding concerned.you only!— Who ever heard of a filial youth that doubted the wisdom of his parents in arranging his marriage?—Or had you perhaps some foolish notion of choosing a wife yourself?—Look what your uncle, my brother, married because he did not consult his father but relied on his own picking!" Chi ended sternly.

"Oh, no, father!" Chin-tzu said resignedly, "I had no intention of doing such a thing! I submit myself to your wishes.— How could

I carelessly put my desires above them? —I only thought..." He paused and his eyes glimpsed a distant dream for a moment, then the habit of a lifetime of obedience to his parents shattered it and he turned silently back to work, the never-ending work of tearing a living from the earth with his two bare hands.—Indeed the idea of selecting his own bride had never entered Chin-tzu's head. It was unthinkable that he, the eldest son, should dare to take a wife without his father's approval.—The father was the absolute monarch of the patriarchal family; he had the power of life and death over his children.—And after all it did not greatly matter what woman they gave him. Like his ancestors he was fated to be a link in a chain rather than an individual, and it were better he should not love his wife too well. Selfish attachment was unfilial and might lead to domestic complications. Marriage was essentially a clan affair. There was no question of two young people making a home for themselves; they were bits of mosiac which must fit into the pattern of the household.—And so the marriage was settled as far as Chin-tzu was concerned.

As for the maid in Hsi Pei Wang, when she was told of what had been arranged for her she made no comment at all about her wedding. Doubtless she would have liked to ask if her future husband were handsome, if he were tall or short, or pockmarked, —but such questions a well-brought-up girl must keep tightly within closed lips or she would be thought unmaidenly.

The bride's family had also named a middleman to act for them, a man called Tang, headman of their village. Together he and Chien sat for hours talking, talking, talking, over the dowry and the gifts to be exchanged, and the rites proper to the occasion. While they congratulated one another on the good bargain each was making for his side the bride and her mother sewed together in their inner courtyard on the red silk wedding garments, and the bridegroom worked in the fields pretending indifference to the preparations going on around him.

Soon all was in readiness and one yellow October day that smelled of wild dates, aromatic and pungent, the Phoenix and Dragon betrothal papers were signed. "Now the affair is settled," said Tang highly pleased, "the betrothal can be announced to all, and then it will be as binding as the wedding."

"Just so, just so," Chien agreed. "Destroy the temples if you will, but break an engagement never. Now I'll take these papers back with me for they must lie three days before Chi's ancestral tablets as a sign your girl will accept her husband's forebears as her own."

"Pray do so, and let us hope there will be peace in the Chi house for those three days, otherwise bad luck might attend the marriage."

With the engagement firmly "buttoned up," the diviner was asked to set the wedding day. Then the groom's family informed the bride's parents of the date and sent them a pair of geese— rented from the wedding shop. Geese were chosen because these birds are ever faithful to their mates, and red "joy" collars were painted round their necks, since a pure white bird would be unlucky at a wedding, which is a "red business," just as a funeral is a "white business." "Now we can rent the wedding chair, and the bead crown," Chi told Clever Needle.

"Yes, but first we must send off the betrothal cakes and the betrothal gifts!"

"Of course," agreed Chi, "and I've hired forty bearers in flowery coats from the wedding shop to carry them!"

They made a brave show these gifts of cloth and jewellery and food, and several tens of bright new silver dollars, on each of which was pasted the red paper character for "double joy," spread out on red lacquer tables for all the neighbours to admire.

"It's a fine procession," whispered Clever Needle watching it start, "longer than usual,—long enough to give us great face."

"Yes," said Chi in an undertone. "I hired more presents than we could afford to buy. Chien will see they are returned later, and they do add splendour and richness!"

"I wish they might have been packed in boxes. The dust of the road will soil them,—and suppose it should rain!"

"It will not rain, woman, look at the sky! Whoever heard of rain at this season? But even if it did we could cover the things with transparent oil papers so nothing would be spoilt, and the neighbours, would still see how much we are sending."

The dowry consisting of everything for the bride's personal use from an ear pick and a tongue scraper to the furniture for her own room was carried to her new home in the same way, but Chi remarked with a chuckle that her bearers numbered only twenty.

Then the day before the wedding the two families feasted their own friends separately. Willow retired early for she must rise at dawn to take her wedding bath, and let her women friends pluck out the fine fringe of short hairs about her forehead. They rolled and twisted them between two threads, and coiffed in the style of a matron, thus signifying her goodbye to girlhood. Primly she sat with her hands folded in her lap while this was done, and while they rouged her cheeks and her eyelids, for her face was wax white, and rubbed a touch of vermilion on her lips and darkened her eyebrows with a brush dipped in ink.

Then they put a mirror in her hand, but it reflected little coquetry from that serious young face. She was not plain, but neither was she beautiful, and already at twenty her mother had taught her that life was a serious business and marriage meant new duties rather than new pleasures.

"Willow, my daughter," she told her, "remember in all things to submit yourself to your husband and to respect his parents so that your life may be peaceful in your new home. The rules of behaviour I have taught you carefully, and do not forget that conversation is the least of a woman's virtues."

Then she led her girl by the hand dressed in her red satin wedding gown to bow before the ancestral tablets for the last time. Thus she made her formal farewell to her old home. "Nevermore," she thought sadly, "may I 'cross the year' under my father's roof, nor return to this house save as a guest."— Presently the red chair sent by Chi arrived to fetch the bride in the midst of gay and noisy confusion. It was a fine chair, brave in red satin embroidered covers and curtains with hanging bead tassels. Chi had stipulated it should be new, though he paid fifty dollars hire instead of twenty five—the price of one that had been used already.—Before it left his house two married women, mothers of sons, searched the chair thoroughly with a lamp to make sure no evil spirits lurked within. Then at the lucky hour which the soothsayer in Hsi Pei Wang had fixed for her to start the bride was led out to the wedding chair, timid and reluctant, weeping loudly,—partly because it was the custom, and also because she was sincerely sad to leave her home.—A girl must marry, of course. An old maid had no place and no consideration. Yet, when she went "out of the door" breaking her home ties, never to return, never to re-knit them, it was natural she should be unhappy. Henceforth she must live as a stranger among strangers until she could make new affections among new kin.

Women attendants tucked her robes neatly around her feet, covered her face with the red satin veil, and put a mirror and an Almanac beside her. Then the curtain was let down and crackers fired as the bearers raised the chair and turned it around three times for luck,—and no one needs more luck than a bride.—So shut up in her red satin box and half smothered in her red satin veil, Willow started for her new home. Banners were carried before her, and wooden fans inscribed with lucky phrases wished her long life and many sons. Gilded trumpets groaned and lighted lanterns showed pale in the daylight.

Her mother standing in the doorway watching her daughter go wiped her tears away with her long sleeves. "Be careful, mother," whispered her youngest daughter. "You will spoil your new gown. Remember it is hired only for the day!"—But the mother did not hear. She watched the bearers bearing her child away, watched until a turn in the road hid them from sight. She had memories of her own journey as a strange bride to a strange house. Sighing heavily she turned back into the lonely home.—"Alas, that a daughter's marriage holds the sadness of departure, while a son's marriage holds only the joy of arrival!"

Meanwhile the Chi family watched the procession coming from afar, winding and twisting along the narrow field paths, and the whole village watched also. At last the chair was at the door and two women lifted the satin curtain and invited the bride to step out. Her trembling feet could scarcely support her as they helped her from the chair. Her robes and veil and beaded crown were heavy and weighted her every movement. It was a hard ordeal for the shy young girl to cross the courtyard filled with strangers for Chi had invited all the neighbours and many guests from other villages to join the merrymaking. Willow could not see the folk for the thick veil still covered her face, but she could hear their comments. "A good lowly maid who walks modestly!" said an old woman's voice,—"Yes, indeed," 'came another, "see her meekly bent head."—The kindly words cheered her.—But there were other and personal remarks on child-bearing which made her blush even beneath the thick folds of her veil.—Presently the two attendant matrons leading the bride warned her that she was near the threshold and should raise her foot to step over a saddle with two apples placed beneath it. This she must do to ensure peace in her new home as by a play of words these things signified peace.

Still supported by her matrons of honour she was led to her bridegroom, and together they bowed before the ancestral tablets in the central room. She knelt with him before his honoured parents, and finally they bowed three times to one another,—the little blindfold bride guided in all her movements by her women. Thus the young couple publicly acknowledged their obligations to past generations, their obedience to the bridegroom's parents set in authority over them, and their new relationship to one another—in the presence of witnesses. So Willow signified her willingness to become a daughter of the house of Chi and cut herself off forever from her own family and clan.

Still veiled, Willow was led into her bedroom and seated upon the *k'ang* beside her bridegroom,—he in the more honourable place on the left. Chin-tzu leaned towards her and raised her veil and for the first time they gazed on one another's faces. —It was an anxious moment.—In fear she looked at him, and in fear she saw him glance at her.—Would he find her ugly?— And would she find him repellent?—But at this "mutual seeing" both were lucky. Willow saw a strong young man with a frank farmer's face, heavy and broad, and yet not coarse or cruel. And she was relieved and even glad. One may trust one's parents, but... And Chin-tzu looking sideways at the girl was well-pleased also. Gentle and meek she looked with modest downcast eyes, and he liked the sweet serenity of her smile and the wide curve of her brow.—Mercifully there was no disappointment on either side as there too often is.

They sat without speaking, shy of one another, while two gilded cups were brought and a little wine from a gilded pitcher poured into each. They drank, and exchanged cups, and poured wine from one into the other. Then both sipped the "Mingled Wine," one of the attendant matrons holding her cup to the lips of the bride, who was too nervous and timid to lift it for herself. After the wine ceremony that "makes the perfect circle," the "sons and grandsons" dumplings were brought in and the young husband and wife ate their first meal together in harmony though the little bride could scarcely do more than nibble a few crumbs. But now that they had shared food and drink in common they were legally wed. Sharing, that signified union, was the essence of the ceremony,—not asking for blessings, not worshipping. No promises were asked or given. The marriage rite required no priests. The ancestors and not the gods must recognize the pact.

Chin-tzu, without addressing a word to Willow, went into the main room to greet the wedding guests. He wore the long silk coat of an official which every man had the right to wear on his marriage day, his forehead was newly shaved, and his freshly plaited queue lengthened by a handsome, red tassel. But the bride remained in her room. She might not join in the general feasting. She must sit quietly on the *k'ang* while strangers came in to "test her temper." They could play all manner of jokes on her and make all kind of embarrassing remarks about her, and now she no longer had the protection of the red satin veil to hide her blushes. They spoke loudly of marriage and birth with the coarse frankness of a land where child-bearing early and often is a woman's first duty. The peasants dwelt much on these matters and they had no false modesty, for, outside field work, they had little else to occupy their minds. But whatever the guest might say or do Willow had been taught that she must not reply nor laugh, nor even raise her eyes, but sit dumb as a doll until the last guest was gone and her husband should return to her.

Yes, a wedding was fun for everybody but the bride. She and she alone of all the crowd might not have a good time, might not join in the gaiety and, however hungry, might not share in the feast though it was many hours since she had eaten a full meal in her own home.

Each guest brought Chi a money gift enclosed in a red joy envelope. Usually it was about equal to the cost of whatever food he ate, or a little less if his appetite was good and he consumed more "happy noodles" and drank more wine than a normal gift would pay for. Neighbours were judged according to the value of their presents. Some were "hundred cash" friends, some "thousand cash friends", and a few like Ma "silver dollar friends." Chi could not help a silent chuckle at the merchant's generous contribution—bigger even than

Chien's. Ma's was certainly a fine "face" gift, but Chi felt the outward value of that silver covered a "cash friendship." "Cut turnips sometimes resemble lotuses!" was Ma's inward comment. Chi might suspect what he liked, but the neighbours would never guess that the bond between the two was copper and not silver.

At the feast Chi acted as host for Chin-tzu, who suitably embarrassed to outward appearance as a young bridegroom should be, stood silent in a corner scratching his head and staring at his father. "Let all come in!" the Elder announced with a grand gesture. "My house is open, and today we refuse food to no man, not even to homeless beggars. Let all have brimming wine-cups and make merry. This is a marriage, and a marriage means grandsons, so let us share our joy with all and sundry!"

"May you soon see three generations under your roof!" cried the guests as they seated themselves eagerly at table. All day long the feasting lasted, and it was late indeed before the last guests were gone and Chin-tzu could return to his bride.

For three days Willow remained in her inner room according to custom. She did not join the family even at meals. She might not speak until, at the end of that time, her mother-in-law gave her permission for the girl was married more closely to the Chi family than to Chin-tzu. His parents governed even the relations between him and his wife, and she must honour them and obey them before even her own man, since if she attempted to tie him to her apron string he would be mercilessly teased. A marriage like theirs, arranged "sight unseen" by their parents and denied enthusiasms, could yet develop deep and strong affection growing with years of common interest and experience. Such a tie indeed bound Chi and Clever Needle themselves together until now "their hearts were within each other." Hot love so often burned itself out quickly in a flame of passion. It was best to begin with a tiny flicker that would grow gently and glow temperately but eternally on the family hearth. So the ages had taught, and experience was seldom wrong.

On the fourth morning Willow waited upon her parents-in-law and worshipped the family gods and the ancestors again, thus cementing her kinship with her new relations. Her position in the household was that of a child to be trained in the duties of life,—

neither mistress in her husband's home, nor yet a servant, but just a daughter-in-law, which was something between the two.

Lucky indeed is the bride who pleases her mother-in-law, and this Willow by her humble and submissive ways succeeded in doing. In fact Clever Needle remarked to Chi at once, "I like our new daughter. She is a good worker and well trained in the proprieties. Never does she forget to give us the morning '*ching an*,' the bow of peace, and she listens silently when I speak to her, whether I use words of praise or blame, Don't forget to give Chien a good present. He has indeed done well by us."— And in her heart she thought, "Had I had a daughter, her pattern would have suited me!"

As for Chin-tzu, he made no comment at all. Love had no place in his marriage. What was there for him to say?—On the fourth morning he was back at work in the fields, sowing the winter wheat. This duty could not be neglected, least of all by a bridegroom who looked forward to being a father in the coming year. A day off to pay his respects to his wife's parents, then settled down to wait to see his children born.

XXI. The Rain Procession

The village women were washing in the stream that flows out of the Black Dragon Spring, born between rocks dyed rainbow colours. They squatted in a long line beating their clothes on stones and rubbing them clean with wisteria pods. The sun threw shadows of these patient homely figures on the wall behind them with as much care over each contour as if it had been the profile of a court beauty. Faded blue trousers, a child's coat grotesquely patched, white cloth stockings, and embroidered ankle-bands were spread out on the grass to dry. Now and then a big white crane flew slowly overhead on heavy wings to alight in the rice fields beyond and catch a protesting frog. Occasionally a donkey passed, happy to cool his hoofs in the fresh running water, or a thirsty flock of goats came down from the hills to drink. It had been a very hot dry summer, and even the spring, with not a drop of rain to feed it, lacked its usual strength.

Day after day the sun burned his way across the sky, and such few clouds as appeared seemed to have no wish to linger. The "small heat" was over now, the "great heat" at its fullness and still no rain fell. Dogs' tongues lolled out. The farmers worked short hours naked to the waist, their trousers rolled above their thighs, and cartwheel straw hats covering their heads. But they could do little to save the crops.

Each afternoon the peasants squatted on their haunches, fans in hand round the dwindling wells and looked up at the enamelled blue sky which all day long radiated heat like slag raked from a furnace. They looked and hoped for rain, but no rain came. Sinister cracks appeared in the fields. The corn drooped exhausted tassels. Even the strong Big Millet heads bent down towards the crumbling earth demanding mercy.

Drought, as the weatherwise farmers knew, was to be expected. For forty two days high winds had blown parching the fields, and all because this year a dozen dragons instead of the usual trio or quartet were in charge of rain distribution. That was a forewarning of a dry season, since a large committee never attends to business as well as a small one. The dragons played about together careless of their responsibilities, or weary of sport and argument, folded up wings and tails, withdrew their claws and dozed peacefully in the shining skies.

From all the villages scattered over the great plain came the sound of rain drums being beaten. Their vibrations crept through the earth and hummed through the air, shaking the images of the gods in the temples from head to foot, and the branches of the trees from fork to tip. "It is useless to expect rain," said the diviner, "there are ten black specks on the sun and the chief dragon, He Whose Face is Dark, has hardened his heart.—He has put one ear against a mountain peak and stopped up the other with his tail. He does not wish to hear."

But for once nobody listened to the old man's warning. It was so many years since drought had come to Hundred Altars that the people could not believe it was coming now.

And yet nothing ever happens for the first time. The old men remembered they had heard their grandfathers tell of a severe drought in the reign of the Emperor Chien Lung more than a hundred years ago. At that time the Emperor, grieving for the thirsty land, journeyed in person to the Black Dragon Spring to pray for rain. At first the god had refused to listen to Majesty kneeling beside the spring in golden robes of office. Then the Emperor ceased to implore politely. In his capacity of Supreme Dragon Sovereign, Son of Heaven and Heir to the Dragon Throne, he gave an ultimatum to the Rain God. Either rain should be sent because the people needed it, or the God should be banished from his temple to the dry cold regions of the Far North. But the Dragon God dwelling comfortably in his marvellous green pool with two tortoises to serve him, continued to defy the Emperor. "Very well," said his Majesty to his courtiers, "I will wait no longer. Place his image in the sedan chair. Give orders that the procession be made ready. He shall start at once!"

No sooner had the cavalcade reached Frog Village, three miles distant beyond Hundred Altars, than the Dragon, hot and uncomfortable in the scorching sun with not a damp scale to his parched person, remembered his cool water with longing. He hastily reconsidered his decision, and rain began to fall. It fell in heavy lances, in torrents, and in sheets. It fell for three whole days. The little streams by the roadside hitherto almost dry, now in full flood, raced recklessly hither and thither over-flowing the fields and the farm yards and turning the village streets into canals deep enough to drown a pig.

Then the peasants begged the Emperor to intercede for them again. "Enough is enough!" they pleaded. "If this downfall continues much longer we shall have floods." So once more the Emperor had to remind the Dragon that he was not behaving as a serious Rain God should. "Thunder of Heaven!" said his irate Majesty, "Have you lost your sense of moderation?"— This time the Dragon needed no second warning. He pushed the clouds away at once and sunshine came again. Then in token of his satisfaction the Emperor ordered him to be carried back to his pool and gave a gift of Imperial yellow tiles to roof his shrine. And the country folk in memory of the flood renamed Frog Village—"The Village that was Drowned by the Dragon."

"Chien Lung was a great sovereign," said Wu the coffin-maker. "If we had such a man on the throne now we could appeal to him again. I have heard tell that the Emperor of today is but a baby and his officials too busy filling their pockets to care what happens to the country."

"Yes," agreed Chien, "People say there are rebellious mutterings in the South. Usually before when trouble has come, it has come from the North. But the unrest now is in the South. It is a bad omen."

When he finished speaking no man disputed his statements, asked a question or leant towards his neighbour with a whispered comment. Each kept his thought within him. Of what use puzzling over rumours? They were fatalists, these peasants, incurious fatalists from long experience. The "will of Heaven" was beyond their power to alter and the wise men of old taught them to accept with patience what they could not change. How otherwise, but for this calm philosophy, could they bear life in a land where for two thousand years there has always been famine somewhere because of drought or flood or revolution as each succeeding dynasty grown corrupt and weak became a falling wall to which some virile adventurer was glad to give a push?

Yet their Confucian viewpoint did not prevent the Elders from suggesting an appeal to the gods. Now that a serious drought threatened. Chi, senior elder, in his father's stead, called the Villagers together and urged them to hold a rain procession and offer a feast to the Black Dragon in hope of bribing him to send the needed rain.

"It has been done since ancient days," he said knowing well that he could use no stronger argument. But processions and feasts cost money and times were hard. The poorer farmers could not afford to contribute in case their prayers were not answered. "But brothers," Chi appealed to them, "think well before you refuse to ask the gods for help. The crops have never been so poor in my life time. They are no higher than a two-year-old child. The water in the wells is an arms-length less than I have ever known it and many of the rocks at the bottom of the Black Dragon Pool now thrust their heads in the dry air."

But the villagers were doubtful. They still believed that rain would come of its own accord in time to save the crops. They still hoped to save their money. They were unable to look farther than from one day to the next. Chi and Chien shook their heads. To see the fields suffer as they were suffering now was hard to bear. "Poor folk," they said to one another, "we do not wish them to endure a famine it is in the power of the gods to spare them."—But the answer to their appeals was always, "Wait,—wait, rain will come of itself."

Then suddenly the mud houses began to crack and the ground to wrinkle like the face of an old crone. And the people were seized with panic overnight. "Order the procession!" they said with one voice. "We will pay!" Now at last they were ready to throw themselves on the mercy of the gods with elemental fierceness.

So Chi and Chien and the other Elders hastened to Trembling Sea and bade him as the parish priest arrange the rain festival in honour of the Black Dragon, according to the old customs followed for centuries.—"I will do my part," Trembling Sea answered willingly, "Do you as Elders summon the magistrate from Pei Yang Ho since from time immemorial a state official must attend a "Paying Tribute to the Gods" to make it efficacious, and lend dignity to the people's prayers."—A messenger was promptly sent and returned with the word that his lordship agreed to come. Then there was much sweeping and garnishing of the temple guest rooms, and promptly at noon the next day the Elders gathered to receive him.

A gaudy escort accompanied the great man. Lictors carrying bundles of rods and beaters with heavy gongs strode ahead, shouting at the tops of their voices to clear the way. The magistrate, dressed in his full robes of office, a long dark gauze gown with embroidered squares back and front to denote his rank, high black satin boots, and an official hat with a button of his grade, and an iridescent feather trailing down his back, was an impressive figure seated in his green cloth sedan chair surrounded by outriders mounted on shaggy Mongol ponies,—a good man too as magistrates went, not a tiger to the people below him and a mouse to the officials above him. Nevertheless he had his little vanities and enjoyed the murmur of admiration and approval from the populace who watched him pass by.

When his procession reached the temple the double gates were flung wide open and his Excellency's chair was carried through the courtyards and set down before the door of the reception room. The great man stepped out and was ushered into the guest hall by Chi and his fellow Elders. Each knew where he should stand to greet the high official, and how many times he should bow, and the Magistrate with great condescension returned the salutations with bows only less deep. Then Chi bade the exalted guest be seated in the place of honour and served him with the inevitable tea. His lordship was an amiable man with dignified and gentlemanly manners and thanked the villagers for his welcome. Indeed much breath was wasted on pleasing phrases between hosts and guest before the Elder had a chance of humbly referring to the reason of the Magistrate's visit.

"We, the unworthy people," Chi said, "are anxious lest our fields be ruined by the drought. Thanks to your fatherly care there will be a rain procession in honour of the Black Dragon God.—May we entreat you to lend your presence to it?"

His honour bowed assent.

In the meantime the cortege was forming in the outer courtyard and when it was ready the magistrate was invited to take his place behind the travelling image of the Black Dragon God, a smaller copy of the large statue that stood upon his altar near the spring at Hei Lung Tan. Even this replica presented a fine appearance. Its shining face was freshly lacquered. A new horsehair beard and moustaches gave it a fierce expression. In addition the image had been presented with a new embroidered robe and crowned with a willow wreath for the willow is a symbol of water. The eight newly married men who acted as bearers for the god's chair wore willow wreaths also.

After preliminary offerings by Trembling Sea at the temple altar, the Magistrate shouted as he prepared to step into his own chair, "Let the god travel!"—The temple bell clanged, gongs were beaten loudly, and incense rose in clouds as the procession started off down the village street for a tour of the countryside, since the people argued that if the Dragon saw the thirsty fields with his own eyes and realized what misery threatened, he would send rain.

Men and boys followed behind while women watched the procession from their doorways. The further it travelled the longer it grew. Farmers from neighbouring villages, anxious to add their prayers to those of Hundred Altars, joined in till the long winding convoy was a carnival scene.—Young men came fantastically dressed as women, or swaggering military heroes or white-faced clowns. Others disguised themselves as ghosts and goblins and were animals. Some carried banners bearing the characters, "Rain, Thunder, Lightning and Wind." Men on stilts hobbled along with the others, humorous or exaggerated masks hiding their faces.

When at last they reached the Black. Dragon's golden-tiled temple on Flowering Eyebrows Hill, the crowd accompanied the god to the edge of his own spring where his chair was set down. Then they climbed to his main shrine above where his "large" image was seated on a throne chair behind the high altar. A tablet of honour giving his title of Dragon God hung above his head. Standing on a lower level around him was his court;—the lesser members of the Ministry of Weather,—the god of Thunder with his bird's head and toes and his hammer in his hand; the master of Rain with his watering can, the Goddess of Lightning with the two mirrors she clashes together, the God of Wind with a bag over his shoulder, and the little imp called the Cloud Pusher—All were, the Dragon God's assistants.

Before the altar the peasants burned prayer scrolls and offered petitions to the accompaniment of a continuous beating of drums and gongs. The diviner, too, had his part in the ceremony. While the people prayed the old man cunningly tickled a bucketful of frogs to make them croak—an unfailing device to bring rain.

It was a long long service, one of those never-ending Eastern ceremonies, but finally the magistrate and the priest and all the folk after him descended the steep stairs to the pool again where the travelling image of the god had been left in his chair, baking in the sunshine as a hint for him to wake up and do his duty. Priest and people knelt beside the water and repeated their petitions:

"O mighty Dragon we have beaten drums, we have lighted incense, yet the land thirsts and the crops fail. Deign out of thy pity to send us rain!"

So for an hour they waited beside him anxiously to watch the rain clouds gather. They looked for an immediate miracle out of the sky. But alas, the mighty Dragon God of the Waters took no notice of their entreaties. He stared unmoved over the parched fields beyond his green pool. The long afternoon drew toward evening. The peasants began to murmur among themselves. There were some among them who had doubted from the start. These unbelievers said:

"It must be that the gods are like unjust officials. They have been bribed by devils and will not hear us."

Now so long as the gods behave themselves the everlasting people are always generous to them. They give them high sounding titles, silk robes, feasts, outings, incense, honours and theatricals. But, when expected blessings are withheld, the gods are punished like mortals who fail in their duties. It is quite logical to worship an image sincerely and to seek vengeance upon it in an angry moment. The one feeling does not exclude the possibility of the other. Strange contradictions exist in all beliefs.

The people had waited long and patiently. They had shouted themselves hoarse with prayers and supplications. They were hungry, hot and tired. They began to think they had spent money for nothing. Presently the growing fury of the crowd voiced itself in the high pitched chorus of the young men, crying in unison; "Dragon God—you have deserted us!—Either you have lost the power you had in the old days or you deliberately turn a deaf ear to our sufferings! Dragon God we have offered you good food in plenty,—and still you scorn us, leaving us hanging between the cliff and the precipice!"

A hand was raised to strike the image, then another and another.

"Spare the god lest you bring his vengeance upon us!" shouted Chi, trying to make himself heard above the roar of the crowd. But no one listened to him, and he stood by helpless, his fists clenched so hard that his nails dug into his hand and his thumb knuckles cracked. The people feeling their last hope gone had a sense of outrage. The crowd lost control. They went up to the image and slapped its face and spat in it, and beat it with their carrying poles. One arm hacked off rolled to the ground. A man kicked it viciously into the pool startling the water-cobblers that crossed and uncrossed their long legs unceasingly in panicked fright.

It was not the first time that a rain procession had ended so. Similar scenes of violence occurred often enough on the banks of the Yellow River—China's Sorrow—when the Rain God there refused to do the people's will. But the shrine of Hundred Altars had never witnessed such a tumult. The fury of the peasants was the fury of patient men deceived, and once it had broken its bounds nothing could control it. In vain Chi shouted: "Are you not ashamed of thus mocking the gods?"—His voice was lost in the cursing and. angry grumblings. No one paid any attention to the Elder. A man shouted at the battered image: "We took you for a god but you are only an old sow's carcass after all and we will leave you to stifle in the furnace of the sun!"— Since the gods were but deified mortals they could suffer heat as mortals did.

Neither the priest nor even the magistrate lifted a hand when the rabble broke out into insults and mockery. They acknowledged the justice of such anger. They knew the frenzy of their fury must burn itself out like the prayer papers and incense sticks smouldering, in the great brazier. When they were ready and no sooner, the villagers accompanied the Magistrate back to the village, still muttering against the god who had not sent the rain needed for their crops.

Ma, to whom the whole ceremony was a farce, smiled sarcastically as he overtook Chi. "Well!" he scoffed. "Your friend the Dragon seems a little deaf today!"

For once Chi turned on him savagely. "Do not insult the gods! Are we children that we should expect them to send rain in an hour! If rain comes in a week we shall be well repaid and fortunate too after this afternoon's work. It was an evil business! When will men learn that when they smite the faces of the gods they only hurt their own hands!"

"Bah!" snorted Ma, "That such a plaster image should send rain would be a miracle indeed!—and there are no such things as miracles!"

Chi looked at his companion steadily, "It may be so," he said slowly with a queer smile, "It may be so,—and it may not be so. — But is it wise to scoff at what you do not understand?"

Juliet Bredon

XXII. Rumours

Chi was right. Rain did come after the procession. But it came too late and it lasted too long. The cobs of Indian corn were already shrunk and shrivelled as a beggar's hand, and such as had not been burned were partly mildewed. Half the red brown heads of the *kao liang* were broken off their stalks by the torrential downpour and beaten into the ground. Only a meagre harvest could be gathered in. The Dragon had his revenge after all.

Ma's distillery, which in normal years worked every day, now worked only one morning out of three, for the Great Millet used in wine making had to be brought from a distance, since there was none to spare from the fields around the village. Cartage cost money. After it was paid on the malt bricks brought from Peking and on the grain as well there was but a narrow margin of profit left for the merchant. But Ma did not want to close down while he could pay expenses. His twelve employees would be thrown out of work if he did that, and work was getting scarcer and scarcer in the countryside. Men came in every day from outlying districts in search of it. They wanted to eat like everybody else. But Hundred Altars could scarcely feed its own people let alone strangers, and they were obliged to move on again.

Meanwhile rumours floated through the countryside. It seemed that the discontent in the South was serious, and the unrest spreading. Carters passing through the village and camel-drivers leading their slow caravans from Peking to the coal mines in the hills brought tidings of astonishing happenings in the distant Yangtsze Valley, Rebellion, they said, had broken out there.

But at first the peasants in their peaceful backwater took these words for idle talk,—echoes of the loose gossip that fills the Peking teashops in summer and the wine shops in winter. None dreamed then how true the rumours were. Still less did they imagine that the disturbances in Wu Chang, a teeming city on the Yangtsze and the hot bed of this new agitation, were the prelude to real revolution. How indeed could people so far from the storm centre guess that? Uprisings and rebellions were part of their traditions. Such insurrections often flared up hotly and as often fizzled, out like damp fire crackers. Within the villagers' own memories the Boxers had overrun the countryside though by good luck the fanatics had not touched Hundred Altars. Their fathers had seen the Emperor's Summer Palace burned in 1860, and their forefathers had lived for centuries under the menace of the northern barbarians.

But in spite of all these trials life went on much as usual. The people still had their eternal right to labour. They always had the hope that trouble would be localized, as indeed it frequently was. After all though the Yangtsze provinces might suffer there might well be peace on the northern plain. Wars, unless fought over their own fields, touched the farmers but little. The old folk song summed up their feeling towards the rhythm of life;—

"When the sun rises I toil,
When the sun sets I rest.
I dig wells for water,
I till the fields for food.
What has the forging of swords to do with me?"

But one evening the *pao shan ti* brought more definite and disturbing news to Hundred Altars.

"I hear from a sure source," he told the group gathered at the inn, "that on the great river the junks are lying idle at the wharves. The merchants have put up their shutters. There is no business doing in the cities. Only the blacksmiths are hard at work at their anvils forging swords,—wide curved broad swords for soldiers who wear white arm bands. I am told these men have taken first one city and then another. They are in league with a group of young men who have the West in their eyes and desire a new order of things. Inner tranquillity, the happy medium, the golden mean that Confucius taught, they declare are out of date. They want a new world and they are greatly daring. I believe they have even torn down the dragon flag of monarchy and trampled upon it. Rumour says that Yuan Shih Kai, the northern general, has been ordered from Honan to protect Peking."

"What are these new people thinking about?" asked one of the distillery workers who had joined the group, his feet still wet and sticky from trampling the grain in the fermenting pit. "What do they really mean to do, and who is to profit by their plans?"

"People say," the *pao shan ti* replied eagerly, "that these young men are doing all this to help us, the 'cotton-clothed.' They proclaim that the land belongs to the people, and that all should be equal, not one rich and another poor. They ask why we should pay taxes to an Emperor who is but a helpless child and a stranger. China for the Chinese is their cry. Why should the Manchus rule the sons of Han?"

This talk to which the village youths listened with interest but not with any real idea of what it was all about, horrified the Elders. Centuries of tradition lay like a heavy weight on their bent backs. Centuries of filial obedience shackled them. They hated change and saw no need for it. Their time-honoured system of local self-government left a large measure of power where it belonged, in the hands of the headmen, the natural leaders of the people. What was this silly talk of upsetting the present established order and giving authority into the hands of men young and therefore unskilled in the conduct of affairs?

"If all you tell is true," sputtered Chi eyeing the *pao shan ti* angrily, "a pretty state of things will come to pass. 'Ask the young they know everything!'—is that the idea? But such news can't be true," he added scratching himself thoughtfully behind the ear. "Tell me only why have they asked General Yuan to come to Peking?"

The appeal to Yuan made Chi wonder if the trouble he denied might even be brewing near at hand. Nobody could answer that question not even the *pao shan ti*.

Next day Ma received a message from his friend Merchant Hu in the city. Hu wrote, though guardedly, about the news. He thought the rebellion started in Wu Chang might be very different from those that had gone before. "Always hitherto," he wrote, "the customs of our country have been undisturbed even though the land changed masters. It was the sovereign of one reigning house or the sovereign of another who held the power. But these new leaders say that no one shall ever mount the throne again. They talk of a 'republic,' a new system of government borrowed from the West. That may mean a revolution will take place in industry no less than

Hundred Altars

in politics. My advice to you therefore is to come into the town and have a talk with me about business affairs."

Ma felt that this advice was good. It coincided with his own ideas. He had long seen visions of a larger life than Hundred Altars could give him. He had long felt it was a mistake to have all his interests centred in one place where drought or flood could cause the crops to fail. And now that a new world was being born where more power might centre in the merchant class he felt city connections would prove valuable. Hu's letter gave him a chance to establish such connections and he meant to take it;

Meeting Chi at the inn one evening a week later he told him that he was leaving for Peking next morning on business.

"Surely from all we hear it is not a wise time to be away from home!" the farmer remarked.

"I have thought of that," Ma answered, "but things are quiet at the moment in Peking and if I go now before trouble comes—should indeed trouble be coming—I shall be able to settle my affairs and be back shortly."

"Things are not what they used to be!" Chi sighed.

"No!" retorted Ma, "and they never were!—Still a new day may be a good day,—we are the largest country in the world, even the people who live across the water admit that! And when we change our ways they say with fear in their hearts that we will be greater and more powerful than they!"

Chi snorted.

"But have we not always been the greatest people?—the greatest country?—whoever doubted that? And as for changing our ways—to what should we change?"

"Pah!—You farmers are ever frightened!—You think only of the land beneath your feet. To gain one must venture! Such a reward as the future holds is worth paying the price of war and unrest for a few years.—You are content with too little!"

"And you want too much!" said Chi bitterly. "The outcome of this rebellion will be endless trouble if many men think as you do, unless the Emperor is able to stamp it out!—Well, the only useful war I know is made with hatchet and chopper against weeds and stones and stubborn earth!"

As usual in arguments between men who see with different eyes the farmer could not convince the merchant nor the merchant convince the farmer.

Ma went to Peking next day, leaving his family in the village. Willing enough himself to take risks, he could not do business with an easy mind if he did not feel his womenfolk were in a safe place and the countryside seemed quiet enough.

When he reached the city, though, he was quick to note signs of unrest. Soldiers on guard were searching people who passed through the gates. There was more than the usual confusion as the traffic flowed in and out. A fat man, whose naked belly showing beneath his half-open coat over-hung his belt in heavy folds of flesh, argued with a corporal. An officer sitting in the stuffy gate-house, drinking tea in his undershirt, was called. Pushing and scuffling ceased at last when the fat man got his bundles through by "thanking" the officer with two silver dollars. Ma, smiling slyly, showed his gratitude in the same way, and turning his back on the crowd hired a cart at a double fare, for the driver was frightened to cross the city. "Suppose they take my mule!" he argued timorously. Who "they" might be he was not sure.—But people in general were not anxious to roam the streets. Their instinct was always to stay at home in uneasy times. Even peddlers, who had little enough to lose, were scarce, and few vendors shouted their wares. Only old women were about, and in the shops Ma noted little of value exposed for sale. "The merchants are afraid of looting," he said to himself with growing discomfort. "There must be trouble afoot!"

He reached Hu's house without adventure just after sundown, and found the trader, too, disturbed.

"No one feels sure of what is coming next," he told Ma. "Just yesterday there was a bomb thrown near the North Temple Market. No one knows who did it or why. Folk say someone was trying to murder General Yuan as he drove down the street. But Yuan escaped and a house was blown up instead of his carriage. 'See that a few heads come off and are paraded through the streets,' was the secret order to the general in command, 'but be sure the heads are unimportant.' Later in the day the heads of a few unfortunate coolies were prominently exhibited and a 'proclamation' renewed the promise of protection for the city and regretted the fact that a small disturbance had occurred. It laid the blame for the affair on certain bad characters roaming the town—But undoubtedly the 'bad characters' are revolutionaries!—Yuan was quite calm. He is a brave man. Yet, I do not envy him his place for all his power and wealth. One party is trying to persuade him to go down to the South and help the revolution, the other urges him to remain here.—Whichever he does he risks having his head parted from his neck."

"Why doesn't the Emperor issue his commands?" Ma asked.

"They say he no longer has any real power, that the Manchu dynasty has exhausted its heavenly mandate to rule and the best and ablest men are reluctant to serve him any more. Yuan seems the only one who stands by him."

"And who is the leader on the other side?"

"One Sun Yat Sen, a country doctor born in a village near Macao, a man educated in Western ways."

"And what manner of man is he?"

"His enemies describe him as a hopeless idealist; an agitator, a leader of revolt, eager for power, stubborn and domineering. His friends speak of his love of his native land, his unselfish struggle against the oppression of the officials, his deep belief in the wisdom of the people and their right to rule themselves. Well, time will show.—And now tell me what of the feeling in the country? What did you see as you came in?" Hu asked, "And what are the people saying?—One hears of men trying to stir up trouble even in the villages."

"I have not seen any in our parts," Ma answered, "True there are rumours, but the farmers are not anxious, except about their crops. This year they have only harvested enough grain for one meal a day."

"The farmers never think of anything but getting their bellies full," said Hu impatiently. "They see no further than their own fields. There's nothing beyond—to them. They do not want to hear about new ways, not even easier ways. Men talk of machines in the countries beyond the water that do the work of several men and would profit us to sell. But the farmers will have none of them. They run their farms just as their great grandfathers ran them."

"True, true," Ma agreed, "I doubt if in our lifetime the peasants will move forward. These new ideas will just come up against the stone wall of their obstinate ignorance, and stop there. But we merchants can be far seeing and profit by the new times. *If these new people get in ...*"

"That is the question," Hu said thoughtfully. "It would seem as if they have won the South, but the North is still hesitating. We merchants hold the money bags and no party can rule long without our help these days. But better wait and see how the Republicans get on before deciding to support them; it is not wise to come out too openly on their side yet. True for the past sixty years the Manchus have crippled trade with the squeezing of their corrupt officials, and the new people might build roads and railways and make taxes lighter. But whether they will win or lose is not certain yet, and it would be a pity to throw in our lot with the wrong party," he ended with a sly twinkle in his eye.

"Still if they win," Ma suggested, "it looks likely that their policy might be good for trade."

"That it does.—But let us wait and see.—And now to our business. At the moment there is little doing in Peking. People, as you saw, are nervous. They will not buy or sell. But I have interests in Tientsin where there might be scope for your talents. For years past foreign merchants have been established there and in the safety of their concessions, they have built up a flourishing commerce in shipping our wool and silk to western countries. I hear some of these white men have a reputation for commercial honesty almost equal to our own. Now I wish to get in touch with them and their trade but I cannot go myself for I am needed to guard my interests here. Would you be willing to go to Tientsin and look into these things? We could share the profits and you might even find it worth while to remain and attend to that end of our joint business.—Of course it would mean risking some capital, but you have done well in Hundred Altars...."

Ma's eyes glinted greedily.

"You are ever long thinking," he said presently. "I accept your proposal on principle. It is better than remaining in Hundred Altars and growing hollow cheeked with the farmers for little silver will be spent there for the next two or three harvests. My manager could run the village business—till I can make other plans."

"Well," said Hu very pleased, "if you are prepared to go to Tientsin, go quickly,—tomorrow is better than the day after.

There may be good fishing while the waters are troubled."

Ma agreed, and when they had talked the matter over more fully and settled everything, he asked about Young Tiger and received a much better account of him than he had dared to hope. The lad had been diligent because he had no chance to be otherwise. Still, no matter the reason, he had not caused trouble and when he was sent for to greet his father, the latter noted with pleasure that his clothes were neat and he no longer had a dirty neck.

The following afternoon accompanied by Hu and Young Tiger and a servant carrying his bedding roll and white pigskin trunk, Ma went to the railway station. He went early, well ahead of train time, but already hundreds of people were there,—a dense crowd fleeing to the shelter of the foreign concessions in Tientsin for the bomb outrage had started a panic in the capital. Many Manchus were leaving—as Hu pointed out to Ma. That was significant. When the ruling people begin to run change is already in sight. The platform was a tempestuous scene, a storm of agitated faces. A tall thin man in a chocolate coloured gown shouted for a compartment for himself and his family, proclaiming that he was an official. But there was no such thing as an empty compartment. Ma after much energetic pushing and jostling managed to squeeze into a corner of a second class carriage with his bundles and thought himself lucky. People hung on to the platforms, sat on the roofs of the cars, climbed to the fender of the engine, even squatted on the coal in the tender.

An hour late by schedule the locomotive began to belch out clouds of deep black smoke and showers of shining sparks from its funnel. Then, giving a sudden jerk, it jolted the cars forward with a violent rattle as buffers bumped against buffers. The express groaning and wheezing went on its way beyond the high grey city walls through the quiet twilight of a limpid evening, leaving a panic of surging people behind who had been unable to get aboard.

"I've really started to be a big merchant now," thought Ma, "at last I've really started."

Juliet Bredon

XXIII. The Great Adventure

Meanwhile those left behind in the capital waited in fear and trembling for the next political move. They did not rise inspired by the promises of the new leaders nor actively espouse the cause of the old. They sat on the fence and found it an uncomfortable seat. Yuan, so far, was master of the situation in Peking, but there were whispers that he was playing his own game and might or might not remain loyal to the throne. If it suited him to keep the city quiet he was strong enough to do so. If not, there might be trouble.

Hu, the merchant, though outwardly calm was inwardly fearful. But Young Tiger did not share his master's anxiety. He revelled in rumours. His idea of living was adventure. The more things happened, even if they were not pleasant things, the more he enjoyed life. He listened with eager ears to the tales of rebellion and of the New China growing up like a mushroom overnight. He longed to get out into the storm centre, to leave the hateful shop, to join the ranks of the Revolutionists, to do anything—anything except what he usually did day after day.

Now, Fate hitherto against him became his fellow conspirator. Work had suddenly slackened after the bomb outrage, for there was practically no trade in the city, and the lad enjoyed his first idle hours since leaving Hundred Altars. What a relief not to spend long days bent over the counter! Oh, if he were only allowed out in the streets to see and hear what was going on!

Then, one afternoon just before darkness fell, pandemonium began to reign throughout the city. Cries, shouting, shooting, fires were everywhere. Some soldiers, breaking out of barracks, had mutinied and were looting. When the news reached the trader's household it created much excitement. "This is bad," said Hu anxiously. "We haven't had anything like this since 1900!"—and he ordered the gate barred immediately and all his people to remain withindoors.—

But a little later when things quieted down he decided it was necessary to have first hand knowledge of what was going on, and decided to send Young Tiger to find out.

Hundred Altars

"A plucky lad he is for all his faults," Hu told himself, "No one will notice a boy of his age. It's safe enough for him to go!" But he took the precaution of telling the lad to wear his oldest coat since a worthless garment is the best protection in time of trouble.

Young Tiger started on his errand with alacrity. He wanted to shout aloud in his newly found freedom, but he knew that would be indiscreet. Freedom at last, freedom to go where he liked even for an hour or two, freedom to mix with all kinds of people without any restraint,—it was glorious. He imagined himself in the midst of the Revolutionary party marching along with men carrying white flags and bristling with swords and spears. Why, there was no telling what he might not see or do!—So he slipped eagerly through the small back gate, lusting for adventure.

But once outside he found the streets strangely disappointing. Occasional furtive figures skulked in lanes otherwise quiet and deserted. Every door was shut tight. Silence everywhere,— except for some crows cawing excitedly in a tree-top. They sensed trouble.

At last he reached the main street outside the Central Gate of the city where the big shops were. Here he saw soldiers dragging valuables off the shelves. The lust for loot had seized them, and not only the soldiers but the riffraff who followed them were equally busy robbing the shops and the homes of the well-to-do.—One man had an embroidered coat over his arm, another carried a piece of carved ivory which he offered for a dollar to a passing foreigner come out out of curiosity to see what was going on. A few frightened ricksha men had taken shelter in alleyways, hoping to escape the notice of the soldiers lest they commandeer them to carry loot.

Young Tiger asked one of the wretched pullers what had happened.

"Aiyah!—Aiyah!" the man answered trembling, "there is much trouble. The soldiers have left their barracks, and turned robbers. No one seems able to control them any more. They are taking what they please—the best merchandise, the prettiest women. Look yonder!" He pointed to a big shop opposite where men carrying lanterns were passing in and out. There was a glimpse of a shadow writhing maliciously against a wall, repeating the movements of a soldier seizing a long-gowned civilian. The shadow began to sway to one side, a shot rang out, and a second shadow half hidden by the first, fell forward on its knees holding out imploring hands.

"Soldiers have no pity," the coolie said, his teeth chattering with fear. "Now run home, lad, if you have the luck to have -a home to run to.—It is not wise for a boy to be on the streets today."

As Young Tiger started back he eyed the soldiers enviously. Not one but had some treasure folded in his coat. "What an easy way to get rich!" he thought, "What a pleasant way to be free!" —He was young enough to feel no fear, neither did pity move him.

When he reached home the tale of the mutiny lost nothing in the telling. "There's a wild crowd of soldiers rushing to and fro.—Some of them are firing their pistols in the air, others are stealing what they please from the shops and houses. It is very dangerous. But, as for me, I pushed myself into the thick of everything and found out all about it."

"Ah, that is serious," said Hu. "There is certainly danger and from what quarter it will come no man can say.—Perhaps it will be our turn next, but luckily we are on a side street and may be overlooked. One thing is sure to happen; the officials will shut the city gates, and no food will come in from the country."

Next morning there was another disturbance, but farther away this time. Still now and then the crack of a single musket shot rang out near at hand. Some man had tried injudiciously to defend his property or his daughter from a straggling soldier who was taking what he could get on his own. Hu became more and more uneasy, indeed everyone lived in a state of great suspense. One asked another: "What shall we do? Is the mob coming this way, and will we all be killed? Where can we run to for safety. Hu answered still with outward calm: "Remain quietly here, it is wisest."—But he called Young Tiger to him again:

"Are you willing to go out into the streets?" he asked. "I want the latest news."

"Yes, master. I am not afraid any more than I was yesterday. I will go."

Nothing could have made him happier than to get out again. The sights of the day before had fired his young imagination. All night long he saw himself looting the rich shops,—picking up whatever he wanted wherever he found it, and in his dreams he heard the rattle of firing and jumped nimbly over dead bodies lying on the ground. He even had a vision of his friend the ricksha man prodded by bayonets as he dragged a wounded soldier with blood dripping from his chest.

Hu would not let him go before late afternoon. "Keep a sharp look out and do not get into trouble," he cautioned, little guessing the wild ideas that seethed in Young Tiger's brain, "and take these few pieces of silver. If you see any food for sale bring back what you can that we may have something fresh to eat in case things do not return to normal for some days," he added pulling money out of the wallet attached to his belt.

Young Tiger took the silver and went into the deserted streets again. He saw neither butcher barrows nor vegetable vendors. Peddling was too dangerous now. Too many tricksters were about who would seize a scrap of green stuff, or filch a piece of meat. But here and there he noticed in passing a door of a provision shop wrenched off its hinges, leaving a free view of empty courtyards or stripped shelves.

Presently he met a band of soldiers. They were looting a big silk store. One man had a roll of rich brocade in his hand. Grinning he held it high above his head, turning it round and round that all might see. "Worth fifty dollars!" he shouted. "Who'll buy?—Who'll buy?"—A scabby legged beggar salvaging a half eaten apple from the gutter almost under the soldier's feet, retorted ironically,—"Keep your silk!—I don't want it."— The soldier laughed.

"Where are we going now? This place is nearly empty!" asked a tall man in an ill-fitting uniform. "To Jade Street, to Jade Street!" came the answering chorus.

Young Tiger watching from a safe corner. noticed a cart, already piled half full of loot, waiting for more treasures. The man in charge receiving an order to move on had trouble with his mule which baulked obstinately, frightened by the strange hubbub surrounding him. The other soldiers bade the man hurry, but the mule refused to move, and the driver belaboured him with a rope without result. "Takes two to start this son of a turtle," he muttered, then seeing Young Tiger he bawled at him, "Here you,—lend a hand!"

The lad stepped up and grabbed the bridle. He had known mules in the village. Ma had eight working in the distillery. This beast recognized a country lad when he smelt him and let Young Tiger lead him forward unprotesting. The corporal in charge of the party noticed the boy. "Making yourself useful, and used to mules I see! Who are you and what are you doing out on the streets today?"

Young Tiger's ears pounded with strange excitement, but he answered meekly that he was just doing nothing and going nowhere.

"Poor work for a strong young man who seems to have brains in his head," the corporal remarked shrilly. "Why don't you turn soldier like the rest of us? We lost a wounded man in our company this morning and we might accept you."—His words were cut short by another soldier who wanted to know where they were going next, and Young Tiger was left to his own thoughts. —These soldiers were real men, not old women in long robes like the merchants, though some of them were mere boys in years, no older than himself. But they were not like any soldier he had ever seen in their neat uniforms of grey cotton. How different from the Pei Yan Ho magistrate's guard of honour. His men had loose jackets decorated with black velvet characters, high velvet boots with baggy trousers tucked into them, wide flapping hats and a fan or an umbrella slung across their backs. Those old-fashioned soldiers fought with twisted spears and rusty pikes, and relied on their gongs and drums and war cries to frighten their enemies. These men had rifles and sharp bayonets attached to their belts.

But both types were alike in that whatever they wanted they took. If it was a cooking pot that they needed they seized it, and if they fancied a maid they had their way with her and no husband or father dared say them nay for they were quick to use cold steel when denied. Soldiers, old or new never deal kindly with the people.

Now that the mule was going peacefully the driver bade Young Tiger roughly to be gone,—"Hey, get out of here you!" he roared. The lad fell back. The corporal, no longer interested in Young Tiger, hastened to join his comrades. Looking enviously after them his unwilling apprentice followed at a distance. It was half dark already. The lanterns shed a sparse reddish glow. The first stars trembled like bits of brilliant bean curd in the black velvet of the evening sky, just as something inside the lad trembled with agitation. He noticed the men had filled their cart now and the weight of it tugged at the mule's shoulders and made his hoofs heavy as if

Hundred Altars

charged with lead. The company straggled off into the purplish twilight.

Presently they paused again making a ring about a cricket peddler at a street corner. The man had come from the country and like a foolish yokel ventured to cry his wares. He carried cages full of chirping crickets slung from, a pole over his shoulders. In a few minutes the soldiers had seized a dozen of his best specimens. The countryman protested loudly, but to no avail. "Shut up ass!" the corporal shouted. "Why cry about such a slight loss?—You should consider yourself lucky—son of a stupid farmer, that we have not taken everything you have and beaten you besides."

The other soldiers laughed roughly at his sally, and the few passersby hurried on unheeding.—Wise men take no sides in soldiers' quarrels.

"And now for a rice bowl!" cried one of the men.

It was easy enough to steal one from the nearest house. Then the group squatted in a gateway for an improvised cricket match.— Young Tiger approached timidly. In his excitement he had unwittingly taken his purse from his belt and held it in his hand. One of the soldiers caught sight of it, and hailed him to join them. They edged over to make room for him in the circle, and no one asked any questions, neither who he was nor whence he came. The sight of money was a free passport to their company. Being themselves men from everywhere and nowhere with records not to be inquired into, they were quite willing, if he spent freely, to accept him into their easy brotherhood as one of their own kind. If he had money he had doubtless stolen it. But if he was willing to spend it he was welcome.

Two crickets evenly matched in size and strength were let loose in the little rice-bowl arena and tickled with straws to .make them fight. Each man backed one of the tiny gladiators with cash, the winners taking the stakes of the losers. Young Tiger punted more heavily than the rest. He had only silver in his purse for one thing, and for another he was determined to make a great display. As he lost continually the soldiers were friendly. —He hardly noticed how fast his money melted away; But when he had bet his last coin he said with an anxious look:

"Now I have lost all the silver my master gave me.—I cannot go back to the shop for he will beat me if I return empty-handed."

One soldier, who had won most of his money and was in a good-humour therefore, said with a loud guffaw: "Ha! You seem to be a stout lad, much too good for shopkeeping!"

"You are right!" Young Tiger assured him boldly. "I am wasted working in a shop, for I'm not afraid to spend money, I am not afraid to die, and I am not afraid to kill!"

The man was only jesting and the earnestness of the boy's reply amused him. The lad had spirit and was well-grown too.

"Why don't you join us?" he suggested half-seriously. "Ours is a good life, we eat and drink and take what we want where ever we go!"

The other soldiers were rising to their feet now, and their leather-soled, shoes made a crunching noise on the hard ground. For a moment Young Tiger stood irresolute—all his training had taught him to despise the profession of arms; now he hankered after it.— "Half of these, chaps are boys like me," he thought. "They can fight and loot why shouldn't I do the same?—I don't want to stay in a dusty *hong* all my life!"—The men started down the street.

"Where are you going?" he called after them.

"Back to the barracks!"

"Then wait—I'll come too!" he shouted and hurried after them. He felt a crazy desire to join them and to be a soldier and forget the degradation of the shop. The excited blood surged gloriously through his body. He was ready to endure anything, to face any sort of death. Besides the die was cast. He could not turn back now even if he changed his mind, for the men would laugh at him. That would be unbearable. Besides, having lost the silver he could not bring himself to go back to Hu. A sudden surge of joy swept over him. Now he had chosen he was free, free—free as he was born to be! In his excitement he began bragging wildly to his new companions.

"I was born in the year of the Tiger and am by nature fierce. War is my destiny. From this day I have no father and mother. From this hour I am free from the slavery of the shop!" He spat viciously as if with that one gesture he rid himself of his old life.

The men grinned, but they were pleased nevertheless that such a stout-spoken young fellow should want to join them. The soldier whom he had helped with the mule and who had left his cart to watch the cricket fight recognized him. "You're the boy who persuaded my mule! I know you—you will be useful, you understand mules!—Doubtless," he added in a loud aside, "his mother was a mule!"

Shouts of laughter greeted this sally, but they did not dampen the lad's ardour—He picked up a cap from the gutter and pulled it low over his eyes as he saw the other men did theirs.—At the barracks a sergeant hailed him—a thin man with a wrinkled skin and an arrow-shaped mouth.

"Who are you, and what are you doing here?"—his voice was fierce and snarling.

The corporal whispered something in his ear.

"What's your name?" his sharp voice barked again.—Young Tiger looked up blinking with surprise at such brusqueness. "Don't know your own name, eh?" he snapped again before the boy could answer. "I can see you are a bright lad! (sarcastically) Well, how old are you?" The curtness of his tone stung like a whip.

"Seventeen!" At last Young Tiger had found his tongue.

"Why do you want to join us?"

"I want to fight," the lad replied boldly. "I am tired of being ordered round."

"You'll be ordered round here just the same. But no matter. You're the type of lad we need!" snapped the sergeant, and bidding a corporal see that Young Tiger was given some kind of uniform and a gun in the morning he swaggered out of the room.

"Well, now you're in with us!" said a comrade laughing. "Be sure to remember to close one eye when you shoot!"

"Why?" asked the boy impudently, "do you always close both?"

The men laughed, then quickly slunk away as the sallow face of an officer looked over Young Tiger's shoulder. "Who is this man?" asked the lieutenant.

"A new recruit, sir!" the corporal answered.

"Send him to bunk in with the rest!"

Young Tiger found himself herded with his new comrades into a big room where men were snoring on heaps of straw. It smelt of cheap cigarettes and dried sweat. He found a corner for himself and lay down in the pitch dark.—It was not cheerful —not what he had expected, but he comforted himself with the thought that now he was a soldier and need never work again. "But I will go forth to wars and do great deeds!"—And so he fell asleep and dreamed of battles where he fought in a brocaded uniform.—He was very young still.

But after a week or two of his new life he was wiser. Soldiering in this day and age was neither colourful nor glorious as in the time of the Three Kingdoms of which the story tellers sang. And as for the excitement, the fighting he had expected— half the time life was duller even than in Hundred Altars. There were no pleasant looting parties. An order had been issued from high quarters that there had been enough looting and it must stop. He now saw the army from the inside out. He hadn't expected a soldier's life to be like this.—Only when he and his comrades got leave now and again and went to a wine shop and the strong spirit began humming in his head like a fly against a window pane, he felt bold and important again.—

At other times he seemed to live to the rhythm of a vast dusty dullness. Soldiers waiting in cold rows in drill fields; the monotony of feet tramping in unison, the ache of his own tired legs stretched to the same step as thousands of other tired legs.

XXIV. The Flight

While Peking seethed with mutiny,—a mutiny that men hinted was ordered by Yuan himself for his own purposes,—life in Hundred Altars went on as usual, serene and untroubled. Whatever the alarms elsewhere, the villagers felt safe and they cared little what happened to others so long as nothing happened to them. The growls and grumblings of city garrisons did not concern country folk. "Where there is nothing precious," they said to themselves, "the Phoenix does not alight; where there is nothing valuable soldiers will not loot."—And for once they were pleased to be poor.

But their confidence was rudely shattered when one day a man came galloping into Hundred Altars on a sweat-drenched donkey to warn them that the Monastery of the Great Awakening only twenty li distance had been ravished by a band of mutinous soldiers who, fearing punishment for their evil deeds in Peking, had escaped outside the gates. "Bandits, dangerous bandits!" ran the whispered comment up and' down the street. "Dangerous indeed— and desperate!" panted the breathless messenger. "They are assembled in a great cave among the hills whence they descended yesterday to loot the temple."

Now the Abbot of the Monastery of the Great Awakening was a man universally respected. He had great piety and even greater learning. His only fault was his scholar's pride of scholarship. It made him arrogant and he scoffed openly when he was told that bad characters were about, asking with mock humility: "Why should they molest a man like me?"

As a matter of fact the corporal leading the mutineers had a rough soldier's admiration for a man of learning and when he heard of the reputation of the Abbot he forbade his men to enter the temple though it was common talk much grain was stored there. He even ordered a placard pasted on the gate warning other marauders who might come after him to leave the place in peace.

"The impudent stupid!" exclaimed the Abbot-scholar as he ordered the protecting paper torn down. "We need no such safeguards from an ignorant soldier—a destroyer! It is an insult that such a man should dare give orders concerning my affairs."

"Despises me, does he!" rasped the corporal when he was told what had been done. "How dare this helpless priest flout my strength! I'll show him who rules in China today!"—He too had his pride, the dangerous pride of an armed leader of armed men, and his words were prophetic of the years to come when the soldiery of rival warlords should teach this bitter lesson to the people and prove to them that the sword was mightier than the pen.

Next morning the corporal ordered his men to harness their stolen mules to their stolen carts and led them back to the monastery. With the butt of his pistol he pounded on the heavy gates. The gateman opened them a crack, unwillingly.

"Fling the doors wide!" ordered the corporal.

But the servant who had caught the spirit of his master answered proudly:

"Only peaceful men can enter here,—and as for forcing your way in we have fifty fierce watchdogs to prevent that!"

For answer the corporal pushed him roughly aside and gave a sharp order to his men. As the watchdogs rushed forward to the attack the men fired, and not a bullet missed.

"No one need fear them any more!" the corporal shouted kicking the prostrate bodies out of his way as he led his troops up the steps to the temple, and swaggered through court after court into the Abbot's room. The priest sat erect at his writing table, his hands folded, finger-tip touching finger-tip, the long sleeves of his robes drooping almost to the floor. His outward attitude of Buddhist calm belied the fear that crept over his heart, and not without reason. "Fool!" hissed the corporal, as his men hustled the scholar roughly out of his red lacquer chair. "Now tell us where your grain is stored!" But helpless as he was the Abbot refused to speak; not even when they beat him would he utter a word. Nevertheless the soldiers found the grain and took it all, loading it on their carts while the gateman gibbering and sobbing was pressed into their service.

When Hundred Altars heard how brutally the respected Abbot had been treated the villagers said to one another, "What can we expect—we ignorant folk, if a scholar is beaten and robbed?"— When the soldiers come this way, as come they will for they know ours is a big village and we have wine though food is scarce, we shall be lucky if they spare our lives!"—Resistance they knew would only make matters worse. The peasants had no arms and the chalk circles that imitated cannon mouths painted on their outer walls would never scare away these modern soldiers. Only a few of the villagers like Wu the coffin-maker dared be optimistic. He stoutly denied the possibility of an attack. "There has been a bad crop this year," he said bravely, "these bandits will be looking for richer loot than they can find in our poor homes."

"Coffins," Liang, already trembling, reminded him, "make excellent firewood for cooking pots."—He was' a coward with a coward's arguments.

"The magistrate will protect us!" said Chien comfortingly.

"Well, he did nothing for the monastery," the blacksmith retorted. "His men all ran away and hid themselves. They are a helpless lot nowadays these officials of ours. You heard what the *pao shan ti* said about them on the Yangtsze! They were good enough in times of peace, and kept order where there was no one to disturb it, but in troubled times like these they seem to have lost the art of ruling.—The soldiers steal and plunder and murder wherever they feel like it."

Next day worse news came. A village to the west had been sacked and people tortured to tell where they had hidden their silver. It seemed the robbers were well organized and that their raids were being carried out systematically in one village after another. The ragtag and the rabble in Hundred Altars accepted the danger philosophically. Families like the Changs had nothing to lose but their lives, and they were no great loss—indeed such people might expect more fortunate re-births. But for the Chis who owned silver it was different; for them flight might be wise.

"I think I will take my family into Peking until things grow quiet here," Chi told Chien, "What do you intend to do?"

"Alas, I have no choice," Chien sighed, "my mother as you know is old and ill. She could not bear the journey, and it is my duty to remain beside her."

"Of course you must," Chi agreed, "but for us it is best to go— Aiyah!—*Mei yao fa tzu!*—There is no help for it."

That same day he spoke his mind to his eldest son.

"Who knows tomorrow these soldiers may attack our village. We had better take what we can into the safety of the city, and when we return, even if the house be burned, the land will still be here and we shall have something saved with which to start life again.—True, we have no relations in Peking, but somehow we shall find a lodging."

Chin-tzu accepted his father's decision without question. It was for the head of the family to judge whether they should go or stay. His word was law for them all.—So when the Elder bade Clever Needle prepare for the journey she too made neither criticism nor complaint but set to work at once superintending the sorting and packing, deciding what must be taken, and what might be left. And Willow, strong again after a recent childbearing, worked beside her quietly and incessantly while her little son slept on the *k'ang*.

Other families were getting ready to go also. The women hurried in and out of one anothers' houses like bees in and out of a hive, consulting neighbours about what to do and how to do it. Their perplexities were mingled with strange expectations. Most of them had never been beyond the next village, and now that they were to set forth upon the great plain and enter the Capital, they were excited and not a little dazed. It was a great wrench for them to leave their homes, the fields they had helped to cultivate, the trees they had seen planted and the friendly hills whose profiles were as familiar to them as. the faces of their own relations,—a wrench to leave them even for a little while. And who could say how soon they might return?

At cockcrow next morning Chi and his sons started harnessing the mules and packing. their belongings on the two long open carts. Warmly dressed in wadded robes one a-top of another for it was a "three coat day," the women and children settled themselves cross-legged on bedding and bundles. Clever Needle with the foreign clock clasped tightly in her arms, Willow holding her month-old son,—wrapped in his father's cast-off coat lest he befoul his own new clothing,—Amah Niu and Little Dragon, were all together in one cart. Chin-tzu and his brother were in charge of the second in which Snow Peach and her two girl children were packed in among kettles and cooking pots and Kwanyin's cumbersome carved wood shrine, and the lacquered pigskin box containing the spirit tablets of the ancestors.

"Drrh, dak, whoa-ho!" shouted Chi whipping the lead-mule who responded by drawing his horse-hair traces taut with a clatter of the iron rings that held them. As he shuffled into his .sheepskin-lined coat even Chi felt they had begun the great adventure of their lives, and as if somehow the earth was falling away beneath their feet.

When they rumbled past Ma's gate they heard a loud sound of weeping from the women's quarters. Clever Needle plucked her husband's sleeve.

"Someone has told Ma's women that the bandits are coming, and with the master away they do not know what to do!"

Though Chi had never quite forgiven Ma for foisting Snow Peach and her children on him he was neither cruel nor unkind, but willing to let the past be past,—except sometimes in his own heart. Hearing Ma's women crying piteously for help his sympathy was roused. Now, if ever, old grudges were best forgotten, and neighbours must stand by neighbours. After all Ma was a fellow villager and local kinship is only less binding than blood relationship. A Chihli man will always aid a Chihli man, a Shantung man a Shantung man, and northerners in general will stand together against southerners. However little love was lost between Chi and Ma in Hundred Altars they must support one another among strangers and in times of stress. Therefore Chi said to his wife:

"Go fetch these neighbours, they can travel with us," and as he spoke a sudden thought struck him.—Here was the solution of the problem of lodging in the city. Ma must return his kindness by sharing shelter with him. Ma would owe him a debt of gratitude for saving his inner household, and for face sake he would pay that debt, if for no other reason. "Bid them order Lung-erh hitch their mules to their own cart,—we have no room in ours for all of them. And tell them to make haste and gather only such things as they need. We must get to the city as quickly as possible, before the guards hear there is trouble in the countryside and close the gates."

Clever Needle found the weeping women huddled helplessly, together in one room. But as she appeared in the doorway dressed for the road, they ceased their sobs and looked up appealingly at her. Before Shui Ching could speak Clever Needle said smiling reassuringly:

"Rest your hearts, the master has sent me to tell you you must come with us.—Get ready what you can!—Quickly, lose no time, or we may find the city gates shut!".

In spite of their joy at her good words and their relief at being taken to safety the women were as troubled now for their possessions as they had been before for their lives.—They looked round them in bewilderment. What should they take?—What should they leave?—Even a cooking-pot became suddenly precious.—"You can't take everything!" said Clever Needle fidgeting nervously after them, "So choose and choose quickly!" —In the end they gathered up only a few personal possessions— clothes and bedding. There was neither space for valuable blackwood In the cart, nor time to pack Ma's precious porcelains. But Shui Ching insisted on bringing Flowering Eyebrows, the singing thrush, in his ivory cage, and her bowl of lilies due to open at New Year, while the two amahs, fussed over their new quilts fearing lest they be soiled by the dust of the road. Lilac Blossom knotted her trinkets into a handkerchief and put on all her best coats one on top of the other, and an old cotton gown over all. Even little Swallow clung to her toys, and the *pi-ba* that her father loved.

The mules accustomed to grinding grain blind-folded made difficulty about being hitched open-eyed into the carts, but at last Bent Neck and Lung-erh succeeded in getting them between the shafts, and Lung-erh guided the creaking cart down the steep stone descent into the street to join the procession.—Only Bent remained behind. He was one with the coffin-maker in scorning the thought of danger coming to such a quiet village. Besides as the workmen and Ma's foreman in the distillery had been called home, he refused to desert his master's property. "If the devils come they come," he muttered, "if they don't they will stay away, but I shall stick to my post until the master bids me leave it."

The road was already crowded with carts for the exodus into Peking had begun. All the morning long the dusty highway was churned and pulverized by hoof and wheel as carts and mules and donkeys plodded over it when the villages emptied themselves into the highway. Everywhere were strange, humorous, and pitiful sights,—scenes to make the heart grieve, and fill it with wonder at the patient endurance of the people.— Neighbours called out to one another asking advice—what to do—where to go?—They seemed to be as one family now, and a family in distress. Fathers or brothers led the mules that drew the long flat carts over the heavily rutted roads. Here and there an old woman sat astride a donkey which her filial son led by the bridle, or a baby peeped out of a panier which in normal times carried manure to the fields.

Ten long weary miles across the plain and the procession came out through the Pass of the White Tiger's Mouth on to the road paved with stone blocks—good for ten years as the saying goes, and bad for ten thousand—that passed the Emperor's Summer Palace, the glazed tiled roofs of its fairy pavilions a-gleam. Beyond rose the pagodas of the Jade Fountain, and in the background the five marble towers of the Temple of the Azure Cloud, while on a drill field close beside the road trumpets blared their orders, and Imperial guardsmen exercised shooting arrows, practising with long lances or galloping to and fro.

Except for the Elder none of the Chi family had seen such wonders and they sat with their mouths open, and their eyes stretched. The imaginative Little Dragon was enthralled. He forgot that his arms were cramped and stiff from holding tightly to the side of the cart, and that his legs were biting with pins and needles. Indeed all the children were almost incredibly patient and good, and accepted their bewildering new surroundings with the adaptability of childhood.

Now the crowd of carts poured into the narrow streets of Hai-tien, the courier's town with its mosque, its pungent Mohammedan smells, its butcher's barrows guarded by a crescent—for many of the carters and carriers were followers of the Prophet. Chi and his sons had hard work to get through the traffic. Some careless drivers striving to overtake and pass each other locked their wooden wheels together, and thus halted the long line of carts. Insults followed and racuous curses,—acid references to the ancestors of men and beasts were exchanged while the carters cracking the whips with their seven foot lashes tied with bright red tassels, encouraged their mules to back out of an entanglement. Now and again too a frightened farm animal accustomed to the quiet of country lanes lost his nerve and put a leg over a long loose trace, or a nose bag tied under a cart fell off, or a bundle cracked open like an overripe melon and spilled its contents on the road.

Dusk was falling by the time Chi and his party reached the city gate. In the gathering twilight its tower looked like the head of a dragon reared high above the grey flanks of the wall that formed the curving body. Pouring in through the narrow entrance were hundreds of travellers like themselves, in carts, on foot, on mule-back, in sedan chairs borne by two or four carriers according to the wealth or dignity of the passenger. Donkeys and other pack animals crowded past with bags of grain or panniers filled with coal. Wheel-barrows creaked along carrying water in barrels or squealing pigs in nets of rope, jostling red bridal chairs and black lacquered coffins,—for men were marrying and burying in haste lest troublous times interfere with their ceremonies later. To add to the confusion soldiers stopped this surging mass of refugees for search or suspicion, and Chi felt nervous and bewildered. He had the peasant's fear of the town and its people whose wily ways were so different from the straightforward habits of the country where men were guided by humble leisurely proprieties. But though his heart felt like water he assumed a bold fearing, creditable enough to one who seldom spoke with strangers, and got through without difficulty.

Once past the guards and inside Peking the little party of exiles followed the great horse road to the Central Gate of the Tartar City. There they passed again through the wall towering forty feet high and apparently impregnable with its loopholes and its mighty towers above heavy wooden gates. Looking at these defences Chi felt a sense of security and comfort. Whatever happened men would be safe, sheltered by these mighty arms. Nothing could penetrate them, not spears, nor arrows, nor even iron bullets. That ideas might did not occur to him—ideas more disturbing to the peaceful rhythm of life than any war-like violence.

Outside the gate they jolted over the famous Beggar's Bridge into a maze of commercial streets where men of the same trade lived side by side, Brass Street, Silver Street, Embroidery Street, —all silent and shuttered now. They had left the crowd of refugees behind them.—A turn east and a second turn south brought them to Little Sheep's Tail Alley, and the trader's gate set in a long stretch of well-built wall. "This merchant must be indeed a man of wealth and standing," the farmer thought as he knocked timidly with his flat hand on the great red lacquer doors of the dignified entrance guarded by two stone lions.

The surly gateman disturbed from a comfortable doze called out:

"Who are you and what do you want?"

"The family of Ma from Hundred Altars seeks admittance."

"We expect no guests at this hour of the evening," the doorkeeper grumbled as he slid open the wooden bolts. "Do you not know that there is unrest in the city and good men stay safe indoors? Only the night watchman whose duty it is to beat the gong from hour to hour walks the streets!—Take your carts yonder to the stable gate," he added pointing to another entrance, "Your womenfolk can wait in my poor room while I call someone."

Chi did as he was told. Scarcely had he rejoined his party than a heavy step crossed the courtyard and Ma himself appeared.

"Enter, enter!" he cried with evident relief as he caught sight of Chi. "I am *indeed* glad to see you.—I myself only got back today from Tientsin, and heard there was trouble in the country."

"You heard rightly—there are robbers who claim to be soldiers come out from the city—so I judged it wise to leave, and hearing your women weeping, and knowing they were alone,

I could but play the part of a neighbour and bring them with me."

"That was truly a friendly act and I am grateful.—But what of my house?" asked Ma anxiously.—"What of my silver?"

"Bent Neck stays in charge," Chi assured him, "He says he will look after everything."

To his surprise Ma still seemed anxious and depressed. The farmer knew that he had left Hundred Altars with high hopes. Things had gone well with him in Tientsin. The future looked rosy. But Chi did not yet know that when he returned full of content he had been met by Trader Hu with a blank grave face and the news that Young Tiger had run away from the shop and joined the army. Hu was frightened at first when the lad failed to return, and then bitterly angry and astonished once he found out the reason. He blamed himself for ever having let the boy go out. "But how could I guess his head was full of such wild thoughts? He was well fed and clothed here and I could not imagine he desired anything more!—And yet I should have known that his heart was never in his work— There was no 'feel' of a real merchant in him."

"The ungrateful snake!"—Ma groaned aloud as he heard the worst. "What madness could have seized him? I gave him everything,—even a chance to learn trade with you!—To think that he should have given up all he had—the wild young hothead!—Well, those who would cover themselves with martial glory often go in need of any other garment."

The blow struck Ma heavily, and he took it harder even than the trader expected. Ma was more than angry, more than grieved. It was not so much his heart that had been hit for there had never been great love lost between him and Young Tiger. His pride received the full force of the blow.—How disgraceful for a respectable merchant to have a soldier son!—The sword had scant respect where the ideal of the race was the scholar.

And on top of this keen disappointment Ma had now to face the prospect that his house with his treasures and pyramid of silver on which he had counted to finance his Tientsin venture were at the mercy of bandits. No wonder if today he was resentful towards life, and felt too old, too beaten and hopeless to make a clean amputation of all that was behind him and start afresh. With a heavy heart he led Chi in to see the trader, and informed Hu of his plight—and how the Elder had been obliged to flee into the city and how out of neighbourly kindness had brought his, Ma's, womenfolk with him.

"Elder Chi is a stranger in the city," Ma added, "He seeks a lodging. Can you advise him where to go?"—Thus tactfully he gave Hu an opening to acknowledge their friendship by helping him to pay his debt of gratitude to Chi in offering to give house room to his neighbours from Hundred Altars.

Chi meanwhile stared about him gawkily, embarrassed by the imposing reception hall. "Rich this trader must be beyond anything I have ever dreamed," he thought. "He looks kindly too for he is fat, and those who have plenty to eat can afford to be kind. But I judge he is proud also, and has the attributes of a sharp city merchant, three hands and two faces."

Hu likewise gauged the farmer. "An honest countryman he looks, trustworthy, and yet not unshrewd."

Hundred Altars

As they bowed to each other, and Chi bowed lower to Hu than he to Chi, each felt a certain sympathy and respect for his vis-a-vis. The clever merchant appreciated the honest farmer. Then he said hospitably:

"You are a friend of Ma's, and he is a friend of mine. If you have no connections in the city I can give shelter here to you and yours."

"But we are many," stammered Chi embarrassed in his gratitude. "Could you find place for us all?"

The merchant smiled, and Ma interposed hastily:

"This is only one of many guest halls. We have crossed but one of twenty courtyards, and there are living quarters without counting."

"Then I thank you elder brother," said Chi accepting the trader's offer with simple dignity. "It will surely be but a matter of a few days, and we have silver to pay for our food," he ended proudly.

"What is offered in friendship need not be weighed upon a balance," replied Hu with a generous gesture.

So it was settled that for the present Chi and his family should stay in the house of Trader Hu.

Juliet Bredon

XXV.　　The Prodigal

No sooner did Ma find himself with Shui Ching, than, scarcely pausing to give her greeting, he burst out with the bad news about Young Tiger.

"I guessed all was not well with the lad when he did not come to the gate to welcome, me,—his mother,—as he should," she stammered. "Foolish lad, foolish and even worse—unfilial! His duty was to stay where you, his father, put him.—How could he be so blind as not to see who filled his rice bowl?—Now what will you do about him?"

"What can I do?—It is a disgrace, a deadly disgrace to have a son turned soldier!"—True, Ma, might have bribed the lad out of the army,—but what would be the use since he had put himself beyond the pale, leaving Ma with no choice but to disown him?

The irresolution in her husband's voice alarmed Shui Ching. She had seen him angry with the lad before, so angry that his rage seemed fit to burst his belly. But when Young Tiger brought scandal and disgrace upon their house that last time in the village, Ma had seemed sure of himself, and ready with another plan when Fate knocked one down. And now he seemed hopeless, dreary, and disillusioned. Even his ardour for success had suddenly gone out of him as if everything was robbed of its worth.

"It is an evil thing that I should have no son now, just when I may prosper and most need one," he complained.

Indeed the most poignant and touching feature of this new tragedy was the fact that it made the Mas childless once again. They both felt that keenly. It started up old memories, painful memories— Shui Ching's failures in her duty, her useless prayers, and their mistakes in choosing Lilac Blossom and the camel-driver's child. It is bad to be unlucky, but it is bitter to be wrong.

Ma seated himself heavily, his shoulders bowed, his lips compressed, his hands held to his throbbing temples.

"There is nothing to be done now," he groaned hopelessly. "We've tried all ways to get a son, and not one succeeds!"

Hundred Altars

"I dare not speak more than a whispered excuse for shame," Shui Ching answered with downcast eyes. "Was the boy mad or did some wild nightmare spirit possess him?—Even though he was born the son of a camel-driver I cannot understand him doing what he did! And yet why blame this foolish youth?— At bottom the fault is mine for never having given you sons of your own."—So in olden days the Emperors took the blame for drought or flood upon themselves, though these disasters were outside their control and they could in no wise be held responsible for them.

"There's no use thinking of that now," said Ma gruffly, the blood rising to his face, "What troubles me is that this will make a new scandal and more talk in Hundred Altars. If my business in Tientsin turns out as well as it promises here is another reason for not returning to the village. To settle among strangers will be easier than to go back to the same place."

Shui Ching made no reply. She came from the country. Her family had been landowners for generations, and her simplicity and goodness were born from close contact with the earth. Whatever happened she could always find contentment in her groove in the village. But for her husband such a thing as a groove was unimaginable, and if his despondency or his energy drove him to accept new ventures her duty was to follow him even in spirit as well as she could. She guessed too that his dark thoughts were darker because of Chi's arrival with his three sons in the trader's house. "He feels," she thought, "that Chi will have another chance to pity him,—and pity is as gall and wormwood to a proud man."—The sight of Little Dragon especially was something Ma desired, at the moment, to avoid. It brought back the old questionings again, if a son had been born to him, if he had had brothers whose sons he might have taken as his own! So many "ifs," so many tricks of fate....

As there was no business doing, Ma spent his days in his own chamber only rousing himself occasionally to talk with Trader Hu. So the time passed slowly by while the city waited, like himself, irresolute. There were undercurrents and rumours of change yet for all those settled in the Trader's household there was no further excitement.

Then one day news came suddenly that Young Tiger had been seriously wounded in a street brawl. He sent a messenger asking if his father would visit him in the barracks where he lay very close to death. It was a grey afternoon, not a glimpse of the sun since morning. The clouds hung so low that they seemed to press like a heavy blanket on the city. Ma's spirits too were grey and dull within him as he followed the messenger to the big barn-like building where the sick soldiers lay, all lousy and dirty on heaps of straw, like broken chairs and tables which had lost their usefulness. No Red Cross or Red Swastika existed then, nor even army hospitals as there are nowadays. Not because men were less pitiful, but because it was not the custom. Soldiers were free-booters. They took their chance. If they were sick or wounded they were dependent upon their comrades for care and kindness.

As Ma walked among the prostrate figures looking for his son he saw a strange sight,—a stranger, a foreigner, a man with a long white beard, carrying tea from one sick soldier to another, bending above the wounded.—Who could this man be?—What was his business among the soldiers?—Just as he was about to ask, Ma came upon Young Tiger lying in a corner covered right up to his. chin with an old blue wadded coat. His mouth was white, and his hair lay in clammy wisps on his forehead.

"Father!" the boy gasped, putting out a feeble hand to clutch Ma's robe, "I have not deserved that you come to me,—-but my strength is gone and I could not come to you to ask your forgiveness.—I am ashamed before you, and my repentence is bitter!" He stopped for breath, and then went on haltingly: "What gnaws at my heart most is that I have brought sorrow to my kind father."—Too well now he realized his folly.

Ma felt his old black anger suddenly melt as he saw the boy's pitiful state.

"Rest your heart, I have come to take you home!"—

But Young Tiger did not hear him, he had fainted away from the effort of trying to speak. Then Ma straightened himself and called out loudly:—"Is there no doctor here who will cure my son?" .

Hearing him call, the strange foreigner came towards him.

"Elder brother," he asked, "what do you need?"—An Irish brogue showed like a ray of sunshine through the thick cloud of his alien speech. "I am a doctor,—can I help you?"

Hundred Altars

"Look at my son," cried Ma wildly, pointing to the boy, "the spirit has left his body.—If you are a skilled physician can you call it back?"

"Aye, that I can though, not for long," the old doctor said and bending down held a bottle of strong smelling liquid under Young Tiger's nose, for no sooner had he looked at the lad than he knew that he was doomed. "But if you wish to speak to your son, let him lie quiet and rest awhile."

So Ma squatted down beside the boy while the doctor went to and fro among the other men who needed him. As his father watched him Young Tiger passed from unconsciousness into a heavy sleep.—Meanwhile seeing a young officer enter the room, Ma rose and went over to him.

"Tell me," he said angrily, "what have you done to my son!"

"He joined us of his own free will," the man replied surlily, "you cannot blame us for what has happened.—Reckless and undisciplined by nature he disobeyed our commands. If you are his father, you should have taught him obedience.—No need to ask what we have done to him!"

Ma flushed deeply with the shame that was put upon him.

"But how has he come to this?—There have been no battles that I have heard tell of?"—he stammered.

"No," the officer answered, "but there was a brawl among the men, and your son, ever violent, attacked a comrade and he in turn stabbed him with his bayonet.—Was it my fault if he could not keep his peace with other men?"—the officer turned on his heel abruptly, and Ma went back to watch over his son.

Young Tiger was still sleeping. Presently the doctor joined Ma who looked up at him curiously, and asked without embarrassment:

"You seem to be the only doctor here, business must be good— are you well paid for your work."—

The doctor knowing the custom of a country where personal questions are polite, answered without embarrassment either and with a queer twinkle in his eye.

"Foreign friends give money for medicine, and I give my work for my Master. He bids me help the humble ones, the cheated ones, the one life stamps upon."

"Then your master is a rich man and he pays you well," said the merchant deeply impressed.

"That He is not, nor does He pay me at all as you count payment, but He has promised me eternal life."

"It is a strange business that does not pay its men except with promises," said Ma incredulous, but he asked no further questions. People who worked without receiving money for their tasks were mad. He had heard it said that certain foreigners did this. It was a part of their strange religion, a religion of pity,— but to Ma such unpaid effort seemed wasteful and foolish. Yet the old man's words gave him a queer sensation, a disturbing chill that flooded his mind with memories of rich men he had known with discontented faces, of one man richer than all others who despite his wealth had starved to death unable to swallow one morsel of all the delicacies his money could buy.— Of shrewd men whose bargains sometimes failed.—But this old white-headed foreigner wore a serene look,—a look of confidence. Why?—Here he was wasting his time and neglecting his business for people who only thought him mad, yet obviously he was happy.

Again the doctor nudged Ma's elbow. Young Tiger's eyelids were fluttering weakly open. Again he was trying to speak, and, seeing that he needed strength for something that he wished to say, the doctor forced a few drops of brandy between his lips.

"Father,—father," he gasped, "I did great wrong when I told you the child of your little wife was not your own.—It was a lie. She was ever faithful to you, and Swallow is your flesh and blood."

Ma's heart was soothed—all the pain and shame passed from him after the boy made his confession. Ma too made a confession to himself. After all perhaps it was his fault. The sins of the young are often to due to lack of right guidance from their elders. Perhaps if he had treated Young Tiger differently, the lad would have acted differently.

The old doctor bent over the boy again.

"He's going fast now," he whispered, "Would you mind," he asked with a quiet wise smile "if I should say a prayer?" Seeing Ma did not respond he went on, "I don't know what the lad is, or what you are,—whether Buddhist or Taoist or Confucian,—or a bit of all three like most Chinese.—But there's one prayer we can say for you and me and the boy together, without hurting anybody's feelings!"—He saw by Ma's face that he did not mind, and folding his hands he prayed aloud:—"Lord of Heaven give us faith and pity and above all a brave heart, so that whatever comes we may bravely bear it, and give us understanding according to our light. And to Thy mercy we confide this boy, knowing Thy ways are best.—Amen."—"Surely that's a prayer that could offend nobody except my dear old bishop," the doctor thought to himself, "and if he could hear me now he'd be tempted to swear at my unorthodoxy."

Young Tiger lay quiet at last.—The old foreigner pulled the old blue coat tenderly over him, covering his face.

Later Ma did not forget the white-haired doctor. He went back to the hospital and thanked him for easing his son's sickness, and once again he asked him why he gave help to people not even of his own race without payment—No Chinese would be fool enough to do that, he thought.

"Well," the old man answered, "I've looked on suffering all my life and thought about it, and wondered why it existed and how it could be helped.—What explanation does the Buddha give;—that all this suffering is the result of desire and must continue till desire shall be wiped out, and we must leave it be that folk may learn by it. And Lao-tzu, he had a grand philosophy that his priests have brought down to charms and talismans, but he says nothing about helping those who are hurt. And Confucius says only to let every man mind his business in his own family. But Christ, my Master, says that all men are brothers and should love their Father and one another, and help each other too, and serve the stranger like their own people, and leave the rest to Him.—So that is why I am about His business. —It seems to me the one way broad enough for all the world."

And when Ma offered him silver the doctor smiled and thanked him, but accepted nothing for himself.

"I need nothing," he said, "but maybe as your Buddhist priests say it is good for you to have the chance of giving, so I will take your silver to buy food and bandages and things that your people here so sorely need."

A man came up to them and called the doctor away then, and Ma did not see him again. But often afterwards he thought of the strange old man who only wanted to help folk, and he always thought of him with a kind of wonder. He was a good man, yes, and one respected a good man. But his ways were strange,—it was difficult to fathom his ways.

The tragic death of his son was not only a great blow to Ma's plans, but his plea for forgiveness made it a grief also. After all the lad had good in him.—Even Shui Ching though she had never cared much for Young Tiger was saddened too. As for Lilac Blossom, now that he had admitted his fault and retracted the wicked story about her, she also could mourn for him sincerely, for he was, the women agreed, the son of the house, and now they need not be ashamed to shed tears openly for him.

XXVI. Exiles

The Chis were doomed to remain exiles in Peking much longer than they expected.—"A few days," the Elder had said hopefully when they first came—But the days stretched into weeks and the weeks into months because soon after their arrival Chien sent a message by a sure hand to say that Hundred Altars had been looted though he and his were not molested.— But the Chi homestead and several other deserted houses had been partly burned, and the bandits were still roaming the neighbourhood. Therefore Chien advised. his friend not to return yet, "for food is scarce—the shops are tightly shuttered. Peddlers dare not come. Frightened people are hiding in the hills, fearful of sleeping in their own homes. Young women are taken by the soldiers. The well-to-do mingle with the poorest clad in rags lest they be tortured to disclose their silver."

When Chi told this news to his host the trader who had taken a personal liking to him quite apart from his duty towards the farmer as a friend of Ma's, begged him to stay on in his house until such time as he could safely leave the city. "Remain under my roof. Why should you go elsewhere?" he urged with genuine hospitality aroused by the Chis quiet unassuming ways. —They never asked more than was offered.—Besides Hu's compound, covering several *mou* of land, was so large that these guests were far enough away in their own courtyard not to interfere with him and his. Clever Needle even had her own kitchen and did her own cooking, in her own way, so there was no excuse for friction with the merchant's wife.

The separation of their domestic problems was doubly fortunate since she and Hu Tai Tai were women of opposite types and the ways of one were not the ways of the other. The rich town woman, mistress of many servants could afford to be generous, but actually was miserly. "That woman for all her money," Clever Needle remarked to Chi, "sees every scrap that comes into her kitchen, and never lets a well-filled bowl go out of it.—Of course one watches things oneself and waste is hateful, but carefulness to such a point... Lucky for us we pay for our own food, especially considering the appetites of Snow Peach and her girls," she added with a little noiseless laugh.

The Chis were grateful guests, but they were human and like everyone else enjoyed criticizing their hosts where they could not be overheard. Theirs was just criticism too. Hu Tai Tai was a hard woman,—hard on her servants, hard, also, on herself.— Life had made her so. The two sons she had borne her husband, the two beings who might have roused her soft and tender side, had died in childhood. Since she lost them she had ever remained aloof from worldly sympathies, wearing a shut face with a strange blankness in it like a piece of white paper from which the writing has been wiped away.

Like many another disappointed mother she found her solace in religion. A virtuous life, she often remarked unctuously, speaks louder than a brazen trumpet. But she was always doing acts of merit rather than of kindness,—providing coffins for the destitute whom charity, given in time, might have kept alive; collecting written characters or printed papers to be burned in temple furnaces thus saving them from desecration; giving away "virtue books."—Not a begging monk left her door without a contribution to insure his prayers. And yet, though she was always busy over her religion, she made life within the house a never-ending misery, accusing even her old amah,—a gaunt horsefaced old woman, with broken teeth and a booming voice,—who had served her faithfully from childhood, of having a thin spun memory and a tongue like a scorpion's tail. Indeed the trader's wife was one of those people capable of raising a tempest of emotion which wore the nerves of others to rags but somehow left her calm and serene standing in the centre of the storm, a martyr and a saint. Had Clever Needle been less tactful there must have been friction, for her hostess was very much the condescending town lady to her country-bred guests, and carefully marked the social distance between them.

Clever Needle felt that Hu Tai Tai, although she sometimes asked the women from Hundred Altars to join her in her own courtyards, looked down upon their rough village ways and, rather than gossip with them, preferred to be in her own room saying her prayers. So the Chi women kept to themselves, playing with the baby grandson who was already more spoiled and pampered than even

Little Dragon had been, or chatting with Shui Ching and Lilac Blossom—the only friends with whom they dared allow themselves any intimacy.

Nor did Chi himself find pleasure among strangers in the city teashops—people, who treated him as an ignorant rustic. So he too stayed at home, just idling, and somehow between eating and sleeping gloomily passed the day until evening came. Indeed the long winter with its endless procession of useless days was not a happy time for the farmer and his family. It wore down their stolid patience, and often great waves of longing surged over them for their home, their neighbours, for the mountains, for anything and anyone that was accustomed, known, and therefore dear. Day after day as Chi thought of home, memories stabbed his heart with longing. Pictures floated before his eyes of the willows like women with streaming hair bending down to the water above the Black Dragon Spring, of the hills lifting their splintered crests to the sky. He seemed to smell the fields, the sweet fragrance of the newly turned earth so different from the sour odours of the city streets. Yonder was firm ground under men's feet, and a plain straightforward life where they toiled day after day, fathered sons, breathed pure air, and in due time lay down to rest in their own land. Here in town men were engrossed in trade or politics and had a thinly disguised contempt for the life of which he was a part—but without which they themselves would not exist.

Chin-tzu and his brother, deep-rooted countrymen like the Elder, were likewise ill at ease in the luxurious comfort of Hu's house with nothing to do from morning until night, and all the time fearful lest they offend someone. There were certain things usual on the farm that they could not do in the city, well-knowing they would displease their hosts who lived by different conventions and expected their guests to follow them also while they dwelt beneath their roof.

Chin-tzu, though there were nights he could not sleep for homesickness and days when he could scarcely swallow his food, sat silent and uncomplaining, adding to the trials of his parents by no spoken word. It was against his stomach to live in another man's house, and against the grain that his clan should accept favours from strangers with high and mighty manners.

Yin-tzu was so restless that he could not stay within the compound. Often he wandered out into the streets and the companions he met at the second-rate teashops did him no good. These fellows laughed at him for a country-bumpkin—so far behind the times that he still wore a queue. "Queues are out of date," they said "among the new men who belong to the new times. We shall soon cut them off by force as our brothers are doing in the Yangtsze Valley." Shamefaced Yin-tzu wrapped his round his head as men did sometimes in the summer for convenience sake, but it took some courage to go home like this.

The Elder was furious. "What manners!" he shouted, looking with disgust at his son's head with the queue twisted round and skewered with a bamboo chopstick. "Since when have we had a Revolutionist in our family?"—He felt the foundations of good custom slipping beneath his feet, and could hardly restrain himself from seizing his son's hair and pulling it down, and slapping the boy to boot to teach him that he was a farmer of humble birth and destiny and not concerned with politics.

Yet when the shutters of the shop were barred against the night Chi looked forward eagerly to the Trader's invitation to join him and Ma in the latter's study. He would listen attentively while they discussed the affairs of the nation, marvelling at the topsy-turvyness of the ideas of the foreigners from the west which Ma and Hu discussed so seriously. He disapproved of them by and large for they did not seem to be practical,—and yet they had a queer attraction for him. He would hear more and yet more, in spite of himself, though he did not understand all of what the two merchants spoke for their outlook was so much wider than any he had imagined and he was used only to the sluggish talk of the village teashop.

Little Dragon, too, usually contrived to spend the evenings with the three older men in Ma's study, slipping in behind his father and earning his welcome by lighting their gurgling waterpipes. What he heard there as he sat listening by impressed him deeply, for he alone of all his family had profited by life in the city. Here was no gawky country lad, but one in whom uncommon aptitudes were discernible. Looking at him grown tall and handsome in his young manhood Ma thought to himself, "No one would ever take him for country born.—He has poise. He belongs to these refined surroundings."—Ma had always been attracted to him, and unconsciously spared no pains to win his confidence.—"What a waste to send such a lad back to the village. Hsü Hsien Sheng can teach him little more—and what future will there be for him there?—If he had been my son I could have given him his chance—" his eyes brightened as a sudden thought struck him. "I wonder,—I wonder if I could call him in as son-in-law and by marrying him to Swallow make him my son and heir now that Young Tiger is gone.—But I don't want Chi to refuse,—that would be embarrassing." The idea thrilled him intensely and his mind roved over the future. He must wait his chance and broach the matter at an opportune moment for farmer-like Chi could not be hurried and resented having to make quick decisions.—But possibly when Chi was ready to return to the village he would need a loan—especially since the red fire cock had crowed over his roofs.—Yes, when Chi was about to go back to Hundred Altars, that would be the time. No hurry, no hurry, for the New Year was at hand when no man liked to worry over future problems.—It was a time for gaiety and joy.

But a dismal New Year it proved for the exiles in Peking. They took little part in the festivities though the Trader's house was swept and garnished and the home altars glittered with gold and silver, and he and his family dressed in rich fur-lined robes received their friends and offered them rich foods.—Ma still mourned Young Tiger for whatever his hopes might be he had no heir now, an irregular position in the eyes of his neighbours, and one with which Hu deeply sympathized. "When I lost my sons I was a lonely man until I found this young nephew you have seen to take their place," Chi too was unhappy. He mourned his fields and his burned home and was bitter that his dreams of making Little Dragon a Degree Scholar was shattered. He had no money now for such a luxury, and besides he had learned since coming to Peking that the old Han Lin examinations were no longer held. They had been abolished several years before by Imperial decree, but the news had never reached Hundred Altars.—That was a blow indeed to old-fashioned folk like himself for whom knowledge began and ended with their beloved Classics.

But a greater blow was yet to fall. In February of that restless year of change 1912, Trader Hu called all who lived under his roof together into his guest hall and announced to them:

Juliet Bredon

"The Emperor has left his throne. There is a republic in our land. The new party holds the city."

This was indeed important news. So new masters had come to rule the country and the city too!

"Has there been fighting in the night?"

"None. It has all been very cleverly arranged without bloodshed here in the North."

It was a strange, an unheard of situation,—a political compromise impossible elsewhere than in the East.—A republican form of government was established by Imperial decree!—The Emperor had willingly stepped down from his dragon throne reserving only his empty title, his splendid home, his shadow court, which the new leaders on behalf of the country promised he should retain in return for his sacrifice of power. In the name of the baby sovereign an edict had been sent out.

"The whole nation is now inclined towards a republican form of government. The Southern and Central provinces first gave clear indication of this desire and the military leaders of the Northern provinces have since given their support to the same cause. It is not fitting that WE should withstand the desires of the nation merely for the glorification of our own house. WE recognize the signs of the age; WE have tested the trend, of popular opinion and WE now with the Emperor at Our Side invest the nation with sovereign power... actuated not only by a hope to bring solace to our subjects who long for the cessation of political tumult, but also by a desire to follow the precepts of the sages of old who taught that political sovereignty rests ultimately with the people."

"Thus," as one wise man sajd, "the throne itself is converted into a bridge to facilitate the transition from the monarchical to the republican form of government. The Emperor remains absolute to the last, and the very republican constitution which involves his own disappearance from political existence is created by the fiat of the sovereign in his last official utterance. Theoretically, the republic is established not by a people in arms acting in opposition to the Imperial will, but by the Emperor acting in august benevolence for the people's good....The heart of the drafter may have quailed when

Hundred Altars

he wrote the words that signified the surrender of the Imperial Power, but the spirit of Mencius guided his hand." Thus the Emperor handed the country over to his people and some ardent spirits regretted his graceful disappearance. They would have liked to have taken his throne from him by force.

So the Republic was sanely and yet dramatically established to the surprise and mystification, of the simple people who saw a president and an emperor live side by side in peace for thirteen years thereafter. Some truly ardent republicans there were and, among them, many who lived to prove the truth of the saying that "Revolutions devour their own children."—Sun Yat Sen, on the contrary became a Chinese Lenin with the reputation of a national saint and sage, an immortal leader before whom forever hovered the dream of a new world carved out of the old—a Utopia where all men were brothers and full fed.

But to the little group gathered in Trader Hu's great hall listening to the fateful words of change no prophetic instinct warned them of what the future might bring. Were these new masters to be trusted as keepers of custom? Chi was uneasy, Hu reserved judgment; Chin-tzu and Yin-tzu understood nothing at all. Only Ma ventured to remark that there might be a good time coming.—"I will not see the best of it, neither will your sons, but your sons' sons may. Surely it is right for the people to rule the land they live in."

Chi's personal reaction to this news of changed conditions was a stronger desire than ever to get back to the country far from politics where change would be less felt. There were hard times ahead for him, but as he said, "To those who have been pushed over a precipice, a rut in the road has no terrors, nor do the destitute feel anxious when the watchman cries, 'Sleep lightly,— robbers are about!' ".

But the winter wore on very long and cold that year and to the exiles waiting for spring to deliver them, it seemed as if it would never end. The weather did not break till the second moon after the New Year. One day it seemed as if the frost would be eternal; the next, as Chi stood out in the courtyard scanning the sky peasant-fashion, he called his wife and showed her a thin dark triangle high above their heads, the wild geese flying northwards following their leader in perfect formation. "They are late this year," she exclaimed with excited pleasure, "but there will be no more cold weather now!" The ground was ready to unfreeze. Spring must be at hand. It would come suddenly any day now as it does in the north where the first warmth brings a wealth of young life and the sun lingers until late afternoon as if unwilling to be gone. Beauty awakes and buds. Naked trees seemed to take life from the air. It was time to sow the spring crops.

Then it seemed to Chi that not one more day could he remain idle in the city, nor one more night sleep under a stranger's roof. But at the same time he realized that no wise man could undertake the return lightly, just at the hour the fancy took him. In the village he would have consulted the diviner. Many a time in the long winter he had missed the fatherly old man's advice and wondered what had happened to him.—But lacking his presence and knowing he must consult some omen for the future, Chi decided to visit the temple of the City God.

It was an imposing temple not so far distant from Hu's house—a temple built like the yamen of a mortal magistrate.— Two huge flagstaffs at the gate, and the principal courtyard filled with people come, like Chi himself, to ask favours of the Spiritual Mandarin. Further back stood the Great Hall where, behind a high wooden railing, sat the figure of the Dignitary dressed in a -long robe and wearing high black satin boots and a scholar's cap. Stands of archaic weapons—square bladed halberds, curved scimitars and pewter maces mounted on long red staves surrounded him and the figures of two lesser officials who inscribe the records in the Book of Life and Death, stood on his right and left hand. A lictor armed with a great stick was ready to mete out punishment to those whose hearts were evil.

Chi lighted a bundle of incense sticks which he bought from an attendant Taoist priest—an old man clad in a long greasy grey robe with his hair fastened on top, of his head by a wooden skewer. For a small fee he interpreted the omens for Chi. "If the heart is perfectly sincere," he mumbled, "then the Spiritual Magistrate will give right guidance. If the smoke of the incense rises directly towards his image you may follow your desire. But if it blows towards the open door then the omens are unfavourable."

Hundred Altars

To his relief Chi watched the smoke from his incense torch go straight up towards the God.—It was a windless day, the kind of day a careful man chooses to consult the omens.—Chi smiled contentedly as he left the shrine. Out in the courtyard two blue butterflies played together round one of the old cypresses. They went up and up as though weaving a garland. "Spring is here, spring is here," Chi muttered to himself, "and the god says —go!"

Even if his house was burned, even if his silver' was nearly spent, no one with the omens in his favour could be downcast.

Juliet Bredon

XXVII.   The Double Son

How right the omens were a second message from Chien soon proved.—"The bandits," he wrote, "have at last cleared away from the countryside and peace reigns once more. So return now for it is time that the fields should be ploughed and the seeds sown."— That was good hearing. The thought of the land lying there waiting for him filled Chi with excitement.

He went at once to tell the news to Clever Needle, making no effort to hide his eagerness. "We shall return and soon now. I will buy a plough and a new shrine for the Kitchen God without which no house is a home, and seed—and," his voice faltered.

"But have you money for all these things?" she blurted out anxiously.

Chi felt the crudity of the question and winced inwardly. Certainly he must borrow somehow, somewhere, to get the absolute necessities to start again. Ma—who was money-lender to the village—seemed his best hope. City usurers would charge him ruinous interest. For several days he pondered how best to ask a loan from the merchant whom he believed would be loath to lend, as he would need his capital for this new venture in Tientsin of which he talked so much.—Meanwhile he told his sons that they would soon go home. The two eldest were almost as pleased as Chi himself, but Little Dragon's sensitive face showed that to him the news gave no joy. It was a blow to his hopes, a sore disappointment to leave the city where in three short months he had learned so much and could learn more. But if he went back to the village, he would be forced to abandon his beloved books and work beside his brothers.

He listened to his father's fiat gravely, uttering no complaint, but across his brow a deep frown settled. Though obedient he was not too young to show his disappointment.

"I know," the Elder, reading his son's heart, said sadly, "that you wish to be a scholar. Yet how can I set your feet on that good path? The Han Lin examinations that were once the gateway to official position exist no longer.... There are new schools, they tell me, but I have no silver to spare for those. Besides, what hope is there in scholarship today?"

Ma, who had come to have a word with Chi, overheard the talk. He might have passed on with both ears closed, but he had plans of his own and did not so choose since he gathered that there had been a clash of wills which might give him the opportunity he sought. Little Dragon, on Ma's arrival, bowed and politely left his elders alone together.

"I should like to have a word with you neighbour," said Ma thoughtfully, unconsciously counting Little Dragon's retreating footsteps, "Let us go to my study where we can speak in private."

When they were comfortably seated there having taken off their long outer gowns and hung them on a peg to save them wear, Chi racked his brains trying to guess what Ma wanted, and how he could best ask for a loan. But to his surprise Ma himself immediately opened the subject.

"I understand you have decided to leave the city," he began, having settled himself squarely and planted his hands heavily on his fat knees.

"Yes," said Chi slowly, "for now I have heard that the bandits are gone and the countryside is quiet again, I do not wish to accept a stranger's hospitality an hour longer than I need."

"And how about Little Dragon?—Will you force him to return with you? I could not help but hear what passed between you a while ago. He has no desire to return it seems,—I always thought he was not like your other lads."

"It can't be helped. There is no other way for him."

"Oh, but there is! Why not send him to the new schools where boys with a love of learning may study things more useful in the new world that is coming than the Classics."

"But what could men learn better?" stammered Chi, a sound Confucianist at heart. "It is not for nothing that our fathers have lived centuries by their light—lived wise and sage lives.— How dare we set them aside?"

"It is not a question of better or worse, but of learning more suited to modern times. The Classics are not enough these days." — He paused and then continued slowly letting each word sink in: "Now perhaps to return to the land is right for you who are no longer young and cannot easily change your ways. And for Chin-tzu and Yin-tzu who are willing to go on working in the fields without ambition like blind-folded mules turning grindstones. But I have always told you Little Dragon is not like your other sons.—Everyone knows it, and if you refuse him this chance for the life he craves people will say you have no love of scholarship."

This was a clever argument. Chi, unlike Ma, cared greatly what people said of him.

"Well, I have no spare silver to pay for such learning now even if I had faith in it. What is the use of knowledge if it is apart from wisdom?" he countered.

"Knowledge is power still.—And I will lend you silver,—all you need."

Chi started in surprise. The peasant is by nature prone to a curious hurtful suspicion in human relationships. Why, puzzled Chi, should Ma make such an offer at a moment when he needs all his capital? This sudden generosity was unnatural. There must be something underneath it,—but what? Chi's mind was not keen enough to see through the suave suggestion of the merchant but he knew the man wanted something or why should he seek him?

"Is this in gratitude for saving your womenfolk?" he asked startled into bluntness.—A sure canny instinct warned him that the surface of Ma's words gave no true reflection of their depths.

Ma answered noncommittally.—Were they not neighbours after all? and generosity between them only natural?—Chi's mouth dropped open with astonishment. Such virtuous words from a man of Ma's character only sharpened his suspicions still further.

"Your offer might be good enough for me, and maybe sounds even too good.—What security would you want?" he inquired carefully. "I am borrowing this money, not taking it as a gift, but I may be long paying it back."

"Oh, scarcely anything..." the merchant paused significantly, and Chi knew his instinct was right. Whatever Ma wanted was well worth the silver he was offering. "Well, what would you say to a mortgage on your fields?" Ma went on, "Oh, just for form's sake, of course!"

"A mortgage on my land!"—A sudden wave of emotion, a desire controlled in time, to strike his neighbour propelled Chi's thoughts out of him.—Mortgage his fields!—a horrible thought to a man such as he, mortgage the land he loved, the land on which he and his ancestors had been born and which his sons and grandsons should till when he had returned into it? Pledge it to another man?—Even to educate a son?—Such a thing had not happened in all the long generations of his family. It was unthinkable—and Ma knew it as well as he himself. This talk about a mortgage was only a blind. Ma really wanted something else—something quite different. So Chi choked down his fury and answered calmly, "No, I cannot mortgage my land, not even if I starve,"—and then fell silent, waiting.

Ma rubbed his hands unctuously over his knees. How should he best say to Chi what he wanted to say? He must be wily, yet bold; and lead up to his wish dexterously.

"You know," he began smoothly, "that I am going to start business in Tientsin. It is a fine city, and it has schools—good schools where they teach what young men these days need to know. Now if you really want the silver, I have another plan. Let me call in your third son, Little Dragon as my son-in-law, and I will educate him. He shall have the best teachers and live in my house and I will make him my heir like an own son, and when the right time comes he shall marry my daughter."

"What is this you ask?" Chi cried out, and he spat on the floor with sudden venom to ease his heart of fury.—So men spit when they see foreigners whom they must greet with smiles on their faces, but inwardly despise.—How dared Ma suggest he part with this dearest son?—But Ma was not dismayed. He had expected this violent reaction at first.

"Surely," he pleaded coaxingly, "you could spare one lad,—you who have three sons! The eldest has already given you a grandson and the second will be married shortly also, and present you with more grandsons than you need.—One boy out of three may well be let go for his own good.—Besides, Clever Needle is a young woman yet and will doubtless bear more children."

"Never will I let Little Dragon go," Chi protested stoutly.

"I understand," Ma continued, "that to beget a scholar is a source of pride, but if he is cut off from scholarship and yet his long fine hands are unfit to grasp a hoe handle firmly, he can neither fulfill his destiny nor be of use."—Ma spoke bitter truth. Little Dragon was totally unsuited to work on the land. If life had been otherwise, if the Emperor had still been on his throne and the old system of literary degrees in force he might have followed in the footsteps of his great grandfather, acquiring knowledge cheaply. But with this new madness for foreign schools, expensive schools,... Chi rose in his agitation, and stalked heavily about the room. No, he would not part with this beloved lad who was in a way his dearest child. He could not bear to see him take another's name and worship at his grave. It was too hard. And yet for the boy's sake... He paused, deep in thought.—Seeing him weakening, Ma tempted him slyly.

"He shall have the best teachers. I will give him every possible chance to succeed. It would be a shame to stifle the lad's love of study. Give him the chance he craves, and he may yet 'pluck a whisker from the beard of Fame.' For this chance he worries all day long. Have you not noticed how pale he is? He will grieve himself to death if you force him to work on the land. Besides, though he will marry my daughter and take my name, when he has learned all the new schools can teach him I plan to send him back to Hundred Altars to manage my affairs there, until..." He meant until his own death or Chi's, —but it was not tactful to "paint the devil on the wall."— "Thus he will be near you, and you will not really lose him. There will be separation only for a few years, and his future will be secure. —Well," he ended rising with the sure knowledge that his last promise had half-persuaded Chi, "think it over, neighbour. There is still a week before you return.—As for the boy, if you let me have him, there is a brilliant career in store for him, I feel sure."

"It is a hard decision," sighed Chi, "before I say the last word I must talk matters over with the boy's mother."

"Oh, women!" sniffed Ma, "When a woman speaks, smile but do not answer."—He was well pleased and sighed with content. At last he felt sure of getting what he wanted.

The more Chi thought, the more he came to believe that Fate spoke through the mouth of the merchant, though he shrewdly suspected Clever Needle would accept Ma's proposal less philosophically, and he knew that the power of a woman in family affairs could not be denied.

"I have been thinking, wife," he said when he told her what Ma wished, "that maybe the boy would thrive and prosper better in

Tientsin for a few years; and we could hold in check our longing to see him for his sake."

At first she would not listen, and argued hotly,—"Of what use is this foreign learning to the son of a farmer ? Will it make him an official? This is the greatest nonsense I ever heard!—Why should you let him learn these new things and new ways—way of which we have scarcely heard, and which do not belong to us? —Has a madness come over you?"

"But if it is the best thing for him,—if it is the only chance he has," Chi said patiently, well knowing how the suggestion of parting with him grieved her. "He pines. You see that yourself."

The best thing for her Little Dragon,—best for him! That phrase repeated itself over and over in her mind in those days of indecision. She knew that sweat and blood and health and youth go into every crop a farmer reaps, and, knowing that, she hesitated to condemn such a son to such a life. Her heart, like his father's, was torn in two. For the sake of the boy's future they must, it seemed, make this bitter bargain.—Besides, if Little Dragon did "cross over" to Ma's house, their sacrifice and his would make it possible for the whole family to begin life anew without a stranglehold of debt around their necks—such a burden as even their little grandson might feel until middle age. With times so hard and the future uncertain they simply dared not refuse Ma's offer. Yet they both felt bitterly that they had been caught full in the collapse of the old regime—and caught unfairly. At last she said to Chi:

"You have spoken dreadful words for a mother to hear, nevertheless I must consent to Ma's request, for I am nothing but a woman and how shall I forbid a thing to which you, the Elder of our family, are ready to agree?—Now send the lad to me, that I may speak with him myself."

But of what they said to one another, these two, so closely knit together, never spoke.

Juliet Bredon

XXVIII. The Return

Their last days in Peking were full days for the Chis. The Elder with Ma's loan of silver in hand was busy bargaining for what was needed to re-stock the farm. Buying was not such a straightforward matter as in the village. No man would give a stranger credit here and an honest countryman must be ever on the watch lest he be cheated by a sharp and greedy shopkeeper.

Clever Needle, meanwhile, visited all the temples in the neighbourhood to pray for Little Dragon's future, lighting candles and incense before Kwanyin the Protectress, and begging her to guard him. Timid by nature she habitually feared to look beyond the day, and now she seemed to see a whole line of tomorrows with strange faces grimacing at her, the first of them big and clear, the others getting smaller and smaller, and they all looked and appeared frightening and seemed to say,—"I am coming,—I am coming. Look out for me!"

To her relief she heard that Ma had decided to return to the village for a time taking his family and Little Dragon with him. So the parting was postponed a little because the merchant must see what had happened to his business and his property and put his trusty steward in charge of his affairs temporarily while he himself should be absent in Tientsin. Later as he had promised Chi, he would send back Little Dragon to safeguard his interests in Hundred Altars. Other men were afraid to launch out in these troubled times, but Ma having his adopted son, felt he could look Fate squarely in the face. Now the merchant was thoroughly content. He had his heart's desire, and strangely enough, it seemed to him quite natural that he should get the boy at last,—the boy, grown tall and graceful, that he had coveted from the day of his birth. There were more ways of fatherhood than in the flesh, and through his exceeding love for the lad, and the lad's love for him, it seemed in some strange way as if Little Dragon had been given to him in a profound and spiritual birth. Shui Ching too shared the master's joy. It occurred to her that the gods had answered her prayers in their own way and their own time. The son she had prayed for on the mountain pilgrimage so long ago was hers at last. And she too thought to herself,—"It is not in the body alone that a child is born."

For more reasons than one Ma decided to sign the betrothal papers quickly. He did not wish to leave too much time for the Chis to brood over the loss of Little Dragon and perhaps change their minds. "Now let us bind our children together with the red cord," he said smiling, "and let it be done at once for delay is useless, and we will marry them as soon as the boy leaves his school."—Being close friends they needed no matchmaker, but Ma was careful to have the binding betrothal contract legally written out, and he spared no expense sending appropriate presents to the Chis. They would be welcome, especially at this time.

And now came the day fixed for the return. The evening before Chi and his sons formally thanked Hu for his kindness, bowing their knees before him in gratitude for the hospitality they had enjoyed all those long winter months.—"We have been quite unworthy," they stammered, and Hu answered politely,

"Do not thank. It was but a small matter."

Meanwhile the women also took leave of their hostess, and Hu Tai Tai was graciously pleased to express regret that they were going. It was all a game of polite phrases, like meeting yesterdays that, being gone, are not of interest any more, but still must be courteously regretted.

Before dawn next day the Chis and Mas packed into their carts again and took their way along the empty early morning streets. The mules looked wonderingly around. They too had taken on town habits of late rising and seemed scarcely able to believe that at such an hour when every living creature was intended to be in shelter and at rest, they were called upon to go out and labour. Snow Peach's girls as they more fully awoke, for they had moved in a sleepy trance so far, began to take an interest in the strange shapes of the dark objects against the faint greying sky; of this tree that looked like a long nosed devil, of that which resembled a stone lion's head; while the older women cheered themselves as best they could with their own talk.

By the time they passed the Summer Palace real morning had come. Now the road grew bad. Moisture rising through the thawing earth turned its surface to greasy mud, thick and wet like melted chocolate. To lighten the carts, the men walked beside their beasts for it was hard pulling. But the mules themselves required little attention, lacking superfluous energy to shy. As Chi plodded on silently he stared ahead and let the animal guide himself. He was thinking much of seed and crops, and laying his plans while with practised eyes he made weather forecasts, observing the omens of the season to come. As for Ma, there was a reflection in his face of the joy with which his heart was turning towards the future.

The miles were very slow and the women, cramped and cold, began to complain of their discomforts. Chi told them sternly to hold their peace. They bumped along beside the flat quiet fields with bordering willows already lightly touched with green. Now the hills came nearer and nearer, and presently the exiles reached the familiar bend in the road, the home turn, and there they glimpsed the roofs of Hundred Altars and the pines like dark plumes above the temple. Now the little company entered the village street peering anxiously around to see what damage had been done, but seeing little because, of the high walls, except here and there a blackened roof with tiles awry.

At their gate the mules slowed up of their own accord, and the women and children unpacked themselves from the carts while a dispirited band of neighbours came out of their houses to watch. Brief greetings were exchanged while the Chis unloaded themselves and their goods. Willow's baby whimpered and struggled. Snow Peach's girls whined and fretted, being chilly and hungry. Clever Needle too was stiff and weary but she hurried into their compound after Chi anxious to see what had happened to their home.

They found two rooms in the outer courtyard more or less intact having walls and roof and doors still standing, though the paper of the windows was torn and stained. Of the side houses on the larger courtyard, one still stood. But the second and the main hall had been partly burned. Most of the good hardwood furniture had been smashed in sheer wantonness by the bandits as they searched without success for silver and valuables. But the *k'angs* were intact and the smoke-swollen oven in the kitchen still usable.—A place to sleep. A place to cook. Having these no situation was hopeless, and the Chis wasted no time grieving over what had been destroyed but set themselves steadfastly to repair the damage. They did not ask much

Hundred Altars

of life, and finding that little snatched from them were not discouraged.

After the noon meal Chi went out into the village. It was good to see the familiar faces of neighbours walking to and fro with their carrying poles over their shoulders and the women going in and out of the houses with sieves or cooking pots they had borrowed,—and best of all to see his old friend Chien, eager to tell him all that had happened.

"After you left," he said, "we waited hoping that our village might be spared. On the horizon we sometimes saw flickering torches as the bandits crept down from the hills to plunder. Sometimes as they came into this valley or that, a small red tongue shot up here and there in the darkness as they set fire to a house.—Then one night when we had not been long asleep Hundred Altars was awakened by yells and shouts and the deafening discharge of jingals. A band of men, perhaps a dozen, perhaps twenty, rushed into the houses. The dogs drowsing in the courtyards on heaps of dry leaves woke with a yelp, and men ran to their doors. For answer the bandits broke open the gates with the butts of their guns, and when they left a house it was stripped bare of everything of value. There was no denying these men. In the darkness there was panic. Shouting, cries, appeals for mercy sounded everywhere.—Pigs squealed and the chickens squawked as the robbers gathered them up tied by the legs.— Some folk tried to seek refuge in the hills. Others fell upon their faces and pleaded for their lives. The bandits entered your house and wantonly broke what they could not take away,—and lucky you left many of your best things with me! One man shrieking with laughter threw his torch into the dry *kao-liang* stalks you had stacked against the east wall. Soon a bright flame leaped in a flash to the roof as the dry corn stalks flamed for a moment and the whirling leaves fell on the tiles. It was near the dawning of another day before they left Hundred Altars, staggering out half drunken on Ma's wine—for Bent Neck had given them all they could drink, and thus they made little search in Ma's place. They emptied the shop shelves, but he managed to save Ma's pyramid of silver, by covering it with earth like a grave mound."

"And the temple?" asked Chi anxiously, "Has harm come to that? I saw that the *Tu Ti*'s shrine was all right as we came along the street."

"Yes, the temple is intact. Trembling Sea learned wisdom from the old Abbot's misfortunes. He was very polite to the soldiers and gave them all he had, and so the place did not suffer. Another piece of luck—the bandits did not trouble our women as they did in so many places.—But old Six Hairs was killed—he would not tell where he had hidden the silver he did not have. And worse still one brutal faced fellow wounded the old diviner so grievously that he died a few days after.—We buried him by the roadside."

"Aiyah!" exclaimed Chi shocked by Chien's last words, "that is ill news! To think of harming such a man!—Had they no respect for his grey hairs?"

"None," said Chien.—There was a moment's silence as they paid an inward tribute of mourning to their old friend, the gentle seer whose occult advice had guided their lives.

"Ah, well," said Chien, "after all we have not been too unlucky. There was little serious conflict, our women are safe, and the fields remain untrampled and inviolate."

"Did other places fare worse?"

"Yes, many did. In Pei Yang Ho several shopkeepers were shot, and women jumped down wells to save their virtue. Whereas some villages lost all their food, thanks to Ma's wine we saved enough to feed us. And many families in other places have had to 'eat their girls'—sell them to buy food, for in famine times no wife or daughter can be weighed in the balance against a measure of grain!—And some men, too poor to buy seed for their fields, have hired themselves out as workers in the city."

"Sad, sad indeed," Chi agreed as he bade Chien farewell and went off to see Ma.

He found him counting over his losses thoughtfully.—It was heart-rending to see the well-stocked shelves of his shop empty. Still the silver, thanks to Bent Neck's ingenuity, was safe.

"You see," Ma said, "how urgent it is for me to build up a new business in Tientsin?—Here we are at the mercy of bandits. Here I am entirely dependent on local crops and 'too far away from the great cauldrons to smell what is cooking in them.' It may well be that the drought and the Revolution are a warning that I have idled too much in these past years, been too content with what I had."

Chi told all this news to Clever Needle, and ended philosophically,—"Let us forget the sadness of the past since we cannot change it, and lose no time in making our house into a home again."

Each day, each hour, was precious since the sooner the house was in order, the sooner work in the fields could begin. True the winter wheat, planted last autumn before they, left, was coming up, but corn and beans and *kao-liang* must be planted. So while Chin-tzu cleaned the well that had become choked with debris, Yin-tzu patched up the outhouse where the mules were stabled, and the women repaired the paper windows. All they could do themselves they did, and Chi called in "The Elephant"—the old carpenter,—for such repairs as they could not make. "I beg you to begin work at once," Chi said, and the old man nodded, "Yes, —but tomorrow, not today." He pointed to the sun that hung like a bronze mirror in a sky that looked like a leather-coloured curtain drawn across the heavens. Not a breath of air stirred. "There's a dust storm coming," he said, "no man can work today."

And he was right. Within two hours the great wind blowing straight down from the Gobi Desert shook the village as a tiger shakes its prey. Even in mid-afternoon the light was so dim that it was impossible to see more than a few yards ahead. The mountains were blotted out. The trees flapped in the wind like loose sails caught slack in a squall. Dust fell from the sky like rain, Soon there was dust, dust everywhere, above and below. Even the inside of the houses was filled with it. Along the window sills each gust of wind piled up new dunes. Choking cinnamon clouds enveloped everything. Tiny particles found their stealthy way into even the rose-wreathed clock which gasped for a few wheezy breaths and then stopped with a sigh.

The high wind did not die down at sunset as these Gobi winds so "often did, but growled and spat past windows and doors all night long. But towards morning it ceased. The new day dawned calm and serene with a clear dome of sky, a golden sun again, and the dark hills back in their places.

The fields cried out for ploughing and the Chi menfolk worked with sweat drenching them, begrudging even the hours required for sleep. The mules, sweat-drenched too, plodded along before the plough, their hoofs sinking into the soft brown earth, the point of the plough dipping in shallow at first, then gradually probing deeper as the trail stretched straight and dark, running in the same direction as it always had since the Mongol hordes swept down and the farmers began to plough in such a way as to make transport across their furrows difficult. The men took turns guiding the plough, there and back, there and back, or walking behind it seeding and packing the seed firmly in. Earth filled their shoes, creeping even through their socks, damp and soothing to their tired feet. Still they laboured gladly for all the idleness in the city was like a sickness which the land alone could heal. And they all burned brown again after the paleness of the city and their hands, grown soft from handling no other tools but chopsticks, hardened and calloused once more, and dirt gathered under their nails. But Chi only laughed and said: "Let it remain, we have no time for washing now."

Even Clever Needle when she had finished working in the house went out to help in the fields, and her daughter-in-law with her, weeding until their shoulders ached with weariness. Chi protested at first. His womenfolk had never worked on the land except rarely at the harvest. His mother never did, nor his grandmother. It was not dignified for well-to-do farm women to toil like men. It made them lose face. But Clever Needle answered briskly:

"We have no money to waste on hired labourers now. Besides, working in the fields is no harder than housework. A hot stove or a hot furrow,—both are the same. There is no work harder than housework."

She knew well enough that, face or no face, unless the women helped the seed would not be sown in time to harvest the next crops, and Chi sighing was forced to agree.—"When the stomach is empty, pride should not be strong," she reminded him.

Thus life resumed its old routine. The troubles of the past year had left few scars. The trees were just as green as before, the sun shone as triumphantly as ever. The familiar surroundings had not darkened because of the bandits' passage, nor sickened because of the people's pain. Not a family but was happy to be home again, their habits re-established, their communion with the earth resumed. They were working again, soon they would be saving again, the Chis with Chin-tzu's marriage in mind, for it was high time he had a wife to cure his restlessness.

And now that the seeds were in and the weeds out, the farmers had leisure, too, to sit and talk again, gathering at the inn in the spring twilights. Every night darkness came, later. The gentle winds in the white pines soughed softly like the incoming tide. The lilacs were in bloom again. The air was perfumed with them. More birds were busy building their nests. More trees unfurled their leafy banners. Already a young willow branch was pushing its way up through the diviner's grave mound like a sword of vengeance as if to comfort the dead and satisfy the sense of justice of the living.

Since he had listened to the talk of city men, Chi began to realize how little his neighbours knew or cared about the real world beyond the horizon. They had not even known for certain that the Emperor had left his throne. Chi asked old Chang what he thought of the Republic, and scratching his nose the old fellow replied: "Republic!—what is that? I have never heard of such a thing!—But I do know the Emperor had a quarrel with a man named Yuan."

Chang knew no more and no less than three quarters of the peasants did about the change of government, and Chi not unnaturally enjoyed showing off his superior knowledge of affairs gained in the Capital. He spoke of "democracy" as he had heard Hu speak,—but the more he talked the less his neighbours understood the difference the Revolution would make to their lives, for they had always enjoyed a very real democracy under the Emperor. They had always been free to govern themselves, to do what they liked and to think what they liked, and to choose their own village leaders. Indifferent as they were to larger issues they were shrewd and watchful in their own affairs, and by no means deficient in practical, intelligence. So they listened to Chi patiently, and then said "Ah!"—with the air of those who feared worse, yet failed to see that things were very changed.

In their scheme of things, except for the District Magistrate, —the Father and Mother Official—the government scarcely touched the life of the village at all. He and he only was the link between them and the higher officials of the province. But the Emperor occupied a special place. A deep Confucian sentiment bound the people to the ruler. He was answerable for them to Heaven as the head of the family was answerable to the gods and the ancestors. The lack of a sovereign to head the new government and intercede for them with Heaven was disturbing, for they had heard vague rumours that the Worship of the Sky at the great open altar in Peking would not take place. "That is the end of everything," the peasants said. With the Emperor gone who would set an example of filial piety, of virtue?—who would safeguard custom and tradition?—Who would justly decide the rights of town and country folk?—and keep foreigners from breaking the ancient boundaries and forcing their way into the land?

The peasants did not understand the ideals of the new leaders and were scarcely aware of the first birthpangs of new China. To them the new men lacked romance and tradition, and were mere visionaries who saw China already a united nation closely welded, while the everlasting people saw themselves as separate communities owing allegiance to the family first, then to the village, and finally, more vaguely, to their province. The country as a whole meant nothing to them. They were concerned with their own lives.

Listening to the usual talk at the inn—the same he had heard all his life, Chi found it unnecessary to lend an attentive ear. The arguments never changed. What was said yesterday would be said tomorrow. His neighbours prided themselves on this faculty; they believed it revealed their unswerving principles. But to Chi it betrayed their limitations. They were the constant peasants, eternally recurring types born to work the land that belonged to them and was "in their blood," as his father had phrased it long ago. They were men of the earth, rising from it and-returning to it, drawing from it their finest qualities, patience, filial piety, and a great serenity. Chi, by some miracle, had become aware of another life, though he still shared theirs. But at such times he felt his sacrifice of Little Dragon was repaid. The boy now had his chance in the wider world.

After a few weeks in Hundred Altars Ma went to Tientsin leaving Little Dragon with his women. He sent for them later when he had established himself in the port city and had a house ready to receive them.—Leaving the village was a big break to Shui Ching and Lilac Blossom. But it had to be, Ma, no matter what he said or what he did, was walking on towards things they could never understand. Shui Ching sometimes seemed to see him stepping blindly over men and heaps of money, walking forward with a queer light in his eyes, walking over days and nights after a phantom, the future. He bade her "follow"; and she nodded her head and followed. She had no other choice.

Little Dragon, too, felt himself beckoned on and he went gladly. But he did not take the parting with his blood parents lightly, and tried his hardest to console his mother. "In leaving," he told her tenderly, "we have the consolation you and I, that I am doing a filial duty."—It was true. The bargain which brought him his heart's desire, added to Chi's face, to his adopted father's face, and to his own. Only the "sorrow of divided paths," soured his happiness. But life is like that,—a strand of mixed motives interwoven, the blue thread of happiness plaited with the red thread of tragedy and pain.

Thinking deeply of these things the boy could not sleep that last night in his old home. He lay on the *k'ang*, his eyes wide open, letting his fancy paint all manner of visions. He tried to recall, one after another the pictures he had seen of strange places, Ma's two lithographs, and the calendars and cigarette advertisements he had seen in Ma's shop and in Peking. Then he lay weaving dreams about the future, and when he ceased to think about his mother's sorrow, he saw his life as a grand triumphal procession through the halls of learning. The golden bird of fortune and adventure flashed into the vision of his mind. Was it an omen that the phoenix was preparing to alight?

Juliet Bredon

XXIX. The Marriage of the Dead

Soon after the Chis returned to Hundred Altars, Snow Peach made inquiries about her daughter, Mei Li, betrothed to Wong Nai Nai s son in Red Temple Village. There were rumours that this hamlet in the hills had suffered much more than Hundred Altars. But Chi, absorbed in his own affairs, had neither time nor energy to find out what had happened to his niece. As the days passed and no message came from the girl, Snow Peach was filled with motherly anxiety. She had never liked the idea of a rearing marriage" anyway, never forgiven her brother-in-law for forcing it.

"You may be indifferent," she said bitterly, "but 1 must know how my daughter fares.—Let me go and see."

Reluctantly he gave her money for donkey hire and she started off astride a thin little beast that stumbled one step in four.— It was a dull grey day, but now and then the sun broke suspiciously through the clouds, sweeping the sides of the hills with livid green light. As the donkey ambled his slow way along the narrow path beside the fields in the direction of the Monastery of the Great Awakening, Snow Peach noticed the crops were thin as if there had not been sufficient seed for a full planting. All the villages bore marks of the bandits' passage. Here stood a charred wall, yonder a tree hacked down ruthlessly for firewoods Few pigs rooted in the roadside garbage. The children digging for roots and greens had pitiful thin bodies and frightened faces.

The temple gates were shut, the path leading to them weed-grown. Evidently pilgrims did not dare to come and pray this year. Beyond, the road led through a grove of trees whose bark had been eaten off in patches by the mules the bandits tethered to them. Similar wounds disfigured the orchards. It would take years to heal them. But they would heal in time. Nature was patient and the peasants learned patience by living close to her.

A few seasons would pass and the scars would cease to show. No one would guess that sorrow and death had passed that way.

Arrived at Red Temple Village where the fragrant green herbage had already sprung high enough to hide the debris of fallen walls and ruined hovels, Snow Peach had no more trouble finding Wong Nai Nai than Chi had three years before. As usual the old woman sat on the threshold of her lop-sided gateway, bending her head low over the faded coat she was re-patching though there was little left of it but former patches. She looked gaunt, and the high lights on her cheek-bones gave her face a ghostly appearance. Snow Peach's heart was filled with fear seeing the poverty about her, and she hurried forward.

"I am the sister-in-law of Elder Chi in Hundred Altars, and the mother of Mei Li—where is my girl?—Is she alive and well?"

"Mei Li is weeding in the fields," the old woman answered looking up at her visitor. "She will return presently—It is hard for her, poor girl, but since my son's death she has had to do it, for I have not the strength."—Her quiet dignity of voice and manner was founded on the knowledge, that, although poor, yet she was respected.

"Your lad is dead!" Snow Peach exclaimed, dismayed.

"Aiyah, he is dead,—shot by the bandits."—Wong Nai Nai wiped her eyes on her sleeve. "He was a good son, a filial son. Mine is an evil fate."

Snow Peach's heart seemed to stop beating. She had no breath to speak,—such misfortune—such misery!—Would her ill-luck never cease?—Presently Wong Nai Nai begged her to enter the house—or rather what was left of it, for only one small room still stood in the courtyard. The two others were charred skeletons—roofless walls with heaps of fallen tiles cluttering the earthen floors.—But the room where they sat was neat and clean, and the old woman served her guest with hot tea, albeit out of a cracked teapot. Snow Peach, now somewhat recovered from the shock, soon found her tongue again, and asked to hear the tale of their misfortunes.

It was the usual story one heard everywhere. The bandits came upon the village suddenly. Many houses they burned. Some women they carried away, and men who refused to show where grain was stored and silver buried they bound with ropes and left to starve.

"Mei Li and I," said Wong Nai Nai, "escaped in the darkness to a cave in the hills, but my son, who remained behind to collect the quilts we needed to protect us from the bitter cold, was caught by the bandits and killed.—Curses on those murderers, the evil fruits of evil roots!—Surely the priests are right in saying that devils possess men sometimes!

"When at last these villains went away we two women were left alone to face the winter. The village was kind to us. When spring came two 'yard uncles' lent a hand in our fields, though they were hard put to it to tend their own. Thus we managed somehow to pass the days, and now we are better off. The winter wheat will be ready for cutting soon. Sometimes I think that in our miseries we were fortunate except for the death of my son.—Others fared worse, they lost sons and fathers too, and all they had, so that , men, women and children were forced to hitch themselves together to the plough like beasts under a yoke."

"And my daughter,—how did she bear these sufferings?" asked Snow Peach anxiously. "And why did you not send to us for help?"

"We could not send a message. No one would walk the roads. Besides we felt, 'big fish, easier caught, would be too busy seeking shelter to trouble about little fish.'—But, despite all, Mei Li is in good health. She should be returning now.—You can judge for yourself."

Wong Nai Nai rose and went to the gate. "Here she comes."

Snow Peach joined her, looking up the road. Yes, there was her girl burdened with a heavy basket, but she carried it like one who did not find such labour heavy. Occasionally she stopped to rest in a mechanical way by a wall or a fallen tree, and then giving the basket another hitch upon her thin arm came steadily on again. The path was steep, and the soil and scenery differed much from the flat surroundings of Hundred Altars. Even the dialects and the customs of the two villages had shades of difference. But this was not extraordinary since customs and speech differ a little every ten miles in China.—And by the serene look on her daughter's face Snow Peach saw as she drew near that the girl was not unhappy. Old Wong Nai Nai treated her kindly, —that was plain from her tone when she spoke of her as a good girl, a dutiful girl, a true daughter. Here was a mother-in-law in a thousand. What a pity the lad had been killed.— It would be doubly difficult to find a bridegroom for a girl already once betrothed. The aura of ill-luck would cling to her. No family wanted such a daughter-in-law.

Hundred Altars

Mei Li coming down the last steps of the rocky path saw her mother standing in the doorway.

"Mother,—oh, mother!"—she cried, "What joy to find you again?—How is your honoured health?—And are my sisters well, and all the household yonder?"

"Yes,—yes,—all are in good health,—and you, my child?"

"Times have been hard and hungry,—but mother," she said turning with a smile to Wong Nai Nai, "has been good to me."

"That is a matter for thanks and thankfulness.—I grieve for her in the loss of her son, your betrothed. Ah, well, things being as they are you must come back with me to your uncle's home.... There is no longer any reason for you to remain here."

Snow Peach could not repress a sigh, half sadness and half satisfaction. She regretted that Mei Li should not have been wed in the house of this kind old woman, but at the same time she knew that Chi, who had arranged this rearing marriage against her will, would be none too pleased to have this niece back on his hands. The wheel of life brought queer revenges.—Of course before taking Mei Li home she must ask Wong Nai Nai's permission,—a mere formality. Unless,—a horrible thought crossed her mind,—unless, the old woman should choose to insist upon a marriage with the dead boy. Such weddings in the spirit world, though not an everyday occurrence, do take place, and to marry Mei Li to his soul would be a natural thing for Wong Nai Nai to ask under the circumstances. She was feeble and in bitter need of a pair of young strong helping hands, and, if she insisted, since the girl was legally betrothed and as much a part of her new family as if actually married, the spirit marriage must take place.—So far the possibility had not been suggested. It might or it might not have entered Wong Nai Nai's mind. Anyway if it had, tact might persuade her to abandon the idea.

"I can see you have no spare food to give that great useless girl of mine," said Snow Peach in a purring voice to Wong Nai Nai, "and though our house is full enough of mouths in these hard times, yet her uncle will not grudge her food. So I would be willing for the sake of your past kindness to take her off your hands at once."

"Indeed I am thankful to you for your offer which does credit to your good heart," Wong Nai Nai rejoined quickly, "but truth to tell I shall be more than glad to keep her and thus make the circle of our ancestral graves complete.—When she is married to my dead son I can adopt a grandson , to worship at his tomb and hers."

"Mei Li, my child,—what do you say to this!" Snow Peach gasped, fighting back her tears.—If the girl refused the marriage something might still be done,—surely she would refuse this cheerless future?—But the girl facing her smiled:

"I have heard of this old custom, my mother, and it seems to me right and good.—What would the village say of a maid who once betrothed came back free again?—And if for no other reason than for the sake of the dead son of this house to which I came as a promised bride I am glad to wed his spirit."

"That is well spoken, daughter," said Wong Nai Nai proudly, "The yard uncle will find you a son, and yours will be an honourable name."

Snow Peach interrupted. "But she is so young, and it is her right to look forward through the years to bearing children.— Think well of the joy of holding your own son in your arms, daughter! I know this good woman here is poor and heeds your strength, but I can get my brother to give her money to hire help.—Think well, daughter, you are deciding for all your life," —and she looked into the face of her girl pleadingly.—It was serene—untroubled by doubt.

"Truly, I have no desire to return with you—half a widow, and disgraced, mother," Mei Li answered soberly, "rather will I stay here and marry the dead. It is far better than to be betrothed again and bear children that people will call 'Trailing Oil Bottles,' for a second husband.—Oh, mother," she burst out finally, "it is my dearest wish!—Wong Nai Nai is kind and good, and I am not wanted in my uncle's house!"

But Snow Peach only wailed again and louder. "I had hoped for better than this for my maid!"

"Be comforted,—be comforted!" said Wong Nai Nai in her gentle voice, "Mei Li is willing, I am willing and your brother-in-law will be pleased to keep the bargain,—it must be cheaper for him to send wedding presents than to feed her all her life," she added with a touch of grim humour. "Besides, the maid is right, any children she might bear would be a living reproach, and only a widowed man would take her anyway!—and what true-hearted woman cares to be a second wife?"

Hundred Altars

Seeing there was nothing to do but let them have their will—unless indeed, for once her brother-in-law should take her part and firmly,—Snow Peach made her farewells, seeing her daughter's quiet face through a mist of tears. And as she mounted the little donkey again and started home her head hung down, she did hot look once over her shoulder to watch the setting sun that dyed the whole west red behind the hills. Her thoughts were full of this strange wedding to be, and though the gruesomeness of it did not strike her, the loneliness and labour of the life to which the girl was condemning herself did. Nor for the moment did she realize that such an example of faithfulness would command more respect for her maid than any rich marriage she might later make. In such surroundings where misery, poverty, life, birth and death are stark realities virtue also rises in clear bold relief and is held at its own value.—None of the pettinesses of complex civilization diminish its dignity.

Home again, Snow Peach did not fail to tell Chi her opinion of the rearing marriage. "A nice mess you have made of my girl's life!" she reproached him.—Chi sighed and answered with consoling of platitudes. He had done his best at the time and so forth;—the kind of words a man says to a woman who is injured and intends to remain injured. "After all," he protested sagely, "Is it so much worse to be married to a man who is dead than to a man who is living?—You and my brother—you shared the same *k'ang* for fifteen years and produced three girls.—Was that an achievement to look back on with pride?"—With such arguments he defended himself, citing cases among their neighbours of living couples who lived as strangers until years later death parted them still as strangers, people like Siamese twins who were tied together but did not know one another.—If such divided unity happened in real life, was there so much loss in a ghostly marriage?

To these words Snow Peach had not the wit to reply. She accepted Fate and shed tears over its cruelties. But if her mother's heart and pride were not comforted, her feminine mind was to some extent distracted with preparations for the phantom wedding.

There were two months of waiting before the right day came to send the presents, and Snow Peach had to admit that in the matter of gifts for her girl, Chi was generous—even though at this time he was hard pressed. Perhaps his conscience pricked him. In any case he gave liberally and what was sent was welcome indeed in the half-ruined home.

Mei Li returned to her uncle's house to enter the red bridal chair at the appointed hour. The wedding finery and show and the good red wedding robe and the bead crown of the bride gave Snow Peach face. The ceremony she did not see, and it was better so. What mother would have cared to watch her daughter with a pale grave face holding the spirit tablet of her dead bridegroom in her hands and bowing to it—watch her following all the rites well and carefully—alone before the assembled company who gathered to recognize her as well and truly wed to the dead son of their neighbour and to enjoy the slender feast which gave a semblance of reality to the proceedings?—It was only the empty shell of a real wedding after all, since even the ceremonial wine cups could not be exchanged, and one of the young pair could taste only the spiritual essence of the mutual feast.

Yet in doing what she believed her duty Mei Li was happy. Hard work had always been her lot, and she did not mind if the cares of the house and the family fell more and more upon her shoulders. Hers to fetch the water from the spring up on the hillside morning and evening in the big iron kettle so heavy that she must rest every few steps as she carried it back. Hers to cook and clean and scrub and mend, to cut wood for her cooking, and to help in the fields and to look after Wong Nai Nai and the little son.—Yet there were compensations,—there always are.—She saw other girls about her marry, and watched their lives with clear eyes undazzled by romance, aware that many living people only seem alive, masks behind which their deadness is concealed, aware that in some mysterious way the spirit of her husband was more vital, more real than theirs as he fulfilled his duties to the past, the present, and the future through her. And as she realized her acceptance of their mutual responsibilities she knew that her marriage was not merely an empty shell. In time she felt no difference between her life and the life of those around her,—She was a wife and a mother as other women were, and very happy in her mother-in-law, and in the little son who carried on the family name. And the neighbours ever spoke good words of the two women.

Even poor Snow Peach became reconciled to her daughter's strange destiny,—at last when she awoke to the pleasant realization of how much face she reaped by Mei Li's virtuous life. After a time she even took a certain pride in telling Mei Li's story over and over again to her gossips.—As the mother of so filial a daughter Snow Peach queened it among women whose daughters disagreed with living husbands, or failed to produce sons.

Juliet Bredon

XXX. Tientsin

Life in Tientsin at first was lonely for Ma—strange and unfriendly after the simple familiarity of Hundred Altars. For all his courage and adaptability it was not easy to settle into the ways of a big modern city where the smoke of many factories made the sky quiver and the streets were full of choking dust, blowing papers, and scraps of wool from torn bales. But the good *feng shui* the old diviner prophesied for him in Hundred Altars followed him to Tientsin.

Whatever he planned prospered. Whatever he touched turned to gold. To increase his luck he worked hard, zestful of life, spending energy generously. Soon he made friends with other merchants to whom he came with recommendations from Hu as a good man with a good name. Even among the foreigners he dealt with he built up the reputation of a straightforward, honest trader, whose policy was small profits and quick returns.

Though fully in sympathy with the Republic the foreigners at first were a little nervous about the change of government. It might break up the solidarity of the family. The day of large credits was over if a man's clan was no longer willing to be responsible for him and his debts. How would the new code affect the high reputation of the Chinese merchant whose word had hitherto been as good as his bonds? The assured and ordered past might for a time give place to faltering uncertainty.— A crumbling of the old moral fibre,—people were afraid of that.

As soon as Ma had hired a warehouse and an office, he also rented a good-sized foreign house with imposing wrought-iron gates. "Such a residence will give you face and increase your credit especially among foreigners," advised Hu, speaking as a man of the world to his country cousin."—Ma would have preferred an old style Chinese dwelling with his women's quarters separate and a quiet garden with lakelets and rock-caves and winding paths between peony terraces hidden behind high walls —a world apart to dream in. He wanted low roofs of heavy tiles and pigeons circling above them with melodious whistles tied under their wings, and most of all he wanted to live in a home that neither over-looked nor was over-

Hundred Altars

looked by its neighbours. Alas! such houses were not readily found in Tientsin especially in the foreign concessions where it was politic for him to reside.

But if to live in a western house with a tin roof painted red and furnished with western furniture was necessary to increase his standing among the local merchants, he was ready to do so, even though he paid a heavy price for his discomfort. He had been taught to believe that no house without a fine garden was decent or respectable, yet the grounds around his expensive barrack consisted only of a small rectangle of beaten earth, like a village threshing floor, just large enough he was told for a game called tennis—a stupid foreign game where people ran to and fro losing their dignity and sweating like field labourers. High narrow buildings overlooked his house on three sides though happily not on the fourth whence good influences came. But as a compensation there was a white-tiled kitchen and three bathrooms with hot and cold running water-tap's which terrified him at first, and parquet floors and bright electric lights.

When he was settled in his new home, Ma bade his womenfolk join him, and bring Little Dragon with them. At first Shui Ching and Lilac Blossom were appalled by the great bare dwelling all under one roof with its staring glass windows. Neither of them had ever seen anything like it. That queer square hall with a staircase in the middle and all the rooms opening off the landing, each separate room set aside for separate use, who ever heard of such a thing? Each member of the family slept alone behind locked doors in a bed made of iron instead of cosily all together on a heated k'ang. One big room was only used for eating. —That was the greatest marvel to women accustomed to eat wherever they happened to be, and the idea of leaving a large room empty except for a few moments twice a day appeared absurd.

The furniture too, though expensive, became less comfortable the longer they lived with it. The soft green plush upholstery yielded flabbily under the pressure of the body's weight. To Shui Ching's mind the chairs and tables were placed curiously askew, one here, another yonder, lacking propriety. Finally the disorder irritated her so much that she changed the arrangement, placing the things decently, in harmony with each other;—the chairs, in pairs, flat against the wall with a teapoy between, and an enamel pink spittoon nearby to accent friendly companionship. The big square table with curved misshapen legs she placed exactly in the centre of the room and the lamp—a hideous atrocity in yellow with prisms of glass dangling around the edge—exactly in the centre of the table. The two green plush sofas were pressed closely against the east and west walls facing one another. Thus the rules of right relationship and geomantic decorum were satisfied.

But Ma was not. "This is a foreign house," he sputtered, "and the furniture must be placed in the foreign way. Please do not interfere with what you cannot understand." And he bade her have everything moved back as before, slipshod and topsy turvy, —but he permitted the spittoons to remain.

Amah Wu of all the women was perhaps the only one to whom the house was a never ending miracle of fearsome delight. She pressed a button—the room was flooded with light. She turned a faucet—water gushed forth. No matter how many times a day she was summoned to bring tea or light a pipe for her mistress it was always, an adventure to cross the highly polished parquet floor. With mincing cat-like steps she made her way, pausing a whole minute before gathering courage to brave the crossing from one small rug to another. The mats had a way of slipping under her just when she hoped she had firm footing.

Still—think how wonderful it was to fill a room with light by the mere turning of a switch. And to talk with people through a wire,—which she imagined as hollow. For Ma had had a telephone installed and talked over it incessantly, pleased as a child with a new toy. But Shui Ching never learned to answer it with any comfort. As soon as she took the receiver in her hand she giggled and was confused. Lilac Blossom frankly pronounced the instrument a "mouthpiece of devils." Who but they could have conceived a voice without a soul?

Not only did Shui Ching feel uprooted but all her housekeeping routine, the little things that made the interest of her life had vanished. A cook ruled in the kitchen who had his own ways,— a man cook. She dared not interfere with him, and if she wanted some dainty to her own liking she was driven to prepare it secretly on a brazier in the bathroom.

Hundred Altars

Luckily, since she had no outside friends, she and Lilac Blossom agreed well together, and the two women passed their endless idle hours in dignity and peace sewing and embroidering. Shui Ching's mother, a noted needle woman, had bequeathed her talent to her daughter, likewise her designs that were miniature pictures with all the lucky emblems worked in them;—the squirrel and the grapes, the bat, the protecting tiger, the Lan Hua orchid, the fragrant cassia blossom, the semi-sacred swastika.

But the women could not sew all day long every day, and Ma finding his wife and Minor Star moping inside four walls and missing the courtyard life and the free and easy neighbourliness of the village, bought a brougham and a little red pony so they might drive out sedately, accompanied by Amah Wu, along the wide paved streets of the foreign concessions. The women thought these deep canyons between unscalable cliffs peopled with human beings far less colourful, far less friendly and intimate than the Peking streets with their low close huddled houses, their carved shop fronts and their thousand smells. When a rare motor car approached they sat in terror in the glass box that threatened to crash around them, while the Number Two *mafoo* jumped nimbly from his seat and clutched the pony's head with all his strength. The chauffeur stopped short usually, grinding his brakes. Horseman and mechanic cursed volubly. "The Father and Mother of a Row" was imminent, as they say in Ireland, until a sergeant of the Municipal Police quietly interposed his bulky person between the disputants, Thus trouble was averted, and the pony with one final plunge of fright went on his way down the main street of the concession,—a queer No-man's land, quite unlike China.

It was all so strange and different from any life Ma's women were aware of, and the change came too late for them to adapt themselves to it. The drives did help to fill the endless afternoons, but in the long evenings they sat lonely in the great house waiting for Ma to come back and musing over their happy home in Hundred Altars. Now, Shui Ching would say to Lilac Blossom, the crepe myrtles must be in flower. Did she remember the cloud of magenta blossom in Chien's courtyard? They had sat beneath it often through the drowsy summer afternoons while the cornfields beyond rustled and shimmered in the heat. Or she would remind the Minor Star of how the soft dusk was falling on the plain with the tender tints of the last sunrays still lingering above the hills. In the misty twilight she seemed to see the farmers returning from their work, their ploughs over their shoulders, and the shepherd boys in patched blue coats driving the sheep and goats home with loud cracks of their long whips. These well-beloved village sights and sounds stuck in her memory, the familiar figures, the spicy smell of *kao-liang* wine pervading the home courtyards, the soft noise of cloth-soled shoes shuffling down the street. They brought tears to her eyes and she turned her head away from the light when Ma came in lest he see she had been weeping, for the master was happy, and expected her to be happy too.—

He had looked forward to the future, and now the future had become a brilliant present for him, though to her it was alien in every way. The only consolation she found in it was Little Dragon. He had shot up tall and slender like an iris leaf, and bore himself with natural dignity and grace. He had grown stronger, too, since he had been to the foreign school with its drill and games, more manly, less girlish than as a child. If only his hair were not cut, but brushed smoothly from his head into a queue, Shui Ching thought he would be as handsome as a young god. But queues were not worn in the new schools which aped foreign styles and foreign manners, and Ma permitted the boy to do as the other students did. He was too wise to dictate the surface details of the lad's life, knowing that, however radical the young, they demand conformity to their own pattern and are as cruel as the old to companions who dare differ from their standards.

To Shui Ching's horror, Ma also insisted that his daughter should have her feet unbound and attend a modern foreign school. It seemed a terrible thing, this breaking of old customs. Besides, unbound feet were so ugly and immodest.—As to educating a girl, what was the use? Shui Ching herself could never read nor write. "Despite my lack of knowledge," she appealed to her husband almost in tears, "have I not proved a capable wife ?—My mother was a wise woman. She taught me things useful for marriage. She counselled me how to serve your parents respectfully so long as they lived, and how to listen amiably to your reproaches whenever it should please you to make them. She trained me well in the preparation of foods to entice your appetite and in all ways to minister to your comfort. What more does a girl need to know?"

But Ma only shook his head.

"When you married me you were taught things suitable for the humdrum life behind the Orchid Door.—But Swallow is to marry Little Dragon,—don't forget that,—and his life will not be like mine was in my young days even though I -have promised to send him back to Hundred Altars for a time. He is learning new ways, and she must learn them also the better to understand her husband's mind and share his life outside the women's courtyards."

Shui Ching regarded Ma mutely outraged. She had rarely been so stirred, so excited, but his word in his own house was law. Swallow was sent to school, and her mother, an unprotesting martyr to the master's will. found the big bare house more lonely, and more silent than ever.

Meanwhile Little Dragon was having his own difficulties at the great school. His first year was none too agreeable, as is usually the case with first years. Everything was unfamiliar and repellent. The boys were divided into classes so that they sat now before one teacher and now before another, and each made different demands on them. Three hours in the afternoon were devoted to Chinese studies. This was a real pleasure, but how different the teaching was from Hsu Hsien Sheng's methods!—He neither questioned nor explained the text. Here the teacher made critical comments on the sacred Classics.

The mornings were devoted to foreign studies under foreign teachers, and at noon a gymnasium instructor, whose trousers ended above his hairy knees, taught rough games, football, basketball and tennis—games that Little Dragon loathed at first, though in time he came to like them, and learned somewhat of fair play and comradeship from them.

Two years later he had gained a certain assurance and experience which enabled him to observe the life about him without prejudice. He could look back with amusement then on his first impressions of the school and see its merits no less than its defects, its strength and its weakness. The huge box of a building with glass-filled holes which let in the light and air so readily was no longer unfriendly and unfamiliar. He could smile at his terror of the shining slippery staircase leading to the upper class rooms and how he had held on tightly to the railing for fear of losing his balance and pitching headlong downwards to the amusement of the city-bred boys.

In those first months, too, his foreign teachers were a puzzle. "I hear they do not use chopsticks in eating, but put their rice directly into their mouth with their knives," he said to an older lad. "Oh, no," came the answer, "they do not eat rice, but large pieces of meat which they cut up themselves with a knife instead of letting the cook chop the food up decently in the kitchen." Only much later when he came to know the barbarians better he learned to respect their motives however much he disliked their customs. The English teacher,—Master of Haste, the boys called him for he was always in a hurry,—had a good heart. But the Master of History was less sympathetic. He reproved the students for eating garlic, saying it smelled badly. Whoever heard of such nonsense?—Every boy knew garlic was healthy and its fragrance clean and wholesome!—Besides these white men did not seem to realize that their own smell was offensive, though their pupils, brought up with a proper respect for the "five relationships" including the bond between a master and his scholars, were too polite to mention it. These foreigners boasted of being a bath-a-day people, and despised those who did not wash their entire bodies every morning. They had other queer peculiarities and prejudices, especially against spitting for which the boys were punished.

So it was only after a long acquaintance that Little Dragon even with his innate Oriental toleration, understood that "within the four seas all men are brethren," and the customs of all nations worthy of respect. Nevertheless it was difficult to deal with men who said what they thought outright and at once, men without subtle politeness or any conception of the importance of face, men who scolded instead of admiring, a boy who proved himself a successful liar, or could deceive people adroitly. They themselves boasted of telling the truth—which was usually unpleasant in its nakedness. Yet at times he could not help wondering if their frankness did not cover deceiving depths. Still he found kindness in them, and devotion to ideals though the ideals were not those of his people.

Hundred Altars

Take for instance their literature. It taught that the highest virtue was not filial piety but the devotion of sex to sex. The first duty of a man was not to his father but to his wife, and for her sake he might abandon all other earthly ties. In times of danger the woman must be saved first; in times of hardship a man must, so far as he was able, bear a double burden.—Preposterous and ridiculous of course! But poets like Wordsworth and Longfellow did appeal to the lad's taste because he felt they understood nature nearly as well as the poets of his own race.

Besides his course of English Classics, Little Dragon picked up curious scraps of learning—the date of the signing of the Magna Charta, the height of the world's highest mountain and the length of its longest river. So that when Ma asked him, "Are you satisfied with your school life?" Little Dragon was able to answer quite sincerely, "Fully satisfied. I certainly increase my knowledge every day. I read our own Classics, and beyond that I study all that has happened in the world."

"Well," answered Ma smiling proudly, "No knowledge is without its use, and Heaven will surely permit you to turn yours to profit."

In his second year Little Dragon made two friends among his class-mates, Peter Chien, son of a well-to-do farmer from a village on the Grand Canal, and Nicholas Tze, a boy from the Yangtsze valley. The two lads had taken foreign names as school names since it was the fashion of the day, and they told Little Dragon, he must do the same. So the name of Anthony was chosen for him in solemn conclave. The three boys were just at an age when everything new and foreign delighted them. They had vanities peculiar to their own race too, harmless vanities such as sleeping in tight cloth socks to keep their feet small, and letting their hair grow half way down their necks. And they talked to one another in the street in their queer clipped English just to show how much they knew.

Yet the curious topsy-turvy medley of old and new was the basis of a deep-rooted friendship. Besides they were pupils of the same teachers and that in itself was a binding relationship.

Outside his two friends Little Dragon's chief interest was music. He had as yet no taste for the modern girls who sought new freedom, and friendships with the other sex. But his love of music led him sometimes to a Christian church where the organ thrilled him. Listening to its noble notes he felt his mind suffused by an intangible floating glow, like the sea on a hot night when every wave breaks into pale foam and mysterious lights rise to the surface of dark waters, gleam, and vanish again into the depths. He became absorbed in strange fluid harmonies that swept over his body with endlessly changing patterns of light and shadow. But when he tried to reproduce what he had heard on Ma's seven stringed lute which the busy merchant neglected nowadays, he found himself suddenly empty, like a sandy cove from which the bright waves have retreated.

Then one day he saw the announcement of a concert of foreign music at a hotel. He begged Ma to take him. Ma, amused at the idea, agreed. Certainly they would go, and Shui Ching and Lilac Blossom and Swallow with them. Never before had the merchant taken his women to a foreign hotel, though he had dined there with business friends. Here was a chance to show his household what a man of the world he had become. Besides, he thought, it might make it easier for Shui Ching to understand her modern educated son and daughter if she saw the new fashioned life in its own setting. But as usual Shui Ching demurred, horrified that the boy and girl, betrothed to one another, should appear together in public before their marriage. Ma insisted, however. Other young people did, children of his business associates.

So he made his plans for the evening, and Shui Ching went protesting while Ma felt greatly elated at his progressiveness. It pleased him to appear broad-minded. He reserved a good table, invited a friend named Chow arid his wife to join them, and ordered Shui Ching to see that Lilac Blossom, Swallow and herself all had new gowns of the latest cut and fashion. "Get the best. I want to see you all look well-dressed," he ordered. "A man of my position does not grudge silver spent on his womenfolk. Their good appearance gives him face."

So they dressed themselves up in their finery to please him,— a duty not unpleasing to themselves.

Swallow had grown into a handsome girl with Ma's strength tempering Lilac Blossom's delicate beauty. She looked well in her apricot silk gown cut close to fit her figure in the latest style. Lilac Blossom, too, had a similar gown, but of dark blue.

Hundred Altars

Only Shui Ching insisted on wearing the conservative pleated black crepe skirt embroidered in circles as a concession to modern fashion, and a dark satin jacket with a high collar trimmed with silver. She disapproved of dresses that outlined the figure.

But then she disapproved of every modern innovation, of women seen in public, of ungraceful unbound feet, of striding steps, of the habits and exactions of crude young people who expected so much and gave so little. At heart she was and always would remain a plain farmer's daughter. As they sat in the lounge Shut Ching held herself erect on the edge of a chair too high for her, her feet dangling several inches above the floor, observing her surroundings with silent ill-concealed disapproval.

More and more people entered through the curious swinging door, so like a cage, so ready to trap those who walked sedately.

Strange foreigners, tall and lean, their eyes blue like spring-water, and big noses sticking out between their sunken cheeks, brought women with them, women with wild hair never smoothed with camellia oil. They talked loudly and had queer loose ways of looking straight at men. Well, they were western barbarians. They knew no better. Twice shocking were some of her own people who copied their crude ways.

The band began to play, and Chow Tai Tai ceased to chatter, but only because she could not make herself heard above the loud persistence of the music.—She and her husband were Cantonese, small eager folk, and great talkers.—Shui Ching's ears throbbed unpleasantly, she wished they were alone; that the master had not seen fit to invite these strangers. But she sat grimly attentive.

Was this what foreigners called music,—this crude blatant noise, this blasphemy of sound? The instruments seemed to be quarrelling among themselves, shouting one another down like the village women when they reviled the street. "Curse you!" roared the base drum to the trombone, "I'll drown you yet!" And the flutes seemed to mock the violins, trilling: "Well, play your tune, and play it well lest when our turn comes, we shall out-do you?"

Shui Ching thought regretfully of the. thin delicate tones her father drew from his serpent bellied san hsien, of the soft plaintive sounds an artist coaxed from a seven stringed lute. That was music,—a silver tracery of sound evoking summer winds and falling waters, and the drifting flight of white-winged birds, and the rustle of falling leaves.

Yet Ma seemed to be enjoying this cacophony of sound. Was he suddenly grown deaf or had he achieved sufficient concentration to listen to the din un-hearing?—And all those other families round her,—were they also impervious to these noises, or were they like herself trying not to show their discomfort?

The music ceased and people clapped their hands together. There was a pause during which the older women like herself sat silent and ill at ease while their daughters smiled with a silly shine in their eyes when young men came to speak to them, and even answered boldly and saucily. They were brilliant slim young creatures in their- rainbow gowns, rouged cheeks and cherry lips.

It was a long tiresome evening and Shui Ching rose without regret at the end of the programme to bid her guests farewell, while Ma summoned the waiter, paid his bill and gave a handsome tip with the air of the most important man in the world.

"It was a wonderful concert," said Chow Tai Tai enthusiastically, "I never knew that men could play so many notes in such a short time!"

Her husband too was full of praise, though he admitted he liked the first part best, before they all began to play together.

"That," said Little Dragon scornfully on the way home, "was very stupid of him—the players had not yet started to play. They were only tuning up."

"Well," Ma admitted, "it all seemed much the same to me.—But you, my son, how did you find this music?"

"Oh, it was rich and good and terribly exciting," Little Dragon responded eagerly. "Did you hear the sweet thin cry of the violin soaring like a bird on wings high above the rest,—calling the others to follow?"

Ma nodded pleasantly. He liked his boy to take an interest in artistic things. It was becoming to the son of a man who could afford to pamper such tastes, and one of the lad's most engaging qualities was his imagination, though none the less Ma judged he had plenty of acumen. The contemplative side of Little Dragon's nature linked him subtly with the scholar-philosophers of the past. Once in Peking Ma remembered finding him in Trader Hu's study writing busily.

Leaning over his shoulder Ma saw that he was composing a poem, and when he asked how long he had been writing, the boy had answered: "A long, long time. You see there are so many things to say about a tree."

Yes, Ma was thoroughly pleased with the evening, and pleased with himself. It might be daring, it might be modern to attend such a concert, but also he was fulfilling part of his duty to Chi, and at the same time following the counsels of the ancient sages who held that a knowledge of music was a part of the education of a gentleman.

Juliet Bredon

XXXI. The Marriage of Little Dragon

After four long years at school Little Dragon graduated. There was a great ceremony, and again Ma dragged Shui Ching unwilling enough, to see their son sit on a high platform and receive a scroll of paper inscribed with his name in queer gold letters,—a paper which proved he had learned everything a man could learn. Undeniably as he sat there he was a lad to be proud of, a figure to please the eye, and his parents were calmly sure the best looking boy in his class. Yes, he was handsome even in the foreign clothes which as young Anthony he had begged Ma to give him for this great occasion. The other boys were to wear foreign clothes for the Commencement Exercises, at least such as could afford them, and Ma understood that the lad wanted to look as much like the others as possible. So there he was on the platform in a blue serge suit, a stiff white collar and a tie with red and yellow spots,—shy and uncomfortable in the strange garments. He had not even asked his mother to make them, but had had them cut and sewn by a man tailor in the town.

The parents listened respectfully to the long dull essays that the stammering lads read out to prove that they were scholars. A foreign teacher called Young Evans, though he looked old, being greatly wrinkled and white of hair, made a long speech bidding the graduated go forth and serve their country well, and right the people's wrongs, and spread knowledge among them, all the usual high falutin talk with which young men are launched on an ungrateful world.

And then Anthony stepped forward and read the class poem which he had been chosen to write. The sight of him, immaculately dressed, his face, collar, nails and shoes shining, inspired Ma to whisper to Shui Ching. "Everyone must find the place where he belongs. No one place can fit us all. The land fits his father like a pair of comfortable old shoes. But Little Dragon is a fine brush that fits into the sheath of scholarship. I would not be surprised if the boy with his good presence and his gift for learning does not one day sit among the new leaders of our country."

After the proud but exhausting day was over, the three drove home together in the glass brougham. Anthony clutched his precious diploma tightly in his hand. He would frame it behind glass as something very precious, and hang it on the wall of his room beside the photographs of his class-mates, just underneath his school pennants.

That evening Ma gave a great dinner in Little Dragon's honour to. all his friends. He had ordered the best feast money could buy. in the most expensive restaurant in Tientsin. It was a banquet of more than sixty courses, and the rare foods were washed down with hot wines and cool liqueurs flavoured with apricots and almonds and rose leaves. Hors d'oeuvres of cakes and jellied eggs and melon seeds were followed by entrees of duck and fish and southern beans, "fragrant sausages," bears' paws, "embroidered vegetables" and fish cones (Chinese caviar) alternating with sweet dishes of sugared fruit blossoms and Canton pears. Then came a series of. soups made of bean curd, pigeon's eggs, rare seaweeds and silver fungus, and again more entrees alternating with entremets, boiled sharks' fins, "golden cash" chicken, ham cured in honey, turnip cakes, lotus leaf puffs, bellies of fat fish, stewed duck's feet, cubes of pheasant in wheaten griddle cakes, black rose soup, "gold and silver" noodles, pigs' elbows, shrimps and eels in sugar and vinegar, and finally "three thread soup," almond milk, and last of all rice.

This feast enabled Ma to show off his scholar son before his merchant friends, and while informing them that he was about to enter business, politely recommended him to their care.

"For now," said Ma proudly, "he is a man and with your help will be an honest merchant, and later, when I am too old for business I beg you will let him sit in your presence as an equal." It was the end of an age which for all its faults at least had good mariners.

Not long afterwards Little Dragon took his place in Ma's office. Those first months of the young man's working life Ma carefully watched over his son, teaching him, letting him shoulder more and more responsibility. Slouched in an easy chair in his comfortable, office with a foreign carpet on the floor to keep the winter chill from his feet, the old merchant sat seemingly taking life easy, but in reality supervising the fortunes of his house with the same keen attention as when he first came to Tientsin.

Juliet Bredon

The outbreak of the World War two years previously proved a golden opportunity for trade, and China had her part and profit in it. It was the first time Ma had felt the influence of a widespread war, and Ma could not understand why this fighting on a distant continent between peoples of the west should fill his pockets with silver. But he accepted with satisfaction the fact that it did, and was not slow to take advantage of the demands for exports in wool and cotton. The warring nations, ground between the upper and nether mill-stones paid liberally for what they wanted yet had neither time nor manpower to produce themselves, and the merchant, grown wily by reason of his city experiences, learned how to extract his full percent and profit in dealing with the foreigners. Moreover he soon saw that Little Dragon was well-fitted to follow in his footsteps,—sound, cautious, conscientious, yet not devoid of honest shrewdness.

Meanwhile in the midst of his own success Little Dragon was much disturbed by letters which he received from his friends Nicholas and Peter. Now that they had tasted freedom and begun to see the world open out before them it was not easy to go back to the limited life whence they had come, and both boys were homesick for the school. The problem of re-adjustment was bound to be difficult.

Peter Chien had gone home a full-fledged engineer, dreaming dreams of changing the face of his own countryside. But his mother, an old woman with an old woman's power in the family councils, set her face against his schemes. "Farm irrigation, nonsense! Village water-works, absurd!"—"Our ancients needed no such things—why should we, their descendants, have the audacity to pretend that we know better!" she exclaimed indignantly.— Besides there was the question of *feng shui*.

She had been told the story of a man who had built a high tower to store water, and it had angered the good spirits of the air, and they cast a blight upon the crops. She had been told too of another young engineer who laying a pipe-line had carelessly dug too deep into the sacred earth and wounded a dragon causing still more dreadful things to happen.

"She does not understand, my mother," Peter wrote in his rather pitiful letter, "and she will not understand. At the suggestion of change she believes the Heavens are going to fall!"

Neither could be blamed, thought Little Dragon sadly with an uneasy premonition that he too might have similar problems to face when he returned to Hundred Altars. For old-fashioned parents the new times were indeed difficult. If they yielded to their boys' plea for modern schooling, the lads came home impatient of restraint and full of impractical ideals that floated like gigantic kites high above the heads of their neighbours. This younger generation seemed to think that the methods of the West would burst suddenly on China like a great light illuminating the darkness of the past. But instead of that these boys found the deep shadows of custom and superstition closing over them again and they became listless and defeated. They neither fitted any longer into the pattern of family life at home nor had the means to usefully put their new knowledge into practise elsewhere.

How sad to hear this strong, brave song of eternal youth, eternally at war with convention, die down into a murmur of discontent. But such experiences at Peter Chien's were common enough,—are common still. Tragic too sometimes when these students of the new, eager to throw over everything that has been done before, return to their villages.

Poor Nicholas Tze felt himself doomed from the very moment that he crossed his father's threshold. By nature an extremist he believed this was the day for young men and young men only. It was their duty to change everything and everybody, to smash old things down and build anew from the foundations. Under the present, system he felt the people worked too hard for too little wage. They ate too little, they had no comforts, they could neither read nor write. He would help them, he would teach them. His mother smiled:

"Not so fast, my son," she said, "perhaps in a hundred years."

But Nicholas tried to ignore the prejudices around him, and turn a deaf ear to the advice of his neighbours, who said: "Let things alone, conform, or at least compromise."

But he answered hotly:—"Why have I been sent to learn better ways if I am expected to forget them now I have come home."

Looking for sympathy. he wrote to Little Dragon of the gloomy poverty of his village, the undernourished elders, the rickety children, the weary workers earning a miserable pittance, hauling at the towing ropes along the canal banks. "All men are created equal," was the gist of his letter, "let us who have been taught this help our people."—Ten years later he would have been a Communist.

When for months and months he did not write again, Little Dragon often wondered what had become of him and feared for him. But it was only long afterwards that he heard from a mutual friend how a mere trifle had put an end to that generous young life.

It happened in this wise. Among the things Nicholas took back with him from Tientsin was a pair of white tennis shoes dear to his heart. They were a last reminder of the life he had left, for he had been forced to give up wearing foreign clothes in the village. It was impractical to replace them. Unfortunately it grieved his mother deeply to see him wearing white shoes, more deeply than he guessed.

"White is the colour of mourning," she reminded him. "If you continue to wear those shoes someone in this house will surely die!"

"That is a silly superstition, mother,—how can white shoes cause death?" Nicholas laughed.

"I have spoken," said his mother sternly. "It is for you to hear. I forbid you to appear in those white shoes again under my roof, if you disobey you will rue it."

But Nicholas did not take his mother's command seriously. He continued to wear the white shoes daily, thinking to prove to her that she was wrong. She was not reasonable, and he would teach her to view new things without prejudice.—But he forgot that the old woman scorned logic. Hers was the intuitive eastern mind and his refusal to obey struck at the root of her deepest feelings. She cried passionately:

"If my son who should obey me, does not do so he lacks the first of all virtues, filial piety!—I am disgraced for having brought him up so ill. It is therefore time for me to die." And, true to her code, that very night she hanged herself.

The boy was heartbroken. The village blamed him, and he blamed himself. There was no longer any place in life for him neither at home where he was ostracized nor anywhere else he might go because the reputation of having caused his mother's death would always follow him. His half westernized ways cut him off his own people, yet he had neither the means nor the connections to join the enlightened new leaders. What was left then? Only the way his mother took. Dying he would regain his face and hers before their neighbours,—-and it would be so much easier to be dead than alive.

The news of this tragedy saddened Little Dragon greatly. So young, so promising his friend had been. When his turn came to go back to his old home he would be cautious, very, very cautious.

Meanwhile a year later Ma judged the time had come for the boy's marriage. At Ma's suggestion Little Dragon sent a letter begging Chi and Clever Needle to be present at the ceremony. But they refused. Again it was autumn and the season of harvest and they could ill-afford to spare the time away from their fields. Besides as Chi replied, "We are village bred, we cannot endure the thought of a journey in the 'fire-breathing monster.' —A train was ever a thing of terror to them, and much as they loved their youngest son neither of the old people relished a journey to a strange city.

Nor, despite his affection for them, was Little Dragon disappointed. It was perhaps better that Clever Needle should not come suddenly in contact with too many modern ways. They would only grieve and baffle her. The young in these days seemed to be perpetually stepping on the toes of the old. Even Shui Ching complained that the new generation made her feel she belonged to the past, and that her own daughter neither needed her nor heeded her advice.

Behind her back Shui Ching knew that Cornelia, as Swallow had re-named herself at school, and her girl-friends irreverently called her "Mother Ming" in teasing reference to the dynasty gone these three hundred years. Some of the youngsters were positively cruel in their lack of filial spirit towards their elders. Two or three refused point blank to marry the men chosen by their parents, and one at least desired a career. She must be a nurse whether her family liked it or not. But Swallow fortunately was biddable enough in larger matters, and content to claim her new social freedom only in details.

On her wedding day for instance she refused to have the "pulling out of hairs," or to adopt the old-fashioned matron's coiffure. Nor would she be washed and anointed with oil or even dressed by women friends, but insisted on taking a cold shower alone in the white tiled bathroom which Shui Ching herself avoided like the plague. "I am no helpless doll," she said smiling, "I can dress myself. My friends all do it nowadays." When Shui Ching protested, Ma only laughed and commanded her to let Swallow be. "We belong to our times but she belongs to hers."—And he even permitted his daughter to wear a pale pink wedding gown—white, colour of mourning was out of the question—instead of the conventional red robe, and upheld her wish to have no match-makers and no teasing of the bride.

Impossible to deny that Swallow was beautiful as she stood ready on her wedding day in her pale pink satin gown combining features of Chinese and Western fashion, her pink chiffon veil, her high-heeled slippers and the long pink silk gloves that ladies wore on these occasions. Neither was she timid with downcast eyes, but frankly gay and merry as gifts were brought to her— hidden gifts wrapped in brown paper as if, thought Shui Ching, the givers were ashamed of them. And well they might be too, for the girls of the younger set sent vases with unclothed figures upon them, lads and maidens playing naked in a garden, and a queer machine with a handle fixed to it that being wound up made strange vulgar noises. How different from the dignified gifts of other days!

"Do I look pretty, mother?" Swallow asked eagerly, "Will I please my husband?"

"That," answered Shui Ching sedately, "depends on how you observe the proprieties.—As for your appearance it is well enough, except for your hair. With that queer bundle at the back of your neck how can anyone tell whether you are a married woman or a maid?"

Swallow laughed merrily:

"I shall wear a golden wedding ring like the foreigners!"

Shui Ching sighed heavily.—Oh, these young people, what would they do next?

Just then the wedding carriage drawn by two piebald ponies and hung with red embroidered satins arrived to fetch the bride. Upheld by Ma the two young people insisted on a new style ceremony which took place in a fashionable restaurant. Here, instead of drinking from the double wine-cups they signed a marriage certificate and sealed it with a special seal. Swallow sat with uncovered face at the wedding breakfast,—for no ceremony whether conducted in ancient or modern style could be complete without a feast.

At the long banquet table all the women were ranged together on one side, all the men on the other. Thus far even the most advanced yielded to compromise. Shui Ching and the older women would have died of shame had any man, even their own husbands, sat beside them at table. But the younger women and even the girls, greatly daring, chatted to the men opposite.

Although there was no teasing of the bride who mingled freely with the guests instead of being decorously tucked out of sight in an inner room, much good advice was given the young couple,— half in earnest, half in joke. There was, too, much whispered talk of sons,—the older women frankly advising Swallow not to give birth to unnecessary daughters but to make haste and bear an heir to her husband's house. Listening, her eyes meeting his, she smiled frankly at him and without shame, and he smiled back at her raising his glass with good wishes. There was more to that wedding than a formal arrangement. The young people had a real liking for one another, and Swallow who was in many ways her father's daughter, felt a pride in her handsome young husband.

Not only Shui Ching but others among the older guests were shocked by this show of intimacy in public. In their young days husbands and wives did not even hang their garments on the same peg nor wash in the same tub let alone look openly at one another. But when in reply to the toast-master's admonition to exact obedience from his wife, Little Dragon replied,

"Your words of wisdom belong to ancient times. But nowadays we young people wish to be friends, not master and slave. We shall walk side by side instead of my striding ahead and my wife faltering behind me!"—The old-fashioned mothers were struck dumb with horror. That light upon their own marriages had never dawned on them.

After the feast the two young people left together for Ma's house in the decorated red landau, open now and wreathed with paper flowers, while their young friends threw handfuls of rice after them. "Fancy wasting rice, the people's food!" Shui Ching heard one elderly woman remark to another. "In my day a child was punished if he dropped so much as a single grain!"—It was her own thought also, and though hurt by the criticism, it was comforting to feel that she was not alone in her opinion of new fangled ways.

Now that Little Dragon was married Ma determined to fulfill his promise to the Chis to send him back to Hundred Altars. But this could not be done at once owing to the press of business in Tientsin. Meanwhile Ma was anxious to know if there was any immediate prospect of a grandson, and he was not disappointed, for in this vital matter Swallow did her duty as well as any old-fashioned bride. Ten months to a day after her modern wedding she gave birth to a fine boy. To Shui Ching's horror, but with Ma's approval, the child was born in a foreign hospital. As he explained to Shui Ching patiently, in such cases the western trained doctors were far better than the old fashioned midwives. "We must think of the child," he said, "remember with what trouble our own daughter was born," he added, knowing that she felt hurt because her privilege of helping to bring the baby into the world had been usurped.

"Did they not try to gouge out his eyes for medicine?" she inquired, when Swallow and the baby were safely home.

"Of course not, mother," Swallow exclaimed laughing. "How can you listen to such silly tales?"

"Look at me now," Shui Ching said disgustedly to Ma, "a grandmother of a foreign born child!—a woman of the new order! Will you never leave me to comfortable old ways?"

Ma laughed,—but Shui Ching was not happy.

She never could keep pace with new fashions and ideas and she and Ma had grown apart in these city years. Once when his horizon was hers she had been able to share his life, and dreams. Now, she lagged far behind. Little Dragon's words came back to her,—"We shall walk side by side as friends, instead of my striding ahead and dragging my wife after me!"—Keep up or drop out useless. Was that the law of life? Were these young people right? Once she had dreamed that in having a son like Little Dragon life would be so beautiful. And in a sense it was. But now he too like Swallow seemed to have turned away from her, his eyes set towards a future she could not share. Alas, she 'eft, her menfolk were leaving her far behind.

XXXII. Little Dragon Comes Home

Through all the many moons that Little Dragon was away from home Clever Needle counted the days of his absence one by one, and worried over him in the distant city so full of dangers. Now at last the day of his return had come as all days come. She went about the house as one in a dream, cleaning, tidying, preparing the welcoming feast for her scholar son, her favourite, her little third-born, her precious youngest.

"He went from me a boy,—he will return a man," she told herself over and over again. How would she find him?—A stranger in strange clothes with foreign manners, who had outgrown home ways and despised home-folk?—And Swallow— the product of a modern school—what would she be like?—Supposing she refused to be guided by the mother of her husband? —Fiercely moral the older woman sat up like a wary censor watching the younger from afar while at the same time her thoughts drew the girl towards her, but anxiously. Tales of the independence of the young had reached even Hundred Altars. This new generation was no longer dutiful, people said. It would not listen with patience to the old. Clever Needle shook her head sadly.—Even the baby grandson born in a foreign hospital, might well be tainted, too, even at his young age. .

Chi, inwardly no less fearful, made clumsy efforts to console her.—"Stop troubling yourself.—Because a thing is new it need not be evil, nor because it is old must it always be good.—Let us be thankful that the lad comes home to live beside us in a neighbouring house."—But Clever Needle, for whom the limits of propriety and behaviour were the rigid limits set in her own girlhood, feared still as she listened to his words.

Late in the afternoon the Chis gathered, dressed in their best, to await the new arrivals in the common room. Chin-tzu and Yin-tzu, well-scrubbed after the day's labour, hung about sheepishly, secretly anxious lest this town brother despise them. Their wives—for both were married and had children—showed their nervousness by shy excited giggles. Snow Peach and her two daughters—plain girls, but with jackets neatly buttoned and sleek pig-tails tied with pink wool for Clever Needle having striven to make their upbringing orderly and mannerly had at last corrected their sloppy ways,—moved excitedly to the door and back again. Even Amah Niu, grown broad-breasted with the years and greying at the temples, was shaken out of her usual placidity as she waited for her milk son. All day long she had asked questions—how would he look—what would he wear?—for rumour said he had been exposed to the contagion of new fashions, even of foreign ways.—And how ought the children to greet him,—should his brother's sons ko-tow?

"Certainly," Chi answered amazed at her question, "Are elders no longer elders, and does not a young generation still owe respect to a senior?"

If the truth be told the neighbours were scarcely less excited than the family. A scholar was coming home. If he had been an old style Han Lin graduate they would have beaten the drums in the temple to greet him. That could scarcely be done for a modern-educated man, a student of curious studies. Still they were proud of him, proud of his learning as such. Hsü Hsien Sheng, still attaching snails to the dragon's tail, summed up village feeling when he remarked proudly:

"Say what you please, this lad whom I started on his career has studied enough now to read all the Classics. They tell me he has a paper saying so.—The rest is inessential."—Thus with a few wise words he wiped away whole civilizations.

On this particular afternoon, this day of home-coming, a windless autumn afternoon with the white pines motionless as obelisks, and the gossip of the poplar leaves silenced for once, the women loitered in their doorways waiting, and the men gathered at the inn watching for the first sight of Chi's son. They talked about him, his adoption, his marriage. To their minds he was a little like one risen from the dead, for he was returning from a new world, a brave new world, whose courage they could neither admire nor understand. For here in Hundred Altars the world was the old world yet, its ideals unaltered, its life still undisturbed. Even in the midst of national turmoil such villages as this remained the strongholds of the ancient civilization. Despite the Revolution nothing was altered as far as the farmers were concerned,—the new government so far had let itself be carried on by the momentum of the old, with the same loose control and the same officials under different names. The changes in the village were not political, but personal. Some of the villagers had cut their queues. A few of the older faces were missing from the company at the inn, and younger ones had taken their places. Village interests still centred in the village.

"When Little Dragon gets back we must not forget to tell him all that has happened since he went away," the farmers said to one another. "We'll warrant our news is far more interesting than anything he ever hears in the city!"

"That's so," said one seriously. "Let's remember what to tell him first.—There's the death of Trembling Sea. I wonder how he'll like the new priest. He's not a bad man, though young."

"People get over that," said the blacksmith dryly. "If I judge him aright Little Dragon will be more shocked by the scandal at the Wu's—that was a dreadful business."

It was indeed.—Scarcely three months had young Wu the coffin-maker's son been dead and buried in one of his father's own coffins, than Wu Sao Sao his widow "jumped" with a man in Pei Yang Ho,—an indecent proceeding which struck at the very foundation of village ideals. Never before had a widow disgraced Hundred Altars and herself by re-marrying, and well might the elders ask each other what the world was coming to! —Just as in the old days they had gloated over Ma's scandal, so now the rough tongues of the village licked over this new titbit. One told another how on the night the woman left for her new husband's home riding a donkey—since a virgin alone has a right to the red chair,—the ghost of poor Wu had followed her with a lantern in his hand to the very door of her new home, —calling her to return to her children and his parents. But she had not listened; "Bad luck will follow her," the village prophesied. As for the new husband, he must be a fool. —A woman who has buried one man is likely to bury another. And even if she should touch a tree in her new home it would be almost certain to die within the year. It was shameful for a woman to leave her husband's parents thus. Yes, bad luck would follow her, and overtake her too!

Such was the narrow critical atmosphere, the restricted world to which Little Dragon stepped back again as he entered the doorway of his old home after his long journey by train and cart, with Swallow close behind him holding the baby in her arms.

Crossing the threshold he bowed low before Chi and Clever Needle. In his heart he remained their son. He still owed them duty and respect and his love for them was unchanged; Only now that he was adopted he no longer called them "father" and "mother" but "uncle" and "aunt." Chi winced a little hearing these new names. But what did they matter after all?—the old affection held. Rising from his chair he put his hands squarely on his son's shoulders.

"It is six long years since I have seen you, six years," he repeated. "You are a man now, taller even than I.—Let me look at you."

As for Clever Needle, she was clinging to his sleeve half tenderly, half frightened. Just to see him there again in the old home was a reward for all her sacrifice in letting him go.—But the next moment she was confused. She could scarcely believe this was her baby, this tall young man with trousers of foreign stuff flapping loosely round his ankles beneath his long gown, his hair unoiled standing up stiff and unruly, his leather-soled foreign shoes clattering noisily on the worn stone slabs of the floor. Standing back at arm's length she stared at him, taking in every detail of his strangely informal clothes. The scholars of her young days had been grave and dignified, slightly stooped, anxious to look older than their age. They wore long silk gowns falling to their heels and tied their trousers neatly over their socks with black ankle bands. Their sleek queues hung below their waists, their heads were covered by tight-fitting black skull caps, their eyes hidden behind tortoiseshell-rimmed spectacles.—Little Dragon hatless, shod in foreign leather shoes....

Her exclamations of surprise embarrassed him and made him feel incongruous in the presence of these farmer parents. It was a trying situation, and he attempted to ease it with a smile.

"Bring in our son," he said to Swallow who was standing patiently beyond the threshold with the baby in her arms, waiting for his word to give her respectful greetings. Surely the sight of the child would re-knit their hearts together!—The fruit of his life,—the "double grandson" as he himself was now the son of "double" parents, born in one house, yet worshipping the ancestors of another!—Everyone must love that baby when they saw him.

Hundred Altars

But Clever Needle was not ready to love his young mother. At the sight of her in a long gown instead of the customary jacket and short trousers,—a long gown with a slit up the side showing more ankle than was necessary yet not more than was attractive, and leaving her unbound feet plainly visible, the older woman could not repress a start. Little Dragon waited uncomfortably for her to say something, but she remained silent thinking with dismay that between herself and her new daughter-in-law there was a gap of a hundred years. How could they ever bridge it? Presently, as if thinking aloud, she said:

"Once your feet were small and dainty. I know you were well brought up here in the village. Oh, I do not blame you,—but Shui Ching,—what has come over her to unbind your feet!"

Instead of hanging her head modestly and not venturing to answer Swallow smiled at her frankly,—"My father wished it. — Besides, the times are changed."

Little Dragon gave his wife a quick look. He foresaw trouble between the two women—both, proud, both loving him tenderly, but one old and set in her ways, and the other young and impatient. It was the duty of the young to yield, and when Little Dragon reminded her, Swallow blushed and bit back further words. They had been sent to Hundred Altars to be near the elders, to comfort them, to make them happy, and their first duty was to conform outwardly at least to their prejudices, even if they seemed out of date. His friends Nicholas and Peter had tried to force new wine into old bottles with disastrous results.

As Little Dragon turned to greet his brothers and receive a welcome from his aunts and cousins, his sisters-in-law and the ever-devoted Amah Niu, Clever Needle took her latest grandson in her arms. He, at least, appeared like any normal healthy child, dressed except for the Buddha cap, as her own Little Dragon used to be. She was pleased and proud that he neither struggled nor cried but turned happily towards her, clutching at her big earrings, gurgling with delight.—How fair he was, how like his father. But she was careful not to praise him lest the jealousy of the spirits be roused.—"And now let me go, you little snatching creature!" she exclaimed at last affectionately as she disengaged his tiny hands and gave him back to his mother, "else how shall I prepare food for your elders!"

Swallow took him lovingly and capably.

"She may be changed outwardly, and her manners are certainly strange," thought the grandmother whose judgment was softened by the maternal gesture, "but her heart is the heart of a good mother.—I hope that we may come to see with the same eyes in what concerns her child, for she will surely fight like a tigress for her baby."

When the meal was ready Clever Needle called the family together, shouting loudly: "The rice is open, the rice is open!"—It sounded like old days, though now her daughters-in-law and Snow Peach's two girls carried the steaming bowls of food to the table in her stead.

As the men crossed the courtyard his father said to Little Dragon, "Well, son, I suppose you have forgotten how to use chopsticks?" But the latter answered half in earnest, half in fun, — "Oh, no, I still find some of the old ways good.—Chopsticks are not half as sharp as forks."

Once they sat down to the feast there was no further talk. One could not eat with full enjoyment and talk with interest at the same time.—What happiness to share a meal in common again! It was almost like a New Year Feast of Re-union. Not one of Little Dragon's favourite dishes had been forgotten, not even succulent morsels of duck wrapped in thin pancakes and seasoned with sauce and garlic,— a rare treat for the Chis.—His mother's cooking waked old memories in the prodigal. "There is no one," he said, looking towards her tenderly, "who can season as well as you!"

Darkness had fallen for two hours before they finished eating. Then the men lingered over their tea-cups talking. They talked of many things, of the great city, of Ma and his success, of the new schools, even of foreigners and their ways. But Clever Needle called Swallow out to the kitchen. It was not proper for her to linger with the menfolk as she seemed tempted to do. Women with women, men with men. Now that they were to live close together the proprieties must be at once established. Besides, Clever Needle wanted to hear things also, not about the glass house called Politics (which did not concern her) but about Shui Ching's life and her new grandson and his ways.

Not until the moon was sailing like a high-prowed junk in the clear heavens did the young couple respectfully bid their elders good night, and walk slowly back to the Ma house.—Every dog barked as they passed down the deserted street, for even dogs knew that good folk seldom wandered abroad after darkness fell.

It was surprising how easily Little Dragon and Swallow slipped back again into the village life; how Little Dragon found patience to bear with the ripe wisdom of old Bent Neck who sometimes treated his new young master as a child; and with the peculiarities of the distillery foreman who knew his customers, and even with his old teacher whose pride in his former pupil was turned somewhat sour by the thought of his modern learning. But when his neighbours failed to understand things which seemed natural enough to him, he could always rely on Swallow's sympathy. She understood, she knew—thanks to Ma's foresight in having sent her to school,—and she too had her difficulties.

With all the good will in the world she and Clever Needle found mutual understanding difficult. The best they could ever hope for was a loving compromise. The older woman could not refrain from carping, and scolding the girl for small thoughtless errors. Only once Swallow grown impatient answered sharply: "If it is your custom, of course I will follow it, but it seems to me foolish!" And Clever Needle remarked bitterly: "Is a mother no longer in authority because the Emperor no longer sits on his throne?"—Swallow ashamed, apologized at once.—Her young husband's words recurred to her with added force. "Remember my mother is growing old," Little Dragon had said, "and that it is very difficult for her to understand our ways of thinking. We have the future, but she leans on the past."

So Swallow, a good girl at heart, attempted to curb her impulsiveness, and in many ways tried hard to please her mother-in-law. For one thing she heeded her husband's request to ask Clever Needle's advice as often as possible—a subtle flattery that pleased the older woman. At her suggestion Swallow laid aside her slit robes that scandalized the village and wore trousers and short jackets as the other women did. But in what concerned her baby she would, as Clever Needle guessed, go her own way. She would wash him every day to Clever Needle's horror, and she would *not* dose him with the weird concoctions in which her mother-in-law and Amah Niu placed their trust,—nor would she suffer them to pierce his ear nor call him a girl's name.

"In many ways he shall be thy parents' grandson," she told her husband smiling, "but in certain ways he shall remain my son!"

So the months passed until at the New Year Ma announced that he would return for the Spring Feast of Ancestors, and again he kept his word.

He came with his women a few days before the holiday and felt as proud as any Roman conqueror returning to a triumph. Now his neighbours should see what manner of man he truly was. Sweet was the recognition of the outside world, but sweeter still the acclaim of Hundred Altars, and sweetest of all the satisfaction he experienced in the respect his son commanded in the village, Ma was a proud and happy man those days, and glad to be in Hundred Altars again—for a while.

Shui Ching was no less pleased to be back in familiar surroundings. But to her surprise she soon found herself missing the comforts of Tientsin. "A *k'ang* is harder than I remembered," she said to Ma as she rose stiffly each morning, "I must be growing old or else the city life has softened me."—"You'll be a modern woman yet," he laughed in answer. "You'll soon despise the sheltered courtyard life."—Shui Ching smiled tenderly at her husband. "Never, oh my master, never."—And she slipped away to prepare the ancestral offerings for the feast.

"Spring Brightness" dawned serene as usual. The early sunshine seemed to throw into relief the figures of the stooped, round-shouldered farmers and their families as they went out to their tombs, the generation of today still chained to the generations of yesterday. They sauntered out in groups, just as they always did, fathers leading the way, wives carrying the provisions, children grave and on their best behaviour—the Chis, the Chiens, the Wongs, the Wus, the Changs, the Liangs, following the zigzag paths to the graves of their ancestors. Here they crossed a square of golden light, a little further on the perfect sharp shadow of a young peach tree blurred their silhouettes. The generation of today was still chained to the generation of yesterday.

Ma headed his group, his son and his son's son in his mother's arms following behind him.

How many other years he and Shui Ching had gone alone, despising themselves, despised by their neighbours. Then they had avoided happier folk, hanging their heads in shame and looking the other way. Now Ma greeted all and sundry. No more embarrassment, just friendliness. As he watched his women unpack the offerings of food and incense and wine, the gold and silver strings of mock money and the white circles of paper cash to crown each grave, he was happy. He noticed with pleasure that the grove of trees around his graves had grown taller. The memorial tablet with its crown of twisted dragons stood firmly upright. The tombs themselves were well-swept and in repair — his son had seen to that.

Now he knelt down to make his offerings, ko-towing nine times. Here were his forefathers, here were his son and his grandson. At last the circle of birth and death was complete since he had forged his link in the chain of creation; At last he shared the deep communion with the past and the future that his neighbours shared. At last he could feel that his life was rounded out. So a man should feel, as he grew old, content to have fulfilled his duty.

"Whatever changes come," he murmured slipping back unconsciously, for all his modern ideas, to the guiding principle of his race: "I have done my share. The ancestors will be cared for by my son, and my son's sons."

www.ingramcontent.com/pod-product-compliance
Lightning Source LLC
Chambersburg PA
CBHW071956110526
44592CB00012B/1107